"This is simply the best book yet written on how the corruption of identity politics insinuated itself into—and then began to reinvent—American academia.... If this book was required reading at every freshman orientation in the country, it would start a revolution. It tells a story that Americans must hear."

   –Shelby Steele

"Bawer scores entertaining points against the insufferable posturing and unreadable prose that pervades identity studies—a lively, cantankerous take-down of a juicy target."

   –Publishers Weekly

"Bawer has written a terrific exposé of the pseudo-academic fad of 'identity studies' courses and programs. I strongly recommend the book."

   –George Leef, *National Review*

"Bawer shines a revealing light on gurus in these fields who run the gamut from odious to merely bizarre.... This is an informative, credible and even shocking book in which all Identity Studies programs are hoisted to justified ridicule by their own intellectually corrupt petards. Read it and—when you stop laughing—weep."

   –Barbara Kay, *The National Post* (Canada)

"Bawer's study bristles with statistics, direct citations of conference presentations, and detailed close readings of major Identity Studies texts. A patient and comprehensive document, it should be required reading for every humanities student at a North American university."

   –Janice Fiamengo, *FrontPage Magazine*

"The developments described by Mr. Bawer will not surprise readers familiar with the campus wars that broke out in the 1980s, when entire departments devoted to these fields began to be established. Where the author's text shines is in explaining their root causes. Identity studies were established during the cultural turmoil of the civil-rights era by militant students demanding academic affirmation of their racial and sexual grievances. They were thus designed at their inception to serve political rather than scholarly ends."

–**Sohrab Ahmari**, *Wall Street Journal*

"This heartfelt and eloquent book from the English-speaking world's bravest cultural critic—funny and deadly serious all at once—should be read by anyone who cares about the fate of liberal learning in the USA."

–**Andrew Ferguson**

"Bawer shows how it pays career dividends to be oppressed rather than to be broadly educated—at least until the public has had enough and finally tunes out this costly and self-destructive deception."

–**Victor Davis Hanson**

"Bruce Bawer is sober, sophisticated, sometimes hilarious, and eminently clear-sighted as he shows us what has become of America's universities.... A riveting and refreshing tour de force."

–**Phyllis Chesler**

"In *The Victims' Revolution* we have, at last, a serious and thorough dissection of identity studies. Anyone with a stake in these fields—from prospective students to their parents to university administrators to professors—should read it."

–**Robert VerBruggen**, *National Review*

ALSO BY

Bruce Bawer

THE VICTIMS' REVOLUTION

THE VICTIMS' REVOLUTION

THE RISE OF IDENTITY STUDIES AND
THE BIRTH OF THE WOKE IDEOLOGY

BRUCE BAWER

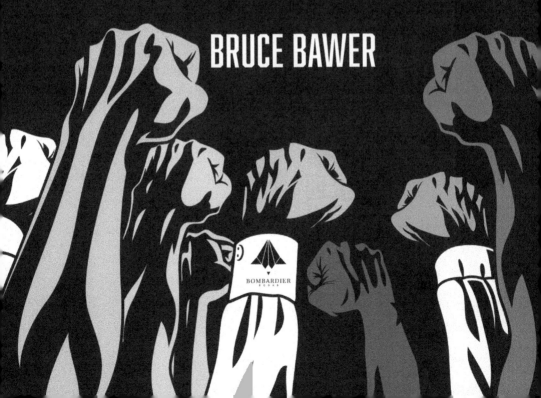

Published by Bombardier Books
An Imprint of Post Hill Press
ISBN: 978-1-63758-814-7
ISBN (eBook): 978-1-63758-815-4

The Victims' Revolution:
The Rise of Identity Studies and the Birth of the Woke Ideology
© 2012 by Bruce Bawer
All Rights Reserved

Cover Design by Matt Margolis
Interior Design by Yoni Limor

BOMBARDIER BOOKS   Post Hill PRESS

Post Hill Press
New York • Nashville
posthillpress.com

Published in the United States of America
1 2 3 4 5 6 7 8 9 10

For Carol

CONTENTS

FOREWORD

I first started reading Bruce Bawer in the 1990s. As well as being one of America's foremost literary critics, he stood out in those days because he was one of less than a handful of gay Americans who were making the case for gay equality rather than gay revolution-ary-ism. With *A Place at the Table: The Gay Individual in American Society* (1993), Bawer was brave enough to show that gay Americans did not necessarily want the radical platforms of the far left who had taken over the movement. Most wanted equality—nothing less and certainly nothing more. In that book, Bawer took on the arguments of religious conservatives and radical leftists alike. Along with the work of Andrew Sullivan, Bawer's work was, in its field, one of the formative works of the 1990s. As was his 1997 work, *Stealing Jesus: How Fundamentalism Betrays Christianity*, a book which showed that Bawer was not afraid to take on people who might have been imagined to be on his own side.

Today the arguments of these books are pretty much accepted by the majority. But that was not always the case. The fact that it is today has much to do with the calm, sensitive intelligence of Bruce Bawer.

So I was already listening. And I was struck afresh in the 2000s when Bawer took what was in some ways an unexpected shift in his focus. After the atrocity of 9/11 and the resulting attacks in Madrid, London, Amsterdam, Bali, and many other cities around the world, a dominant tendency emerged with which to ignore the issue of Islamic fundamentalism. Or at least to wish it away. Most commonplace of all was the desire of Europeans to refuse to admit that there was any connection between the increased immigration of the post-war period and the rise in intolerant Islam among certain members of its immigrant populations. Again, at this period of two decades distance, the connection between a population and its actions might seem obvious. But it was not so then. Or if it was, it required an unusual courage to point it out.

Once again, Bawer turned out to be that person. Just as he had gone for the jugular of Christian fundamentalism, so now he went for Islamic fundamentalism, a consistency that is not rewarded among all of what used to be called the "right-thinking people." His book, *While Europe Slept: How Radical Islam Is Destroying the West from Within* (2006), was a devastating, ground-breaking explanation of how mass immigration—especially mass Muslim immigration—into Europe was in the process of fundamentally altering these societies. In the years since, others—including the present writer—have taken up some of these arguments. But Bawer was one of the earliest pioneers, and undoubtedly paid a certain price for being one of the first people to state the obvious in a society that did not want the obvious to be stated. *While Europe Slept* was an exceptionally important book. It broke a taboo—a bubble of wishful thinking. It said what was politically incorrect but nevertheless true.

And why should he not have said it? After all, there was no inconsistency between Bawer's work from the 1990s and that of the 2000s. Quite the opposite. Why should someone who had seen the rise of anti-gay hate crime in Europe keep pretending that this was not by then an immigrant-led phenomenon? Bigotries change, as do the people acting on them. Threats to liberal society change. Sometimes they come from one direction. Sometimes from another. The crocodiles nearest to the boat are not always the same. It requires a mind of dexterous perseverance to keep identifying that fact, wherever it comes from and whatever the brickbats that may result.

So it is with the present volume. Today there can hardly be anyone in the Western world who has not at least heard of the term "woke." It would have been a good thing if they had heard of it earlier. Who knows, perhaps we would have been able to cut it off at an earlier moment. Had more people read Bawer, then we would have done. I read *The Victims Revolution* when it came out in 2012 and was immediately struck by the depth and precision of the intellectual surgery Bawer had performed, as well as the firsthand accounts of wading through this task that make the book so compelling.

Since the 1970s, American universities had been fostering a culture of "grievance studies," a culture in which "women's studies," "black studies," "queer studies," and others first emerged and then came to dominate. It became a truism for anyone in the know that any discipline that had "studies" in the name was not doing the thing it was claiming to do. To the best of my knowledge, no one has ever dared to present a course in "astrophysics studies." It either is the thing or it is not. But these crock non-disciplines metastasized everywhere in America. And it became a truism of the American academy that whenever a professor retired who had actual knowledge of an actual discipline they began to be replaced by the "studies" professors.

Of course, the students produced from this ought to have been utterly unemployable. Many conservatives in particular complacently pretended that they would be, and that after their lesbian dance majors at Berkeley, these students would crash into the cold hard reality of the labor market. The joke turned out to be on those telling it because today the studies people have found plenty of jobs open to them. Whole industries in fact. Not least in the HR departments of major corporations, and most of what used to pass for the media. In the process, we have seen the rise of that remarkable thing that Bawer identifies in this book: the complete inversion—among much else—of what used to be the American spirit.

That spirit used to be characterized by a respect for bravery. For striding toward the frontiers. For dealing with your lot and also trying to improve it. Only in recent decades has the American—and by extension of American influence in the West—spirit been turned into a spirit that seems to deify the most "oppressed" person in the room. Or at least the person who claims, or pretends, to be the most oppressed person in the room. The space for charlatanry that this opens up has often been remarked upon. The devastation on a society that it wrecks has sadly been more slowly noted.

Today this whole movement tends to be known as "woke." But as so many times before, it was Bawer who saw it coming, tried to warn the public of what was coming toward them, and what they might do to dismantle it. Too few people paid attention, alas, and the corruption of American higher education has continued apace.

Still, there is a virtue in being ahead of the curve. It gives other people courage. It provides untold numbers of other people with enlightenment about the issues coming their way. In time, whole cultures can be woken up. But that requires prophets. And prophets—while often said to be unrecognized—should, wherever possible, be celebrated. I am delighted to see this 10th anniversary edition of *The Victims Revolution* in print. I hope it is no disrespect to Bawer if I say that I hope a 20th anniversary edition is not needed.

Douglas Murray
New York 2022

PREFACE
The Closing of the Liberal Mind

It is my sense that most Americans today, whether they call themselves conservatives, liberals, or moderates, realize that something exceedingly important in the fabric of American society has been imperiled by the developments of the last few decades. They deplore the degradation of our culture, the polarization of our politics, and the coarsening of public debate. They understand that somewhere along the way, we lost the sensible centrism that, within living memory, defined the American public square. They understand that American history, which until not very long ago was a remarkable account of gradual progress toward the full realization of the nation's founding values, has taken a wrong turn. But while Americans lament the loss of shared national values, many of them may not recognize the intimate connection between this loss and the changes that have taken place in American higher education over the last generation or so—changes, specifically, in the teaching of the humanities and social sciences, that have eventuated in the rejection, indeed the demonization, of the very ideas that once defined the sensible center.

"What is it that holds a nation together?" asked Arthur Schlesinger Jr., the celebrated liberal historian, in a new 1998 foreword to his 1991 book, *The Disuniting of America*. He proceeded to reflect on the "fragility of national cohesion," serving up a long list of countries that were then (and still are) "in ethnic or religious turmoil." Even Canada, "long…considered the most sensible and placid of nations," faced the possibility of splitting in two because of tensions between its English- and French-speaking citizens. Schlesinger quoted author Michael Ignatieff on the Canadian question: "If one of the top five developed nations on earth can't make a federal, multi-ethnic state work, who else can?"

As Schlesinger observed, "[t]he answer to that increasingly vital question has been, at least until recently, the United States." For two centuries, America accomplished something that would have previously seemed impossible: the creation, as Schlesinger put it, "of a brand-new national identity by individuals who, in forsaking old loyalties and joining to make new lives, melted away ethnic differences." Hector St. John de Crèvecoeur, author of *Letters from an American Farmer* (1782), described Americans as "a new race of men"—a race that, paradoxically, had nothing to do with race.

To point out the miraculous nature of this accomplishment—its utter lack of precedent in all of human history—is not to deny, among other things, the mistreatment of Native Americans and the blight of slavery and racism. It is simply to note that, in a world where violent intergroup enmity and conflict have been the rule rather than the exception, America found a way for increasingly diverse groups of people to live together not only in peace but with a strong sense of shared identity—an identity founded not on ethnicity but on a commitment to the values of individual liberty, dignity, and equality articulated in the Declaration of Independence and the Constitution. America, as envisioned by its founders and understood by the overwhelming majority of its citizens, was, in an international context, and in a now outdated sense of the word, a supremely liberal conception.

In 1944 the Swedish writer Gunnar Myrdal marveled at the fact that Americans of every ethnicity, religion, and color shared a more "explicitly expressed system of general ideals" than the people of any other country in the Western world. Although American society had yet to live up to the full meaning of its creed—"that all men are created equal, that they are endowed by their Creator with certain unalienable Rights, that among these are Life, Liberty and the pursuit of Happiness"—it was in fact the very thing that made moral progress in America not only possible but inevitable. To quote Schlesinger again: "the Creed held out hope even for those most brutally excluded by the white majority" and "act[ed] as the spur forever goading white Americans to live up to their proclaimed principles.... 'America,' Myrdal said, 'is continuously struggling for its soul.'"

One of the most magnificent examples of America's struggles for its soul was the civil rights movement of the mid-twentieth century. The goal of that movement could not have been more consistent with America's founding ideals—which was why it ultimately succeeded. But that bright success was not without its downside. The most disastrous by-product of the civil rights movement was multiculturalism, a philosophy that teaches, as Schlesinger put it, "that America is not a nation of individuals at all but a nation of groups." For two centuries, Americans had been held together by a shared sense of national identity, a belief in individual liberty, and a vision of full equality—even though that vision, as many Americans acknowledged, had yet to be fully realized. Yet just when the complete attainment of that vision seemed to lie within our grasp, the very idea of a shared identity began to be challenged, condemned, dismantled—and replaced by a new conception, founded not on individual rights and liberties but on the claims of group identity and culture. This new ideology, as Schlesinger recognized, represented a betrayal of true liberalism, a rejection of the idea of a sensible center, and a profound danger to the sense of unity that had made America uniquely strong, prosperous, and free.

Schlesinger was, it should be emphasized, an icon among liberals, a two-time winner of the Pulitzer Prize and the author of books that had helped shape social and political thought at the height of the American Century. The great chronicler and defender of Democratic presidents, in particular Franklin D. Roosevelt, he was also the author of an influential 1949 treatise called *The Vital Center*, in which he argued for a strong and vigorous democratic liberalism as an alternative to the then formidable temptations of communism. *The Disuniting of America* came as a kind of dismal coda to that book. It was published at a time when American campuses were in an uproar over the rise of multiculturalism and identity studies, and in it he warned his fellow liberals that the looming cult of victimhood, while posing as a liberal crusade, was actually an anti-liberal virus that threatened to destroy the very foundations of American democracy.

Schlesinger himself might not have put it this way, but what the new academic groupthink really represented was nothing less than the closing of the liberal mind. Armed with a new sense of mission and moral superiority, the new academic elites simultaneously balkanized and politicized the study of society and culture and wrapped their Gramscian Marxist critiques in an impenetrable jargon that only they could understand. They no longer listened to traditional liberals and held conservatives in utter contempt. Meanwhile, the multicultural dogma spread throughout society, transforming the way people think, speak, and act on a wide range of issues.

In previous books, I have examined some of the consequences of this phenomenon. *While Europe Slept* indicted the refusal of liberals in Europe and the U.S. to defend liberal principles in the face of Islamic radicalism. *Surrender* documented the abandonment of their commitment to free speech in the name of multicultural sensitivity. In this book, I have attempted to go to the root of the problem—the academy, the font of the perfidious multicultural idea and the setting in which it is implanted into the minds of American youth.

Schlesinger understood the crucial role of education in a democracy, especially one as volatile and changing as ours. He understood the importance of the "sensible center" in maintaining our strength and stability and keeping the country on the right path. And he understood the role of traditional liberal education in communicating, preserving, and building upon the sensible, centrist American values that he cherished. He made a great point of the fact that primary and secondary schools, by instilling civic values in young people, were a critical element in the perpetuation of a shared national identity.

Higher education is obviously no less important. And the fact is—as many liberals themselves have acknowledged—that over the course of the last few decades, it has become the captive of a kind of thinking that imperils the American idea, and the American contract, as we have known them for more than two centuries. Among those who have most eloquently articulated the nature of this peril was the University of Chicago philosopher Allan Bloom, who, twenty-five years ago, in a pathbreaking book later described by Camille Paglia as "the first shot in the culture wars," warned that the intellectual relativism that was taking over the academy—and that claimed to represent greater openness—was, in fact, leading to what he called "the closing of the American mind." At its best, Bloom argued, liberal education had been founded on a belief in rationality and objective truth, in vigorous and free inquiry, and in the importance of encountering the great ideas and the great books; now, however, the university—and, in turn, the culture as a whole—was increasingly under the sway of relativistic thinking and rigid political ideas that represented, ultimately, a menace to American democracy. One result of this relativism is identity studies. The problem, to be sure, is not simply a pathological fixation on group identity, but a preoccupation with the historical grievances of certain groups, combined with a virulent hostility to America, which is consistently cast as the prime villain in the histories of these groups and the world at large. If you or I had set out to invent an ideology capable of utterly destroying the America of the Declaration, the Constitution, and the melting pot, we could scarcely have done better.

The ideas that have increasingly dominated American universities since the sixties have followed the graduates of those institutions out into the larger society. The results are all around us, from workplaces where an innocuous statement can brand one as a bigot and destroy one's career to election campaigns in which legitimate criticism of a black or female candidate can be discounted as "racist" or "sexist" instead of being addressed on its merits. Yet those ideas themselves, and the form in which they are presented in thousands of classrooms around the United States, remain an almost complete mystery to a great many otherwise well-informed and responsible citizens.

This needs to change. Americans who care about the future of their country—especially parents who care what their children are being taught—need to know what is going on within those ivory towers. They need to be aware of the truly toxic changes that the revolution has wrought in the seemingly innocuous classrooms behind those ivied walls.

A quarter century ago, Bloom's warning was widely dismissed as a reactionary screed. In fact, it was prescient—prophetic. The sad truth is that the triumph of identity studies—and of the dogmas on which those studies are based—diminishes our sense of human possibility, and threatens to further impoverish our already diminished culture. Attention must be paid.

INTRODUCTION
to the Tenth Anniversary Edition

Disney, which brought you *Bambi* and *The Little Mermaid*, creates a female Muslim superhero named "Ms. Marvel" and a robot who asks a transgender man for advice on female sanitary products. Larry Elder, a black GOP candidate for governor of California, is smeared by the *Los Angeles Times* as "the black face of white supremacy" for preaching a message essentially identical to that of Martin Luther King, Jr. When an eighty-year-old woman complains to her local YMCA about a biological male lurking in the women's locker room, *she's* banned for being a transphobe. The Hachette publishing group cancels the memoirs of our most acclaimed living movie director because of discredited, decades-old molestation charges. The Biden Administration sets down strict vaccination rules for those entering the country with legitimate visas, but exempts people crossing the southern border illegally.

All this insanity didn't come out of nowhere. Since the 1960s, as I describe in chapter one of this book, the study of literature and other fields in the humanities and social sciences has been gradually transformed into something very different—and extremely distressing. An increasing focus on group identity—and on the strict division of humankind into oppressor groups and victim groups—

fed the growth of such disciplines as Women's Studies, Black Studies, Queer Studies, and Chicano Studies. I'm not alone in calling them "grievance studies," and in considering them to be inimical to the serious study of human beings as complex individuals with a variety of virtues and defects.

This book is about those "grievance studies." In preparing it, I read voluminously in these fields, attended conferences, sat in on classes, and performed interviews. I knew that I was taking on: not just the entire American higher-education establishment but also the elite media that are its ideological allies. So it shouldn't have come as a surprise when the *New York Times Book Review* ran—on its front page, no less—a loftily dismissive account of my book by a purported education expert who, calling it "out of date," claimed that identity studies represented "a shrinking sector of academic life" and that his "younger colleagues" at a certain Ivy League college were "returning to close readings of literary classics."

Those familiar with—and critical of—the actual situation in academia recognized this as a lie, and praised *The Victims' Revolution* as truth-telling, plain and simple. Calling it "indispensable," Peter Wood, president of the National Association of Scholars, theorized that the *Times* had judged the book "too important to ignore," hence the dishonest review. George Leef of the James G. Martin Center for Academic Renewal agreed. "It's revealing," Leef wrote, "that the NYT editor realized that the book couldn't be ignored, but had to be panned." And Hoover Institution fellow Bruce Thornton called the *Times* review "a textbook illustration of how the academic establishment goes after anyone who exposes the corruption of a reactionary, failing institution."

As it turned out, *The Victims' Revolution* wasn't only right on the money about what was going on at America's most respected colleges. It was prescient. I don't know of any other book from 2012 that so much as hinted at what the world of 2022 might look like. But to read *The Victims' Revolution* is to see pretty much every crazy social development of the last decade in chrysalis. "The future of America," I wrote in its last sentence, "hangs in the balance." My point was that what was being taught widely on America's campuses wouldn't be confined to those campuses for long. Unfortunately, I was right. The ideological toxins at the heart of identity studies escaped the academy like a virus escaping a Chinese lab. The general culture was infected. And suddenly the world was turned upside down.

*　　*　　*

To borrow from the current lexicon, the world went woke. It happened because college graduates who'd been marinated in identity studies introduced the cockamamie concepts they'd picked up in class into their new workplaces and communities. Women's Studies? The #metoo movement, which started by bringing down serial sex offenders like Hollywood producer Harvey Weinstein, was soon ruining the lives of men who'd done next to nothing. The vengeful hysteria of many #metoo activists stunned more than a few observers—but wouldn't have surprised anyone who'd read in my Women's Studies chapter about students being fed grotesquely exaggerated rape statistics and being taught to regard men (Western men, anyway) as predatory and violent by nature.

Black Studies? The year 2018 saw the publication of *White Fragility* by Robin DiAngelo, who argued that all whites are eternally guilty of race hatred and all blacks are their eternal victims. The following year saw the publication of *How to Be an Antiracist* by Black Studies graduate Ibram X. Kendi and the introduction of the *New York Times*'s 1619 Project, which attributes the American founding to racism. And 2020 saw the death of a criminal named George Floyd, who became an internationally famous martyr and *casus belli*. Suddenly, Critical Race Theory was everywhere, including in primary-school syllabi. For most Americans, it was all new and baffling; but every bit of it was all straight out of Black Studies, which had been founded by race hustlers skilled at guilt-tripping whites—precisely the talent to which both DiAngelo and Kendi owe their success.

Chicano Studies? Donald Trump's call for a border wall was cheered by American workers who'd seen no wage growth for decades owing to job competition from illegals—but it sparked outrage not only among these illegals' employers but also among the innumerable college graduates who'd learned in Chicano Studies class-rooms to view the U.S. as an illegal occupier of "Aztlán"—that is, the regions once been ruled by Spain and then by Mexico—and to regard Chicanos, therefore, as America's dispossessed, having far more of a right to live in the U.S. than any native-born citizen.

Queer Studies? When *The Victims' Revolution* came out, gender dysphoria was an exceedingly rare phenomenon. A few years later, claims of transgender identity had become a trendy lifestyle choice and the supposed right of people to be recognized as members of the opposite sex (or of any one of dozens of other gender-identity categories) had become sacred. This and other recent unsettling developments are natural outgrowths of queer theory, which, as can be seen in my chapter on Queer Studies, is far less concerned with studying sexual orientation than with celebrating gender.

There are other obvious continuities between identity studies and current social trends. The poisonous racism of Whiteness Studies, which a decade ago was almost entirely confined to the classroom, has gone mainstream, with white children being incul-cated with self-hatred and black children being trained to see themselves as victims. (Robin DiAngelo, note well, is a leading Whiteness Studies figure.) Similarly, the reality series and fash-ion-magazine covers that celebrate the morbidly obese can be traced directly to the medically perilous claims of Fat Studies.

In short, the book I published in 2012 about certain unset-tling tendencies on American campuses is no longer just about the academy. It's a guidebook to—and a genealogy of—the most noxious of the strange new ideas that now suffuse our mainstream culture. How lamentable it is that conservatives, moderates, and classical liberals weren't able to keep these ideas from taking over the colleges and universities; and how alarming it is that the sensible majority of citizens weren't able to keep them from conquering society at large, where they are now reshaping our culture and rewiring our children's minds.

As Fifth Circuit Judge James C. Ho said in a September 2022 speech announcing that he would no longer be hiring law clerks from Yale—where these lethal new ideas are particularly prevalent—"Our whole country has become a campus."

*   *   *

The question before us today, of course, is what to do now that these toxins have escaped into the mainstream.

To begin with, it's important to recognize that this isn't a minor or fleeting development that you or I can hope to ignore, keeping our heads down until the freak parade passes by. These changes have already begun to take root and won't get uprooted unless the sane and hitherto silent majority of the public resolves to give them the heave-ho.

And how to do that? For one thing, speak up every time you interact with somebody whom you suspect of being a party to this madness. What does your family doctor think, for instance, about giving hormone blockers to children? Ask her. If you don't like her answer, challenge her on it. And if she stands her ground, tell her you consider her to have betrayed her Hippocratic oath, and then walk away and find another doctor.

Remember that the main reason why so many teachers, school psychologists, endocrinologists, surgeons, and other professionals are going along with trans ideology is not that they believe it: it's that they're taking what is, at the moment, the easy route, because virtually all the pressure they're feeling is coming from the woke side. They need to know that there are more people who oppose this insanity than who support it, and that those opponents can exert pressure, too—and that if they want to preserve their livelihoods, they'd better do what's right. Some of the most inspiring videos I've seen in the last couple of years have been of school board meetings at which parents have eloquently challenged the woke politics that schools have been shoving down their children's throats. If every parent could be that involved, the problems we face would be very quickly and dramatically diminished. Be one of those parents. If you don't like what your school board members are saying, vote them off. If necessary, run for school board yourself. If these pedagogical practices aren't nipped in the bud when your kids are still small, it may already be too late to scrub the nonsense out of their brains.

In fact, you could do worse than to get informed, and get involved, in electoral politics at all levels, from City Council on up. It's not enough to vote for candidates who don't parrot the woke agenda. Find candidates who are gutsy enough to oppose it passionately. And if such candidates don't seem to be on offer in your neck of the woods, run yourself—or talk a like-minded friend into running. This is our country, and the only way to take it back from the woke brigade is to do so one elective office at a time.

Of course, institutions of higher education continue to be Ground Zero for all this drivel. Are you an alumnus of a college that's gone woke? Do you nonetheless still send that college a check every year? If so, why? Have you ever picked up the phone to complain to the college president, or written a letter to the board of trustees, to criticize the ideological direction that your alma mater has taken? Have you threatened to cut it off financially?

Another crucial point about colleges. However appealing it might seem in the very short term, don't let your babies grow up to be Yalies. It astonishes me that friends of mine who know very well—and deplore—what's going on at Ivy League colleges nonetheless brag excitedly about their kids being admitted to these places. Are you one of those parents? If so, ask yourself what's more important to you: the actual education your kid will get, or the purported cachet of a Harvard or Stanford diploma?

Don't listen to me. Listen to Roger Kimball, editor of the *New Criterion* (and a Yale graduate), who wrote recently: "The educational establishment in its highest reaches is today a cesspool, contaminating the society it had been, at great expense, created to nurture. Still, parents are willing to climb naked over broken bottles and impoverish themselves to send their children to this cauldron of iniquity." Or listen to Isaac Morehouse of the Institute for Humane Studies, who's turned off not just by the Ivies but by almost all American colleges: "I can't count the number of parents I've talked with who recognize that college is one of the worst places to learn and degrees are one of the weakest ways to try to get hired, but who still needlessly bite the bullet and send their kid anyway—even though a college diploma nowadays "only proves that you were willing to follow the crowd."

Keep in mind that a generation or so from now, either wokeism will have been vanquished, in which case diplomas handed out by the most ideologically corroded universities and colleges in the 2010s and 20s will be sources not of pride but of embarrassment, or it will have followed its natural course of development, resulting in something not unlike the Reign of Terror—in which case your highly credentialed but hopelessly brainwashed kid will eventually be the next sucker in line for the gallows. If you do want your kids to get a real education, find a state college that still hasn't gone fully woke. Or try Hillsdale College, whose 2022 commencement speaker was Jordan Peterson. Then there's St. John's College in Maryland, famous for its Great Books program. Another promising new option is the University of Austin, which was founded by Bari Weiss—a liberal lesbian who left the editorial board of the *New York Times* because she wasn't woke enough for her fellow editors and which is dedicated to "the fearless pursuit of truth."

As you may know, even many units of the U.S. military have succumbed to woke ideology. So if your kid wants to join the service, do some research. Will they be using boot camp to build your kid's character, self-discipline, strength, and resilience, or to produce a woke warrior? If the latter, advise your kid against taking that route—and write letters to the appropriate military officials explaining exactly why they'll be denied the opportunity to indoctrinate your offspring.

And what about you? Has your employer ever brought in some consultant to subject you and your colleagues to a lecture about systematic racism or sexism? Did you feel that you had no choice other than to bite your tongue and get through it? Well, if it happens again, discuss it beforehand with your colleagues. Almost certainly, most of them feel pretty much the way you do. There's strength in numbers. Often employers arrange these lectures in the first place because one or two employees pushed them to do it. If the majority of employees refuse to participate in such nonsense, it'll stop.

Do you feel insufficiently skilled to take on woke thinking? Let me assure you that you're not. These people are mediocrities, and their ideas are absurd. But if you want to sharpen your thoughts—well, for one thing, read this book carefully. Take notes. Then move on to books like Gad Saad's *The Parasitic Mind* (2020), Abigail Shrier's *Irreversible Damage* (2020), Helen Joyce's *Trans* (2021), Vivek Ramaswamyi's *Woke, Inc.* (2021), Andy Ngo's *Unmasked* (2021), Douglas Murray's *The Madness of Crowds* (2019) and *The War on the West* (2022), and James Lindsay's *Race Marxism* (2022). Valuable interviews with and presentations by all of these writers can be found online, as can podcasts, such as *Triggernometry*, *The Saad Truth*, and *The Rubin Report*, on which woke ideology is discussed from sensible perspectives. And what about the legacy media? If you read *The New York Times* every day, or watch CNN regularly, you can easily be deluded into thinking that you're absolutely alone in your opposition to woke ideology. Put that thought out of your mind. It may seem impossible—it may sound like an outrageous exaggeration—but it's true: most of the nation's legacy media organs—including the *Times*, CNN, the *Washington Post*, the *Los Angeles Times*, MSNBC, the network news divisions, and the Associated Press—are now little more than propaganda organs, marching in near-lockstep to push the same woke narrative. Fortunately, their role as go-to places for reliable news and fact-based commentary is increasingly being supplanted by a raft of first-rate online media. And allow me to underscore that this isn't about left vs. right; it's about ideology vs. truth. By the way, if I use the term legacy media (or, sometimes, corporate media) instead of mainstream media, it's because those media are yesterday's news. Every day they diminish in power and importance. Every day they're less and less mainstream.

And that's an important point to keep in mind. Even though woke ideology may seem at times to have conquered Western civilization, its hold on our institutions is still relatively fragile, and its supporters, however loud and aggressive, make up a small minority. To be sure, small minorities can transform a society. As late as February 1917, the Bolsheviks numbered only about 20,000; eight months later, they pulled off the October Revolution, subjecting the largest country in the world to a Communist tyranny that would not collapse until 72 years later. In the 1932 German elections, the Nazis won only 37.3% of the vote—but that was enough to give them an iron grip on the nation that was not loosened until the Allies marched in thirteen years later.

But there's only one way for a small minority of totalitarian ideologues to win in the long term—and that's if the reasonable, common-sense majority allows itself to be scared into silence. So if this woke madness is affecting your life in any way, that means that there are people in your life who are pushing it. And the only response to that is to push back—and push back hard.

CHAPTER 1
The Victims' Revolution

It's March 2010, and I'm at the University of California, Berkeley, for the annual Cultural Studies Association Conference. It is, to a large extent, a gathering of youth—of graduate students and very junior faculty.

At one session a long-haired, fine-featured young man named Stephen, who reminds me a bit of the actor Matthew Gray Gubler on *Criminal Minds*, gives a talk in which he criticizes homeowners for "participating in global capitalism." There's plenty of rhetoric about "the hegemony of absolute space," "ontological security," and so on. But his point is clear: "We have no claim to our families' property." Though he acknowledges his own fantasy of a two-story house "with a wraparound porch," he recoils at his own dream. "When we succumb to pity for an old woman losing her house," he insists, "we abandon social justice," since we are buying into the idea of an "individual's monopolistic right" over a space.

Another young speaker, Mimi, is here to talk about that iconic 1972 photo of a little girl running naked and terrified from a South Vietnamese napalm attack. Mimi notes that the girl, Kim Phúc, has forgiven the United States and is now traveling around the country celebrating American freedom. This angers Mimi, for whom that old photo conveys such a powerful anti-American message. What happens to the message, she asks, when the girl grows up to do such a terrible thing? Phúc's "loving embrace of America," charges Mimi, "seems a betrayal of the photo." What, she asks, are we "as theorists" to make of the fact that Phúc "appears not to feel anger when we think she should"?

Then there's a young woman named Michelle, whose paper carries the title "Towards a Green Marxist Cultural Studies: Notes on Value and Human Domination over Nature." Pretty highfalutin. But when she opens her mouth she sounds like a parody of a Valley girl: "Um, I'm like a grad student at UC Davis?" Michelle says that the "critique of capitalism has faded in significance"; in reaction, she's "sort of reviving a Gramscian-style Marxism." She describes global warming as "sort of, like, a crisis, in the human relationship to nature?" and as "a natural result of the human alienation from nature under capitalism." She cites several authorities who speak of "a sort of, like, physical or spatial alienation?" but adds that she intends to go beyond them.

It soon becomes obvious that these young people are, for the most part, smart upper-middle-class kids, probably from the suburbs, with little real-world experience and even less in the way of serious education. It's clear that their familiarity with history, literature, philosophy, or any other traditional field of learning is at best rudimentary. What they have is ideology and the jargon to go with it. And they have the arrogance of innocents who really have no clue how little they know. One after another of them pronounces with an imperial air of authority on things about which they plainly know next to nothing.

I find my heart going out to them. They've been trained to parrot jargon, to regurgitate bullet points about Western imperialism, colonialism, and capitalism—and to think that this is what it means to be educated. After spending a couple of days listening to them, I can see how easy it must have been for these kids—who have never known any other critical language—to pick this one up and mimic it. Indeed, once you've gone to a few of these sessions, you discover that you can do the same thing with ease yourself. You don't need to have actually *learned* anything, and it certainly has nothing to do with actual social or cultural analysis.

What makes the whole thing unfortunate is that some of these young people have reasonably worthy topics that they want to explore. But they're prisoners of a mind-set and jargon that make it all but impossible for them to say anything fresh or insightful about their experiences and observations. They've been trained to reduce the rich complexities and ambiguities of human life to simple formulas about oppressors and oppressed, capitalists and workers, Western imperialists and their non-Western victims. And when they encounter a reality that doesn't fit this paradigm, they don't know how to deal with it, other than to make statements that are demonstrably untrue. Nor do they realize how America-centric they are: despite their rote anti-American rhetoric, most of the things they have to say only make even the remotest kind of sense within an American context.

Then there's the disorienting admixture, in many of these kids' presentations, of ludicrously pretentious postmodern jargon and an informal, semiliterate English, full of "likes" and "you knows" and "kind ofs" and mispronounced words (in the midst of all his fancy academic rhetoric, young Stephen pronounces *analogous* "an-AL-o-jos") that seem more appropriate to a high school cafeteria than a professional conference. Indeed, the whole event is suffused by a surprising callowness, a lack of the kind of mature professional discipline that I had assumed all grad students still learned to practice, despite the ideological sea change of the last generation or two. (It is not irrelevant that when I showed up to register on the first day of the Cultural Studies Association Conference, I was the only male wearing a suit jacket; I quickly stuffed it into a bag.)

Once upon a time there was something called history. And something else called philosophy. And there was also literature, and with it came literary scholarship, literary history, and literary criticism. And there were art and music, and, to complement them, art history and music criticism and so forth. All these fields of inquiry, and others, fell under the umbrella term "humanities," or "arts and humanities" (the "arts" part included art and music, "humanities" the rest). The word *humanities* came into common use in the mid-twentieth century and designated a sphere of intellectual inquiry that, strictly speaking, was not to be confused, on the one hand, with the arts, which were about pure creativity, or, on the other hand, with the social sciences, such as sociology, economics, and political science, which, like the natural sciences (among them biology, chemistry, and physics), sought to establish hard facts by means of statistical research and the like.

By contrast, the humanities allowed for subjective reactions and interpretations: no single analysis of the *Iliad* or judgment about the root causes of the Civil War would ever be universally recognized as definitive and all-encompassing; the humanities were not about data, formulas, and equations, but rather about pursuing an open-ended conversation in which there was always the possibility of fresh insights and perspectives. In the broadest sense, the natural sciences, social sciences, and humanities all shared a single focus—the meaning of human existence—but while the sciences sought to quantify reality, the humanities concerned themselves with ultimately unquantifiable experiences, observations, responses, and interpretations.

In the late 1970s I was an undergraduate English major at a large state university; in the early 1980s I was a graduate student in the same subject at the same school. Though the department in which I studied was generally considered one of the best in the country, and was indeed excellent in many respects, by my final year of graduate study I had grown cynical about certain aspects of the academy and decided I didn't want to spend the rest of my life in it. In the classroom there was noble talk about the beauty of poetry, the incomparable value of belles lettres as an ornament of civilization, and the solemn obligation of the scholar to produce and preserve reliable texts of the great works of literature and the profound duty of the critic to separate the wheat from the chaff. Meanwhile the corridors and faculty lounges swarmed with ruthless young careerist professors on the make and cynical older professors who were jaded by the whole game and desperate to retire.

It was, in short, no golden age. But in the midst of it all there were still the humanities at (or close to) their finest—the literature, the expertise, the learning. Several of my professors were first-rate, though their critical methods varied dramatically. I took a number of courses, for example, with the Pulitzer Prize-winning poet Louis Simpson, who, in one class meeting that I still recall vividly, leaned back in his chair, put his feet up on the desk, sighed, "Ah, what to say about this book?"—the book, which he then riffed through absently, was Virginia Woolf's *To the Lighthouse*—and for the next hour and fifteen minutes mesmerized us (or me, anyway) with what, for all its eloquence and incisiveness, came off as an utterly casual, effortless, and off-the-cuff account of the novel, how it affected him as a reader and how Woolf had managed to achieve that effect. Simpson (who in 1975, improbable as it sounds nowadays, had made the bestseller lists with a book about Ezra Pound, T. S. Eliot, and William Carlos Williams) was nothing less than brilliant. This, I remember thinking, is why I came to college. I suppose you would call him an impressionistic critic.

There were other approaches. Richard Levin, an expert in Elizabethan drama, taught us how to look at the plays of that period as if through a microscope, outlining their multiple plots and understanding how they were woven together to contribute to the works' overall impact. And there were the New Critics, who showed us what made great poems great by going through them line by line, examining and relishing the subtleties of language. All these methods, however different, went hand in hand—for they were all about appreciating the work. None of these teachers ever forgot that we were all there for one reason: because we loved literature and wanted to understand better what made us love it. We were acolytes, not priests.

That was what the humanities were about—then.

There were, to be sure, warning clouds on the horizon. One or two professors in the department, for instance, practiced the chic, relatively new activity known as deconstruction, which had come over from France by way of the Yale English department. I steered clear of them. It didn't take an extensive look at the major works of deconstructionist criticism—from its founder, Jacques Derrida, and its chief American exponent, Paul de Man, on down—to realize that this stuff just wasn't for me. The pretentious, jargon-filled rhetoric, which seemed designed to diminish great authors and their writings while exalting the deconstructionist himself, had nothing whatsoever to do with the reasons why I had been drawn to the study of literature. Indeed the whole enterprise was entirely unconnected to the appreciation of aesthetic or literary value. But deconstruction was only the beginning. At some point, something called the New Historicism also entered the scene. It, too, left me cold, and for essentially the same reasons.

Then there was feminist criticism. The idea, I gathered, was that all of Western literature had been written by authors unconsciously imbued with notions of male superiority that had warped their views of humanity—and that the literature therefore had to be examined anew through the eyes of the modern women's movement. It was while I was a graduate student that the faculty members in my department began to debate whether it should permit the teaching of feminist criticism or not. The feminists won.

After I received my Ph.D. I left the academy, and was increasingly glad I had done so. For as the years went by, the discipline in which I had earned my degree looked less and less like what it had been, and more and more like some grotesque parody of academic activity. The idea of aesthetic merit, which had been at the heart of the whole thing, all but evaporated: increasingly, even the greatest literary works were treated as mere texts that had no more or less intrinsic value than a phone book or shopping list.

At the same time, similar developments were taking place in English departments across the nation. And not just in English departments; much the same thing was happening throughout the humanities. Once upon a time students had majored in English because they'd loved reading; or they'd studied philosophy because they loved grappling with ideas about the meaning of life; or they'd studied history because, well, they loved history. If you went into science, including social science, it was because you were interested in learning and discovering hard facts about the nature of the universe or the human animal; if you went into the humanities, it was because you were interested in exploring ideas, values, and questions of character and developing your aesthetic taste and critical judgment. The idea was to learn how to use language to formulate subtle perceptions about life, to capture the complex tensions of a historical moment, to convey your own innermost feelings or describe your most intimate relationships.

All this had been jettisoned. The humanities had been, above all, *human*—but now, in the name of the dreadful project known as postmodernism, they were replaced by something dehumanized, artificial, mechanical. While old-fashioned analytical philosophy, which had viewed itself as a search for truth, struggled on, it became increasingly overshadowed by fashionable new philosophical approaches (often headquartered not in philosophy departments but in English and other disciplines) that preached that there was no such thing as objective truth. Meanwhile history was corrupted by a new hostility toward the West and toward master narratives centering on great, pivotal figures (too often male and white), and by a new tendency to reduce the rich drama of the human story to a series of dreary, repetitious lessons about groups, power, and oppression. As for English students, instead of learning to appreciate the genius of great authors, they were being told that there was no such thing as genius or greatness. Literary works were now simply fields on which to play language games and wage political battles that had little or no intrinsic connection to the works themselves. Graduate students in English who once would have learned to perform "close readings" of literary texts, which enhanced their understanding of the ways in which a skillful use of language and structure creates an aesthetic effect, now learned absolutely nothing about such matters. Instead they were trained to mimic their teachers' vapid rhetoric about, as Daphne Patai puts it in the book *Theory's Empire*, "subversion, demystification, transgression, violence, fissures, decentered subjects, fragmentation, dismantling master narratives, and so on."

These activities were all self-referential dead ends—closed systems that had nothing to do with anything beyond themselves. Though they pretended to be politically radical, they had as little connection with the politics of the real world as with the aesthetic values of the works supposedly under consideration. The whole enterprise, briefly put, was intellectually barren. It posed as political, even revolutionary, but it was all just lingo, jargon, shop talk. As Mark Bauerlein, an English professor at Emory, has put it, the verbiage of the postmodern humanities is nothing more than "catechism learning," a set of "axioms to be assimilated before one is inducted into the professoriate." Once you've picked it up, you're ready to go: you don't need to do any in-depth research or critical thinking; all you need to do is to keep slinging the same rhetoric.

What exactly is postmodernism? The Canadian poet David Solway has explained it just about as succinctly as is humanly possible. After complaining (justifiably) that the word "has come to mean just about anything we want it to mean"—that it has "become a cowcatcher term sweeping all query and objection before it," a word that "punctuates the longueurs of flaccid thinking and insecure conceptualizing"—Solway sets out "to chart the etiology of [the] cognitive disease" known as postmodernism. He traces its roots to the anthropologist Franz Boas, who, in an effort to study exotic cultures without prejudice, found it useful to take the position that no culture is superior to any other. Thus was born the notion of cultural relativity, which also informs the works of other pioneering anthropologists such as Bronislaw Malinowski, Ruth Benedict, and Margaret Mead.

What these thinkers, along with such pivotal figures as the structural anthropologist Claude Lévi-Strauss and the anthropologist Clifford Geertz, have in common is that they rejected, or at least cast doubt on, "the universality of Western norms and principles." This "caustic suspicion," writes Solway, "has gradually but decisively penetrated into the Zeitgeist of the West, culminating in the amorphous yet potent cultural amalgam of postmodernism"—the conviction that "[w]e live in a world without reliable truths or transcendent possibilities, without epiphanies, without absolute values, without teleology and without durable meanings." What follows from this— and what makes postmodernism so decadent and so dangerous—is that it compels one (for example) to reject the universality of such values as individual liberty and to believe that "[t]here are no barbarians, only different forms of civilized man."

In retrospect, it eventually became clear to me that the period during which I had studied English had been a time of revolution in humanities education. In his 2007 book, *Education's End*, Yale professor Anthony T. Kronman would describe the transformation

I had experienced as the second of two major shifts in the history of American higher education. In the infancy of American colleges and universities, a period Kronman called the "age of piety," professors had focused on the Greek and Roman classics and on instruction in the Christian faith, the goal being to provide a "moral and spiritual education" that would illuminate for students the meaning and purpose of human life. In the first great shift, which took place after the Civil War, this "age of piety" gave way to an "age of secular humanism," when the larger questions about the meaning of human life that had formerly been at the center of all higher education became the special province of the humanities—namely, "literature, philosophy, history, classics, and the fine arts."

For Kronman, this period—during which higher education in America became democratic "to a greater degree than at any other time or place in human history"—was a golden age during which humanities departments were not simply focused on "the transmission of knowledge" but were also forums "for the exploration of life's mystery and meaning through the careful but critical reading of the great works of literary and philosophical imagination that we have inherited from the past."

Separate departments of philosophy first started to appear in the 1880s; English departments began to be founded soon afterward, followed by departments of German, French, and other foreign languages. While these developments were under way in the humanities, another major area of study, the social sciences, was taking shape alongside the natural sciences. While sharing the humanities' concern about observing and analyzing human society, social scientists strove to approach the subject by means of analytical methods that would be as objective as possible, as opposed to the more subjective approaches found in the humanities.

The second shift—the one I witnessed as a student of English—had its roots in the developments of the late 1960s. Mainly in response to student activism, the "age of secular humanism" began to give way to a third phase during which the humanities ceased to be concerned with larger questions about life. If during the "age of secular humanism" the humanities had sought to help students in their quest to understand the common condition of humankind, in this new phase the humanities questioned the very notion of human nature and replaced it with the assumption—influenced by such postmodernists as the French philosopher Michel Foucault (1926–84)—that our thoughts about human behavior, our statements about the nature of man, and in fact all ideas of whatever kind are nothing more or less than assertions of power. (We will return to Foucault at greater length in the chapter on Queer Studies, which Foucault helped shape, and which, in the form of Queer Theory, has in turn infiltrated all the other "identity studies" to a greater or lesser degree.)

At the same time, humanities professors, envious of the certitude that their colleagues in the natural and social sciences were able to attain as the result of research, began to impose upon the humanities a "research ideal" that was at odds with the traditional essence of the humanities—thereby, in Kronman's words, "trad[ing] a valuable and distinctive authority for one based upon values they can never hope to realize to anything like the degree their colleagues in the natural and social sciences" could. As the traditional modes of contemplating the meaning of life were abandoned, moreover, they were replaced by New Left politics and by a relativistic, nihilistic mode of thought that denied the very reality of aesthetic merit and objective truth. The very values that the humanities had previously exalted were now disparaged as weapons in an ongoing struggle by straight white Western males to retain power, preserve oppression, and keep capitalist, imperialist, and colonialist systems in place.

Once, the humanities had been concerned with the true, the good, and the beautiful; now they were preoccupied with an evil triumvirate of isms—colonialism, imperialism, capitalism—and with a three-headed monster of victimhood: class, race, and gender oppression. Once, the purpose of the humanities had been to introduce students to the glories of Western civilization, thought, and art—to enhance students' respect, even reverence, for the cultural heritage of the West; now the humanities sought to unmask the West as a perpetrator of injustice around the globe. Once, the great poets, authors, philosophers, historians, and artists of the Western canon had been heroes whose portraits and statues adorned university campuses; now they were to be viewed with a jaundiced eye—for most of them were, after all, Dead

White Heterosexual Males, and therefore, by definition, members of an oppressive Establishment.

As the post-sixties era wore on, deconstruction proved to be the harbinger of a much larger and more amorphous creature called Theory, which addressed itself not only to literary works but to texts of all kinds as well as to every imaginable variety of cultural phenomenon, high or low—TV sitcoms, roller derby, line dancing, porn—and which, drawing on a range of ideas from sociology, anthropology, linguistics, and political philosophy, was fixated on the idea that texts were unstable. Yet despite its heady pedigree, it must be said that the use of the word *theory* to describe what humanities professors have been practicing for the last generation or so is wildly misleading: what these professors are doing is not theoretical in any remotely scientific sense; what they are doing, rather, is pulling handfuls of jargon out of an ideological grab bag and tossing them at whatever cultural or artistic phenomenon they are pretending to analyze.

The point of this activity, which is not unlike slapping a political sticker on a signpost, is not to tease out the secrets of artistic mastery but simply to "prove"—repetitively, endlessly—certain facile, reductive, and invariably left-wing points about the nature of power and oppression. In this new version of the humanities, all of Western civilization is not analyzed through the use of reason or judged according to aesthetic standards that have been developed over centuries; rather, it is viewed through prisms of race, class, and gender, and is hailed or condemned in accordance with certain political checklists.

The result is what John M. Ellis, author of *Against Deconstruction*, calls the "theory cult," whose members, he suggests, can be recognized "not by their analytical skill but by the standardized qualities of their attitudes," and who in all their "work" go "through similar motions to come to similar conclusions." "Theory," Ellis contends, is not "about exploration but about conformity," and its arcane language "identifies those who speak it as insiders and those who do not as old-fashioned outsiders who lack the required level of sophistication" even as it "serves as a protective device in that its remoteness from ordinary speech camouflages triviality or absurdity." Ellis notes that the "titles of conference papers" by members of the theory cult "are full of verbal tricks and gyrations"—though, as we shall see in the course of this book, one might more correctly say that they offer endless variations on the same old tired verbal tricks and gyrations. As Patai and Wilfrido Corral point out in *Theory's Empire*, the practitioners of Theory "have managed to adopt just about every defect in writing that George Orwell identified in his 1946 essay 'Politics and the English Language.'"

*   *   *

One of the leading critics of postmodern humanities education is Alan Charles Kors, a veteran professor of history at the University of Pennsylvania who specializes in seventeenth- and eighteenth-century intellectual history and is the editor of the monumental four-volume *History of the Enlightenment*. Kors is also the cofounder of the Foundation for Individual Rights in Education (FIRE), an organization whose declared mission is "to defend and sustain individual rights at America's colleges and universities." When, over lunch in Philadelphia in the spring of 2010, I asked him which books, in his view, had most influenced the way in which the humanities are taught today, he answered readily, saying that three specific works were responsible "nearly in toto" for the political mentality that undergirds the humanities today: Antonio Gramsci's *Prison Notebooks*; Paulo Freire's *Pedagogy of the Oppressed*; and Frantz Fanon's *The Wretched of the Earth*. In order to get a clearer picture of the way today's humanities students are being taught to think, it will be useful to take a brief look at each of these works.

Born in 1891, Antonio Gramsci was a Sardinian Marxist who cofounded the Italian Communist Party in 1921 and was imprisoned by Mussolini from 1926 to 1934. (He died in 1937.) The thirty-three notebooks he kept during his years behind bars are his principal legacy. He is especially celebrated for his introduction of the concept of hegemony, which occupies a central place in the humanities today. Hegemony is an extremely useful notion for critics of democratic capitalism, because it enables them to make that system sound worse than totalitarian dictatorship.

The premise is this. In a country such as those run by Stalin and

Hitler during Gramsci's own lifetime, government power is palpable, explicit, naked. It is clear that the people living under such a system are not free. In a country like today's United States, by contrast, people think they *are* free. But according to Gramsci, that freedom is an illusion. They, too, are oppressed. The difference is that the power that keeps them in line is invisible. Indeed, to a large extent the people themselves are the unconscious instruments of their own oppression—for they have unwittingly internalized, and unwittingly obey, the unwritten rules by which their supposedly free society operates. This unseen structure of power, in Gramsci's view, is even more potent than the structures of power in a totalitarian dictatorship, precisely because its invisibility makes it harder to recognize and therefore harder to resist. Thus people living in America today are even less free than were the people who lived in the Soviet Union under Stalin.

The inanity of all this is obvious. America has no death camps, no secret police arresting enemies of the people in the middle of the night and spiriting them away to places where they are tortured, held clandestinely for years, and/or executed without trial. But the patent absurdity of Gramsci's concept did not prevent post-sixties humanities professors from making it a centerpiece of their political philosophies. The idea of hegemony provided American professors with a language in which to denounce the democratic West, and especially America, as the very essence of evil—this at a time when the gulags were still in business and Mao was murdering millions.

On to Paulo Freire, who was born in 1921 in Recife, Brazil, studied law and philosophy, and then worked, in turn, as a teacher of underprivileged children, a government official, and a university administrator. In the latter capacity, he organized a program to teach illiterate laborers to read and write, an act for which he was imprisoned. After his release, he lived in Bolivia and Chile and worked for the United Nations. *Pedagogy of the Oppressed*, published in 1968, brought him international renown. In 1980, after stints at Harvard and with the World Council of Churches, he returned to his homeland, where he became active in the Workers' Party and ended up as secretary of education for the city of São Paolo. He died in 1997 but remains a major influence on pedagogy throughout the Western world.

In an incisive 2009 essay for *City Journal*, education expert

Sol Stern sums up Freire's doleful impact on American education, noting that since the 1970 appearance of *Pedagogy of the Oppressed* in English, the book "has achieved near-iconic status in America's teacher-training programs." It is "one of the most frequently assigned texts" in "Philosophy of Education" courses at top education schools; when Stern met recently with participants in the New York Teaching Fellows program, he found that *Pedagogy of the Oppressed*; was "the one book that the fellows had to read in full." To read this alleged classic of education is a stunning experience—for it turns out to be nothing but one long stretch of Marxist agitprop that has nothing useful whatsoever to say about actual teaching. As Stern observes, it

> mentions none of the issues that troubled educa-tion reformers throughout the twentieth century: testing, standards, curriculum, the role of parents, how to organize schools, what subjects should be taught in various grades, how best to train teachers, the most effective way of teaching disadvantaged students. This ed-school bestseller is, instead, a Utopian political tract calling for the overthrow of capitalist hegemony and the creation of classless societies. Teachers who adopt its pernicious ideas risk harming their students—and ironically, their most disadvantaged students will suffer the most.

Indeed, Freire rejects conventional education as, in his own words, a process of "narration" and a "practice of domination" in which students are obliged to "memorize mechanically the narrated content" and are encouraged to think of themselves in an "individ-ualistic" way and not "as members of an oppressed class." Freire's world is one populated solely by the "oppressors" and the "oppressed," and in his book he does little more than insist repeatedly that the "oppressed" should not actually be *taught*, in the old-fashioned sense, but should rather be helped to recognize their own "oppression" and encouraged to resist it.

In short, they should be subjected to what in the 1960s went by the name of consciousness-raising. Freire also insists repeatedly that "the pedagogy of the oppressed...must be forged *with*, not *for*, the oppressed...in the incessant struggle to regain their humanity"; that both teachers and students must be "simultaneously teachers *and* students"; and that a "revolutionary leader" (for at some point in the book, he ceases, for the most part, to label the figures he is talking about "teachers" and "students" and instead begins talking about revolutionary leaders and the revolution's foot soldiers) should be not a "master" but a "comrade." Needless to say, what Freire is talking about here is not pedagogy but propagandizing—intellectuals "teaching" the masses about the latter's own lives and "liberating" them from their "false perception," thereby turning the students into "Subjects [which Freire capitalizes] of the transformation."

What Freire has to offer, then, is a program not of education, or of liberal reform, but of indoctrination in the name of revolutionary "liberation." He defends violence and terror by redefining them: oppression itself, he argues, is violence and terror; for the oppressed to resist it actively, in however bloody a manner, does not constitute violence or terror, for "[v]iolence is initiated by those who oppress" and "[i]t is not the helpless...who initiate terror" but their oppressors. His book is packed with words that have become familiar slogans in the humanities today: *dialogue, communication, solidarity.* He is an open admirer of Lenin, whom he approvingly cites to the effect that "[w]ithout a revolutionary theory there can be no revolutionary movement."

He is also a fan of Mao: it is no coincidence that his book— published in the midst of China's Cultural Revolution, during which countless practitioners of traditional pedagogy were murdered— emphasizes the importance of "cultural revolution." (Indeed, Freire explicitly hails Mao's actions, which, he makes clear, are consistent with his own "educational" program.) Freire likewise celebrates Fidel Castro, calling "Castro and his comrades...an eminently dialogical leadership group" who "identified with the people who endured the brutal violence of the Batista dictatorship." The Cuban Revolution, Freire writes,

> required bravery on the part of the leaders to
> love the people sufficiently to be willing to sacri-

fice themselves for them. It required courageous witness by the leaders to recommence after each disaster, moved by undying hope in a future victory which (because forged together *with* the people) would belong not to the leaders alone, but to the leaders *and* the people.

And let's not forget Che Guevara, whom Freire quotes at reverential length, eulogizing the bloodthirsty Argentinean for his "*communion* with the people," his "almost evangelical language," and his "deep capacity for love and communication." Freire does note that Guevara's own experience showed that some oppressed people's "natural fear of freedom may lead them to denounce the revolutionary leaders" and even to desert or "betray...the cause," and that Guevara "recogniz[ed] the necessity of punishing the deserter in order to preserve the cohesion and discipline of the group." This would seem to be Freire's euphemistic way of acknowledging Guevara's mass execution of those whom he considered insufficiently attentive "students" of his "pedagogy."

As Stern points out, Freire's "declaration in *Pedagogy of the Oppressed* that there 'was no such thing as a neutral education' became a mantra for leftist professors" of the 1970s and thereafter "who could use it to justify proselytizing for America-hating causes in the college classroom." Even the literary critic Gerald Graff, a star of the PC academy and certainly no conservative, has deplored Freire's influence, asking: "What right do we have to be the self-appointed political conscience of our students?" Stern underscores one irony: that Freire's approach to education hasn't been taken up at all by his "favorite revolutionary regimes, like China and Cuba," where "the brightest students are controlled, disciplined, and stuffed with content knowledge for the sake of national goals—and the production of more industrial managers, engineers, and scientists." No; only in the West have students been led down Freire's primrose path.

Then there's Frantz Fanon. Born in Martinique in 1925, Fanon became a psychiatrist, worked in Algeria during the rebellion against the French, and died of leukemia in 1961 in a Washington, D.C., hospital. *The Wretched of the Earth* was published that same year with a preface by Jean-Paul Sartre, who sums up the book's basic dichotomy: over here the people of the West, who are by definition colonizers and therefore evil, and over there the non-Western "natives," who are by definition exploited colonists and are therefore virtuous.

This tidy world picture ignores the fact that many Western nations have never been colonial powers and that many non-Western nations have. Fanon's worldview leaves no room for, say, non-Western powers that have sold people into slavery or oppressed women. Indeed his ideas about European imperialism and non-Western colonial subjects, and of the relationship between the two, are based entirely on his experiences in Algeria, which are not necessarily representative of anything. Yet he serves up a book full of generalizations that are plainly meant to apply to *every* colonial or postcolonial situation. In his world, Western "settlers" are always aggressors, non-Western "natives" always victims.

He makes ludicrous blanket statements about revolution, idealistically predicting that non-Western "natives" who carry out wars of "liberation" from Western colonial powers will then proceed to establish harmonious governments in which they will not allow themselves to be oppressed by their own, for they will have learned better: "When the people have taken violent part in the national liberation they will allow no one to set themselves up as 'liberators.' They [will] take good care not to place their future, their destinies or the fate of their country in the hands of a living god." He further assures us that "[t]he African people and indeed all under-developed peoples, contrary to common belief, very quickly build up a social and political consciousness." Indeed, after a revolution by the non-Western colonial subjects of Western powers, "the people [will] join in the new rhythm of the nation, in their mud huts and in their dreams. Under their breath and from their hearts' core they [will] sing endless songs of praise to the glorious fighters." They will, furthermore, "proceed in an atmosphere of solemnity to cleanse and purify the face of the nation.... In a veritable collective ecstasy, families which have always been traditional enemies [will] decide to rub out old scores and to forgive and forget. There [will be] numerous reconciliations. Long-buried but unforgettable hatreds [will be] brought to life once more, so that they may more surely be rooted out." It is curious that while the history of postcolonial Africa has proved Fanon's predictions spectacularly wrong, he continues to be regarded in the West as an oracle.

Like Freire, moreover, Fanon writes sympathetically about the violence of "natives," arguing that it

> constitutes their only work, invests their characters with positive and creative qualities. The practice of violence binds them together as a whole, since each individual forms a violent link in the great chain, a part of the great organism of violence which has surged upwards in reaction to the settler's violence in the beginning.... At the level of individuals, violence is a cleansing force. It frees the native from his inferiority complex and from his despair and inaction; it makes him fearless and restores his self-respect.

Fanon also shares Freire's high regard for Castro, who, he writes, "took over power in Cuba, and gave it to the people." America, he laments, "has decided to strangle the Cuban people mercilessly. But this will be difficult. The people will suffer, but they will conquer." Such empty sloganeering is ubiquitous in *The Wretched of the Earth*.

Far from encouraging the creation of wealth and stability by building up a middle class in former colonies, Fanon insists that "it is absolutely necessary to oppose vigorously and definitively the birth of a national bourgeoisie and a privileged caste." Indeed, he calls for the stamping out of whatever bourgeoisie does exist "because, literally, it is good for nothing"—it "express[es] its mediocrity in its profits, its achievements and in its thought" and "tries to hide this mediocrity...by chromium plating on big American cars, by holidays on the Riviera and week-ends in neon-lit nightclubs." That's right—Fanon calls not for *expanding* the bourgeoisie but for destroying it, because "the bourgeois phase in the history of under-developed countries is a completely useless phase," and "[r] ich people...are nothing more than flesh-eating animals, jackals and vultures which wallow in the people's blood."

Fanon's prescription for postcolonial society echoes Freire's: "We ought to uplift the people; we must develop their brains, fill them with ideas, change them and make them into human beings.... [P]olitical education means opening their minds, awakening them, and allowing the birth of their intelligence; as [leftist Martinican writer Aimé] Césaire said, it is 'to invent souls.'" In short, non-Westerners are not "human beings" and do not have "souls" until "we"—the *good* Westerners—fill their heads with political philosophy. Fanon does not hide the fact that he is talking here about indoctrination in left-wing collectivist ideology: "the leaders of the ring realize that the various groups must be enlightened; that they must be educated and indoctrinated; and that an army and a central authority must be created."

The fantasy-spinning continues: "The masses should know that the government and the party are at their service.... Nobody, neither leader nor rank-and-file, can hold back the truth. The search for truth in local attitudes is a collective affair." And: "The nation does not exist except in a programme which has been worked out by revolutionary leaders and taken up with full understanding and enthusiasm by the masses." It is striking to read this dangerous drivel—so thoroughly disconnected from reality—alongside somebody like Orwell, who was a genuine student of human nature and who recognized the catastrophic foolishness of such delusions.

Gramsci, Freire, Fanon: these three men's influence on the teaching of the humanities today has been nothing less than a disaster. They've infected it with contempt for the West, which is identified not with freedom and prosperity but with capitalism, colonialism, and imperialism—all of which are seen as unmitigated evils. Meanwhile left-wing collectivist systems, however horrendous their track records, are presented as worthy of admiration. (It is common in the humanities today to refer, as Fanon does, not to "democracy" and "Communism" but to "capitalism" and "socialism.")

Whereas American humanities education once focused on introducing students to the great achievements of Western civilization and to the universal values that make it unique in human history, the goal now is to discredit the West's legacy. In humanities departments today, it is an article of faith that all civilizations are equal—except for Western civilization, which, students learn, is unique only in the degree of its greed, brutality, and lust for power. There are, of course, dozens of other figures—most of them European, many of them French, and nearly all of them, curiously, members of that otherwise discredited species, the Dead White Male—who have exercised a major influence upon the humanities today. We can begin with the fathers of social science, Karl Marx and Max Weber (author of *The Protestant Ethic and the Spirit of Capitalism*) in Germany and Émile Durkheim in France, the latter two being the founders of sociology; and with the Hungarian Marxist Georg Lukács. A group of several German Marxists who thrived between the world wars and who are called the "Frankfurt School" because of their association with the Frankfurt Institute of Social Research—among them Max Horkheimer; Theodor Adorno; Walter Benjamin, author of the influential essay "The Work of Art in the Age of Mechanical Reproduction"; and Herbert Marcuse ("father of the New Left"), an idol of both Abbie Hoffman and Angela Davis who lived to support the Viet Cong—had an immense impact on postmodern literary criticism.

There are other important Marxists, such as Louis Althusser and Frederic Jameson, as well as several writers who are categorized as structuralists (though some later graduated to poststructuralists) because of their preoccupation with the idea of language as a system of signs: Ferdinand de Saussure, the germinal Swiss semiotician who introduced the popular terms *signified* and *signifier*; Claude Lévi-Strauss, the French father of modern anthropology; the psychologist Jacques Lacan; and the French author Roland Barthes, who in *Mythologies* set out to expose what he saw as bourgeois cultural myths. And then there are the poststructuralists, who moved beyond the basic structuralist preoccupation with signs in a variety of directions—among them Derrida, who invented deconstruction, and Foucault and Judith Butler, with whom we will spend some time later. There is no need at this point to examine most of these writers' work in detail, or to isolate at length the wide-ranging, and invariably abstruse, ways in which each of them affected the humanities in our time. But there are two men, both Americans (of a sort, anyway), whose role in reshaping the teaching of the humanities we should pause over.

One of them is Edward Said (1935–2003), whose major contribution to the humanities today can be summed up in a single word: *Orientalism*. His 1978 book of that name made Said—who grew up in an affluent Cairo family and later, as a longtime member of the Columbia University faculty, identified himself as a Palestinian—an academic superstar. His book's thesis is relatively straightforward: that Westerners' perceptions of Oriental cultures have been shaped almost entirely by generations of Western "experts" who viewed those cultures through Western eyes and whose accounts of them were therefore colored by prejudice and condescension. These "experts," according to Said, fostered certain romantic, patronizing notions of Oriental cultures that in turn were used to justify colonialism and oppression. Said argued that instead of listening to these "experts," however knowledgeable, Westerners eager to know the truth about Oriental cultures should listen to Oriental peoples themselves.

Said's book caused an upheaval in the study of Oriental cultures, especially the Arabic and Muslim cultures of the Middle and Near East. In one fell swoop, it scrapped the credibility of distinguished scholars who had encyclopedic knowledge of those cultures. It also had the effect of silencing criticism by Western academics of even the most egregious aspects of those cultures—for what Western readers took away from *Orientalism* was the conviction that *any* criticism by a Westerner of *any* aspect of a non-Western culture was, by its very nature, illegitimate. Instead of thinking critically about other cultures—that is to say, judging them by Western standards—Westerners should approach even their most disturbing attributes with humility and respect, seeking to understand and sympathize.

The argument of *Orientalism* lies at the foundation of two insidious and interlocking postmodern disciplines: Postcolonial Studies, which purports to examine the lingering legacy of Western colonialism in various non-Western societies, and Subaltern Studies, which focuses more narrowly on the postcolonial societies of South Asia.

The word *subaltern*, which was used by Gramsci to describe people oppressed because of their membership in some group or other, was given new prominence by the India-born and largely U.S.-educated Columbia professor Gayatri Chakravorty Spivak in a founding document of postcolonialism, the 1988 essay "Can the Subaltern Speak?" One of Spivak's major arguments, which has been endlessly recycled in the contemporary humanities, is that when we choose to tell the "real" truth about an oppressed group we run the danger of "essentialism"—that is, of overgeneralizing about the group in question and thereby ignoring the fact that some members of that group, being at the same time members of *other* groups, experience their own special kinds of oppression that should not be overlooked. Repetitive hand-wringing about this alleged problem constitutes a very large proportion of the "work" done throughout the humanities today.

I will not focus at length in this book on Postcolonial or Subaltern Studies, but it is worth pointing out here that all sorts of countries have been colonies and colonized, and the effect of colonialism on colonies has not always been entirely negative. Yet Postcolonial and Subaltern Studies attend exclusively to Western colonizers of non-Western colonies and consistently view this colonialism as negative, indeed evil, painting all colonizers with the same brush. The supposed purpose of Postcolonial and Subaltern Studies is to give voice to the formerly colonized, who are seen by definition as having been silenced under the colonizers' sway. This unsilencing supposedly entails washing away as fully as possible the traces of the colonizer and allowing the authentic but long-suppressed voice of the colonized, or subaltern, to ring out—although in fact the most justly celebrated postcolonial authors (such as V. S. Naipaul) have plainly profited by their study of the colonizers' literature and, more broadly, by their education in the colonizers' culture.

What Said has done for the Western study of Arabic and Islamic cultures, Howard Zinn (1922–2010) has done for the study of American history. In the 1997 film *Good Will Hunting*, one sign of the supposedly nonconformist brilliance of the eponymous hero, a drastically underachieving, emotionally troubled young janitor at MIT played by Matt Damon, is his enthusiasm for Zinn's 1980 book *A People's History of the United States*. "If you want to read a real history book," Damon's character spits out at one point, "read Howard Zinn's *A People's History of the United States*. That book will knock you on your ass." The implication here is that Zinn's book is obscure and noncanonical, the kind of book only an offbeat genius would know about. In fact it is the most influential history of America in our time, selling more than a hundred thousand copies every year. It is virtually impossible to visit an American university bookstore without running across high stacks of copies of Zinn's book on the shelves of required reading for history courses.

As with Said's *Orientalism*, the thesis of *A People's History of the United States* is relatively straightforward: namely, everything they told you is a lie, or at best a half-truth. American history, according to Zinn, is nothing to be proud of; on the contrary, it is nothing more than one long, disgraceful record of oppression, genocide, and exploitation. Zinn, a Marxist, did a magnificent job of selectively telling the story of America in such a way as to make it look, indeed, like a trail of horrors. For students with little or no knowledge of history, American or otherwise, Zinn's book is dangerously powerful propaganda.

What Zinn never tells his innocent young readers is that every country's past is full of horrors, and that as the histories of countries go, America's is, in fact, extremely admirable and inspiring. Eager as Zinn is to catalog America's sins, he is equally eager to dodge the fact that what sets America apart is not its transgressions but its readiness and ability to face up to them, clean up its act, and become more faithful to its founding principles. America had slavery, but so did (and do) many other countries; what makes America special is that it fought one of the bloodiest wars in human history to *free* its slaves. America's abiding offense is racism, for which it was routinely attacked by European intellectuals for generations; yet in 2009 America—to the astonishment of European critics in whose eyes American racism was an incurable chronic disorder—became the first Western country to have a black head of state or government. Zinn is a fierce enemy of capitalism, the sins of which he itemizes tirelessly, but he's equally fierce in his admiration of Marx and Lenin, the fruits of whose ideas—Russia's gulag, Mao's Cultural Revolution—he is careful to leave all but entirely off his readers' radar.

Indeed, both Said and Zinn make a point of dropping down the memory hole the very best attributes of America—those that not only have made America the freest and most prosperous nation in human history, but also have positively transformed much of the rest of the world—while also deep-sixing the monstrous reality of communism. America's Declaration of Independence and Constitution articulated ideas about individual liberty, human rights, and equality that have reshaped human civilization, and America's example of standing up to one form of totalitarianism after another in the name not only of Americans' but of other people's liberty has inspired men and women around the world, bringing to its shores generation after generation of freedom-loving immigrants; but when Said and Zinn allude to these facts, it is only to mock them as sentimental lies.

One of the pillars of "Theory," and indeed of all postmodern busy-work, is a sociological concept that goes by the name of social constructionism. This concept places language at the center of everything, insisting that language is always and intrinsically unstable and that it plays a far more crucial role in life than has ever been recognized. Building on this proposition, social constructionism argues that many aspects of human experience that we ordinarily think of as parts of nature are in reality human constructions, brought into being by the act of naming, and that the primary goal of pedagogy should be to expose this fact and to identify the invariably nefarious reasons why these constructions have been put into place. To put it a bit differently, social constructionism, in essence, exaggerates to the point of absurdity a valid, simple, and commonsensical observation: namely, that some concepts are so much a part of everyday life that we can easily make the mistake of thinking of them as if they're as natural as the sun, moon, and stars—even though they are, in fact, human inventions, products of the imagination. One example is the concept of money; another is the concept of "king" or "president."

This is an uncomplicated observation and can also be a useful one. What social constructionism does is to push it farther—exactly how far varies from one social constructionist to another. Some very influential members of the breed take it so far as to argue that certain phenomena that most of us, on reflection, would identify as part of nature, and not merely social constructions, simply did not exist before they were named—so that, for example, there was no such thing as homosexuality before the word *homosexual* was coined in the late 1800s, no anthrax before Pasteur, and no battered babies until that term was first used in 1962. (Daphne Patai and Noretta Koertge, in their 1994 book, *Professing Feminism*, attribute these latter two convictions to the French sociologist Bruno Latour and the Canadian philosopher Ian Hacking respectively.)

There are other concepts that figure prominently in the humanities today, and that will consequently figure in this book. Here are some of the more important ones:

- NEOLIBERALISM: After the Berlin Wall came down, some Western academics began to feel a bit self-conscious about condemning capitalism. So instead they started condemning "neoliberalism." Or, sometimes, "market fundamentalism," "consumer culture," "corporatist culture," or "brand-name culture." What is being condemned here? Answer: individual liberty, free markets, privatization, deregulation, and minimal intervention by the state in private affairs.

- GAZE: Postmodernism, especially when it takes the form of identity studies, has taken from Jean-Paul Sartre a preoccupation with the "gaze." The idea is that when another person—the "Other"—looks at you, you're suddenly aware of yourself as the object of that person's thoughts, which are out of your control; as a result, instead of feeling free to define yourself, you may experience that person's "gaze" as exerting power over you, redefining you, robbing you of your right to define yourself. You may even, Sartre argued, feel "enslaved" by the Other's gaze. In identity studies, such logic is often used to depict harmless glances as despotic acts.

- PROBLEMATIZE: One problem with *problematize* is that definitions vary considerably. Foucault said problematization was the "totality of discursive and non-discursive practices that introduces something into the play of the true and false and constitute[s] it as an object for thought (whether in the form of moral reflection, scientific knowledge, political analysis, etc.)." Many use the word in such a way as to suggest that it means "to frame a matter or situation in such a way as to expose inherent problems in it that are not immediately obvious." In 2000, a contributor to a Women's Studies message board attempted to illustrate the proper use of the word by saying that to "problematize reproductive choice," for instance, is to ask: "What *are* the sociopolitical/economic conditions that surround the emergence of the concept called 'choice'?" Other message board contributors suggested that in most contexts *problematize* could be replaced, without any significant loss in meaning, with *discuss*.

- INTERROGATE: Traditional readers read books; postmodernists interrogate texts. The idea is that a literary work should not be regarded with unthinking respect and awe, but should rather be approached as if it were a suspect brought in for questioning. The fallacious premise here, of course, is that before postmodernism, nobody read critically or analytically. (One can also, by the way, speak of "interrogating" a concept.) This word, too, can often be replaced with *discuss*.

- DESTABILIZE: Postmodernists view all forms of discourse prior to postmodernism as being fixed and stable—or as being characterized by an illusion of fixity and stability. In their view, all texts are in fact unstable, incomplete, and ultimately unknowable, as is the world they purport to represent; in their own texts, they seek to underscore these attributes—to frustrate any expectation of, and dispel any illusion of, stability, either in other texts or in the world around them. The premise is that by destabilizing texts, one can keep the reader alert to the instability, uncertainty, and unknow-ability of absolutely everything.

- INTERVENTION: Critics don't just write about a text or art work or topic anymore—they *intervene* in it, a word used because it takes the focus off the work and puts it on the critic, and because it makes it sound as if the critic is actu-ally bringing about some kind of change. When the jacket copy for a recent book of academic criticism described it as "an important intervention in contemporary linguistic and semiotic debate," "intervention in" essentially meant "contri-bution to." Of course, *intervene*, like *problematize* and *inter-rogate*, can also usually be replaced with *discuss*.

- REIFICATION: Reification is kind of like abstraction, only in the other direction—in other words, it means viewing (intentionally or not) or treating (deliberately or not) an abstract concept as if it were a material object, or a human creation as a part of nature. The term, which was popular with Marx, Lukács, and the Frankfurt School, is obviously popular with social constructionists, since they're preoc-cupied with the difference between the natural and the man-made.

There is, needless to say, a lot more jargon where this came from, some of which will come up along the way.

In the age of secular humanism, students were encouraged think crit-ically and speak for themselves as individuals, to find their own paths in life and form their own tastes, values, and sensibilities. In the post-modern humanities, every person is, by virtue of accidents of sex, skin color, and sexual orientation, a member of a group for whom the rich, delicate complexities of life are reduced to pseudoscientific rhetoric about oppression, collective grievances, experiences of victimhood, and hegemonic power. Indeed, humanities students today learn that all of life is about power, whether economic, political, or social. In today's world, they're told, the West holds all the cards (the humanities establishment has yet to acknowledge that this is less and less true), and in the West, straight white men hold all the cards (never mind the post-sixties institutionalization of preferences at almost every level of society for almost everybody *but* straight white men).

The chief objective of the humanities now is to use "Theory" to uncover the workings of that power, the better to combat it in the name of those groups that are purportedly oppressed. This has proved to be a slippery slope. Once humanities professors decided to embrace a notion of the humanities that had at its center the thesis that straight white Western men are all oppressors, and that all others are victims, the door opened to any number of humanities "disciplines" purporting to address, and redress, the supposed silencing of an increasingly wide range of victim groups. After blacks came women and Latinos, then gays, transsexuals, the disabled, the overweight, and so forth. These and other self-identified victim groups are now the subjects of their own academic fields, which may be said to straddle the humanities and social sciences. Rooted in movements—the civil rights movement, the women's movement—that were, at least at the outset, reasonable efforts to secure equal rights, these fields of "study" became possessed by a narrow, irrational fixation on alleged patterns of hegemonic power and oppression. The words *race*, *gender*, and *class*, the holy trinity of humanities studies in our time, are especially crucial in these identity studies disciplines. Much of what is said and written in these fields consists of little more than the ritual recital of these words, the incessant assertion of the paramount importance of these three so-called "categories of analysis." In every form of identity studies, there are books and articles aplenty in which concern about these categories is endlessly articulated. Recent years have seen the publication of such titles as *Race, Class, and Gender: An Anthology; Race, Class, and Gender in the United States; Experiencing Race, Class, and Gender in the United States; Gender, Race, and Class in Media; Inequality: Classic Readings in Race, Class, and Gender; The Inequality Reader: Contemporary and Foundational Reading in Race, Class, and Gender; Invisible Privilege: A Memoir about Race, Class, and Gender; Social Stratification: Class,*

Race, and Gender in Sociological Perspective; *Prejudice: Attitudes about Race, Class, and Gender*. Sometimes *sexuality* or *sexual orientation* is added to the triad: *Understanding Race, Class, Gender, and Sexuality*; *Understanding Diversity: An Introduction to Class, Race, Gender, and Sexual Orientation*; *The Social Construction of Difference and Inequality: Race, Class, Gender, and Sexuality*.

When any two or more of these "categories of analysis" come together, you're dealing with something called *intersectionality*. Part of the idea of intersectionality is that when you're "analyzing" oppression, it's important not to isolate one category but to look at all of them so that you can see how the different forms of oppression work together. This is the thrust of such recent books as *The Intersectional Approach: Transforming the Academy Through Race, Class, and Gender*; *The Intersection of Race, Class, and Gender*; *Identities and Inequalities: Exploring the Intersections of Race, Class, Gender, and Sexuality*; and *Emerging Intersections: Race, Class, and Gender in Theory, Policy, and Practice*. The way in which academics today think about intersection is illustrated neatly by Paula Rothenberg, author of *Race, Class, and Gender in the United States*, who writes that "[m]any of us have come to understand that talking about gender without talking about race and class or talking about race without bringing in class and gender is simply another way of obscuring reality instead of coming to terms with it. Many of us have come to believe that using race, class, and gender simultaneously as categories for analyzing reality provides us, at least at this historical moment, with the most adequate and comprehensive understanding of why things occur and whose interests they serve." Flip through the most popular humanities and social science textbooks, anthologies, and journals published in the last couple of decades and you will find countless variations on these two sentences.

A key tenet of intersectionality is that the oppression experienced by someone who is the object of more than one kind of oppression (say, a black lesbian) is worse, and more complicated, than that experienced by someone who is the object of only one kind (such as a gay white man, a straight black man, or a straight white woman). Being oppressed for one's identity as black, female, and gay, in other words, is more than just the sum of three different oppressions; it is a distinct experience that needs to be described and understood on its own terms. While much of the rhetoric in the humanities today consists of ritual reiterations of the importance of race, class, and gender, much of it also consists of ritual assertions of the importance of intersectionality—or ritual complaints about an insufficient attention to intersectionality.

For example, at a session called "Bodies in Question" at the 2010 conference of the National Women's Studies Association, one participant worried aloud that Queer Studies "deemphasizes the importance of race." Another fretted that "white queers" don't think enough about how their whiteness informs their notion of queerness. A third complained that "texts addressing issues of race in Queer Studies are marginalized." Panelists and audience members spoke of "the critique of whiteness in Queer Studies," "the intersecting nature of oppression," and "the multiple ways in which people are oppressed." It was observed that "white people can position themselves as oppressed" without recognizing the privilege they enjoy on account of their race. "It is important," we were told, for "queers" who are white "to recognize and interrogate" how their whiteness affects their view of what it means to be queer. In short, the same point was made over and over again, phrased in a multitude of ways, and everybody involved seemed to think that—or at least acted as if—complex ideas and fresh insights were being exchanged.

The mentality engendered by the academic preoccupation with victim groups is reflected in a statement by geographer Gillian Rose in her 1993 book, *Feminism and Geography*: "In the dominant culture of the West now, a white bourgeois heterosexual man is valued over a black working-class lesbian woman." Really? In employment decisions? In university admissions? Rose purports to be able to describe the way in which a "white bourgeois heterosexual man perceives other people who are not like him"—from his position of power, she says confidently, he views them "only in relation to himself." (Note that even as we are expected to accept that a white bourgeois heterosexual man is incapable of perceiving those who are unlike him except in relation to himself, we are expected at the same time to accept that Gillian Rose knows how all white bourgeois heterosexual men think.)

According to the mentality of an ideologically orthodox academic like Rose, all white bourgeois heterosexual men are by definition powerful, while those who are nonwhite, nonheterosexual, and nonmale are by definition powerless. While Rose feels "marginalized in geography as a woman," she feels obliged to apologize for being "empowered by my whiteness." She says that although she is a member of the academy, "I still do not feel part of it" because she is a woman with a working-class background who, as a student, never felt "quite as good as the confident bourgeois men (and often women) I studied with."

Rose is head of the Geography Department at the Open University and has taught at the universities of London and Edinburgh. And yet she genuinely seems to believe that while she enjoys a certain unfair power because of her race, this power is canceled out by her class and gender. In fact, unless the academic settings in which she has worked are bizarre exceptions to the rule, the truth is almost certainly the opposite. In the academy, members of supposed victim groups enjoy considerable privilege. And the more "oppressed" you supposedly are, the more privilege you receive.

On one level, Rose certainly realizes that as a professor at a major university she enjoys a good deal more power than most people—white, male, or whatever. But on another level she seems honestly to think that she is oppressed. So convinced is she of this that it would be useless to try to explain to her that this reduction of human relations to certain ultratidy notions of group oppression results in an outrageously crude picture of the world. If one felt obliged, for argument's sake, to accept her view that human relations are purely a matter of group power and group oppression, one might at least try to persuade her that plenty of people are oppressed—or ignored, mocked, or looked down upon—for reasons other than race, class, gender, or sexual orientation. What, for example, about the short, old, fat, and unattractive? What about those with psychiatric disorders, chronic illnesses, physical handicaps, mental retardation? What about the bald and bespectacled?

The list can go on and on. One would think that making this point would be a good way of getting people like Gillian Rose to stop thinking in terms of a handful of narrow categories and to look at human experience in a more complex, nuanced way, viewing every person as an individual and every situation on its own terms. No; what has happened is that, as a result of such observations, the number of approved "categories of analysis" has, quite simply, multiplied. So it is that we now have disciplines such as Fat Studies and Disability (or "Crip") Studies. One particularly striking aspect of a development like Crip Studies is that the language has come full circle. Over the years, beginning around the 1960s, the "correct" label for people with physical disabilities became increasingly "sensitive"—or, at least, that was the idea—and, at every stage, those who had failed to keep up with the latest advances in terminology were taken to task for their insensitivity. So it was that *crippled* gave way to *handicapped*, which gave way to *disabled*, which in turn gave way to terms like *physically challenged, differently abled*, and *handicapable*. But what happened then, at the end of this process? Academics "reclaimed" the word *cripple*, now shortened to *crip*—restoring to its place of honor the word that had previously been considered the ugliest way possible of describing the thing it refers to.

I have divided this book into chapters, each devoted to a different kind of identity studies. But it must be emphasized that in practice all of these things tend to blend into one another. All of them are preoccupied with race, gender, and class; being (for example) black and gay gives you extra points in Women's Studies, just as being female and black gives you extra points in Queer Studies. Some of these disciplines, moreover, aren't always focused on exactly what you expect them to be focused on: look, for instance, at the *Feminist Teacher Anthology*, a collection of essays from the journal *Feminist Teacher*, and you can get the impression that Women's Studies pays at least as much attention to homosexuality as to female gender; meanwhile, Queer Studies, as we shall see, is certainly more interested in "Queer Theory" than it is in homosexual orientation as such. Sometimes it can seem as if specifically gay-related material has been pushed out of Queer Studies by Queer Theory and has settled instead largely in Women's Studies, thereby, to a considerable extent, pushing out feminism, which, in turn, has bled out into Cultural Studies in a big way.

In the pages that follow I will be focusing on four "identity studies" that, taken together, give a good picture of what postmodernism has wrought in the humanities and social sciences: Women's Studies (also known as Gender Studies); Black Studies (which also goes by such names as Africana Studies and African American Studies); Queer Studies (not quite the same thing as Gay and Lesbian Studies); and Chicano Studies (nowadays usually called Chicana and Chicano Studies, or—no kidding—Chican@ Studies). I will also devote a separate chapter to several other "studies."

Stephen wants to have a house someday—a perfectly admirable ambition—yet has been taught to despise (or to profess to despise) his own dream. Mimi, though by all indications a beneficiary of every blessing twenty-first-century American life has to offer, has been imbued by her professors with a reflexive contempt for her country. And Michelle has learned all the Marxist jargon but would appear to be utterly clueless about the nightmarish reality of Marxist societies. These are the children of the revolution—the upheaval in humanities education that brought down the age of secular humanism in the university. Along with all their fellow students of various postmodern "studies," these young people have been shaped by teachers—or by the students of teachers— who, in their own time, were shaped by the radical politics of the 1960s. Indeed, many of those teachers *became* teachers precisely because they wanted to help form a new generation of Marxists, anticapitalists, and anti-Americans. Those teachers took on the higher education establishment of their day, with its distinctive approaches and curricula—and they won. What have they done with their victory? Here's what.

CHAPTER 2
Gilligan's Island: Women's Studies

The setting: Town Hall in New York City on the evening of April 30, 1971. The event: a debate about "Women's Liberation," occasioned by Norman Mailer s new book, *The Prisoner of Sex*, and featuring Mailer himself as moderator. His gruff, snarky opening remarks are followed by four talks in widely differing styles—an earnest, deadly dry presentation of the feminist ideology of the day by Jacqueline Ceballos, a commissar-like representative of the National Organization for Women; a barbed, witty attack on Mailer, the nuclear family, and much else (not to mention praise for Mao Zedong's "analysis of society") by the glamorous Australian author Germaine Greer, who's riding high with her bestselling *The Female Eunuch*, and whose irreverence and unabashed sexiness set her apart from other superstars of Women's Lib, a movement already notorious for its humorlessness; a sober, dispassionate analysis of seventies feminism by New York intellectual doyenne Diana Trilling, a voice for reason and pre-New Left liberalism; and *Village Voice* scribe Jill Johnston.

Johnston's contribution? Apparently channeling Gertrude Stein, she provides a dose of far-out performance art, telling the audience of upper-middle-class Manhattanites: "All women are lesbians except those who don't know it, naturally. They are but don't know it yet. I am a woman and therefore a lesbian. I am a woman who is a lesbian because I am a woman and a woman who loves herself naturally." Warning that "unless a woman be born again, she cannot see the Kingdom of Goddess," Johnston speaks of "the gay gay gayness of being gay" and describes lesbianism itself (not lesbian rights) as a movement: "Until all women are lesbians there can be no true political revolution." When Mailer cuts her off for exceeding her allotted time, Johnston joins two other women in a group hug and then a lusty roll on the floor. Mailer is irked: "Either play with the team or pick up your marbles and go home," he growls at Johnston. "Come on, Jill, be a lady." "What's the matter, Mailer," she snaps back, "you threatened because you got a woman you can't fuck?" "Hey, cunty," he replies, "I've been threatened all my life."

As the evening progresses, the salty language flows freely. One has a sense that at least some of the participants (excluding the ladylike Trilling) are having fun getting away with the use of gutter language at a respectable place like Town Hall, something that would have been unimaginable only a few years earlier. Indeed, you can cut the sixties atmosphere with a knife. Ceballos, Greer, and Johnston are plainly convinced that they're on the cutting edge of history, that they're in fact *making* history, preparing the ground for a social upheaval of extraordinary dimensions; they're also convinced that they are, in a word, oppressed. When Trilling, the voice of the older generation, disagrees with something Greer has said, the stunningly elegant Greer—the very picture of self-assured, jet-set privilege—purrs chidingly that "oppressed people always argue with each other" (to which Trilling neatly lobs back: "I don't feel as oppressed as you do"). Mailer, for his part, dismisses the feminists' line as "just old socialism": "It isn't just a simple matter of men tyrannizing women." Among those who take part in the Q&A are Betty Friedan, author of the Women's Lib manifesto *The Feminine Mystique*, and New York intellectuals Susan Sontag, Cynthia Ozick, and Elizabeth Hardwick, all eager to get in their two cents. Viewed on film forty years later, the spectacle of these people passionately exchanging ideas—and, for all the blue language and lesbian antics, there are, in fact, real ideas being exchanged here—constitutes a nostalgic reminder that there once was, indeed, such a thing as a New York intellectual scene, and that Mailer and his women were stars, of a sort, whose opinions actually mattered. Even forty years later, one can feel the electricity in the air, the rage, the sense that the entire social order is at stake: at several points, audience members jump to their feet, shout furiously at the stage, and stomp out.

For anybody who lived through the sixties, this debate, immortalized on celluloid under the title *Town Bloody Hall*, makes the whole moment in history come flooding back: Archie Bunker and *Maude*, "male chauvinists" and bra burners, Helen Reddy's hit-cum-anthem "I Am Woman" and the birth of the honorific (and magazine) *Ms.* Johnston's high jinks, meanwhile, underscore the fact that yesterday's shock is today's bore, and the failure of the participants to get their knickers in a twist over Mailer's deployment of the C-word reminds one that in 1971, for all the radicalism on display at events like this, today's familiar, reflexive PC constraints did not yet apply. (Nowadays, of course, Mailer's suggestion that Johnston act like "a lady" would be more than enough to arouse feminist ire.) Given all the passionate talk about oppression and equality by Greer, Sontag, and company, moreover, the twenty-first-century viewer of *Town Bloody Hall* cannot help noticing something that perhaps nobody even thought about that evening: every last one of the panelists and Q&A participants was white.

The setting: the Sheraton Denver Downtown Hotel on the morning of Thursday, November 11, 2010. It's the first day of the thirty-first annual conference of the National Women's Studies Association, which has dubbed this year's gathering "Difficult Dialogues II." (The 2009 conference, in Atlanta, was called "Difficult Dialogues.") Near the front of the program, which contains no fewer than 218 closely printed, double-column pages, is a statement of welcome by the association's outgoing president, Beverly Guy-Sheftall, who reminds us of the NWSA's commitment to "sharing the latest intersectional feminist scholarship" and to "building a vibrant multi-racial, multiethnic feminist community." Guy-Sheftall's face stares out from the page. She's black. Later in the program, there's a picture of the NWSA's incoming president, Bonnie Thornton Dill. She's black, too, and in addition to being the chair (not *chairman*, of course) of the Department of Women's Studies at the University of Maryland, she's the founding director of that institution's "Consortium on Race, Gender and Ethnicity." Closing the program, one notices that in the picture on the cover, which shows part of an enthusiastic audience at (one assumes) some earlier NWSA conclave, most of the faces are nonwhite.

Welcome to twenty-first-century feminism—and Women's Studies—in which the key word is *intersectionality*. Intersectionality is, to be sure, a key concept throughout identity studies nowadays, but nowhere does it play a bigger role than in Women's Studies. (In a vivid demonstration of this fact, all but one of the five main "session themes"—"Indigenous Feminisms," "Complicating the Queer," "The Politics of Nations," "'Outsider' Feminisms," and "The Critical and the Creative"—point away from women's rights itself.) This conference will go on for four days, each lasting from early morning to early evening, and will include a total of 349 sessions, often several dozen at a time, including panels, roundtables, workshops, and plenary sessions. Among the attractions are a large exhibit hall filled with elaborate displays by book publishers (some three dozen authors will be signing their books) and a "recovery/sharing room for those in recovery and/or coping with addictions." (For the duration, by the way, the Sheraton has graciously relabeled the men's rooms in the sprawling conference area as "gender-neutral.")

The sheer hugeness of this event serves as a powerful reminder that in the decades since that now quaint-seeming Town Hall debate, ground zero for feminism has shifted from the salons and auditoriums of New York (and perhaps one or two other metropolises) to campuses around the country. Indeed, Women's Studies is now by far the biggest of all identity studies. At the same time, however, it's the one that most often appears to have the least to do with its ostensible subject. To attend a Women's Studies convention is to feel lightyears removed from the laser-focused feminism of *Town Bloody Hall*—for in this brave new world, the once-singular imperative of universal sisterly solidarity has been diluted and distorted, complicated and compromised by a variety of postmodern impulses, such as Queer Theory, postcolonialism, and transnational feminism, as well as by a host of competing oppressions and victimol-ogies, so that the focus is often at least as much on race, class, and sexual orientation as on the battle of the sexes. The leading figures are not privileged white writers like Greer and Friedan but nonwhite, multidisciplinary academics like Gloria Anzaldúa (Queer, Cultural, Chicano) and bell hooks (Black), both of whom published books in 1981 that helped reorient the focus of Women's Studies: Anzaldúa's anthology *This Bridge Called My Back: Writings by Radical Women of Color* and hooks's *Ain't I a Woman?* "Feminism," wrote hooks in that book, serving up a definition that at once repudiated Greer, Friedan, and other pioneers and helped establish a new way of thinking, "is a commitment to eradicating the ideology of domination that perme-ates western culture on various levels—sex, race, and class...and a commitment to reorganizing society so that the self-development of people can take precedence over imperialism, economic expansion, and material desires." Note that this definition, while broadening feminism's topical concerns, also narrows its geographical bound-aries, excluding from its purview women in the non-Western world.

And let's not forget social constructionism, which figures in all identity studies but plays an especially significant role in Women's Studies—after all, a key tenet of the discipline is that gender itself is a social construction. But Women's Studies deploys social construc-tionism in a highly selective and self-serving way: as Patai and Koertge note, "It's as if everything they dislike about 'women' gets dismissed as social construction, while all the rest is the Real Thing. As for men, most everything about them is not socially constructed, since that would, in some sense, let them off the hook, so men get heavy doses of essentialist attributions while the students imagine they're espousing a straight constructionist line of analysis."

Foucault's notion of hegemony—the claim that power in a democracy like America is more potent than power in a dictatorship because it's invisible—is also a critical element of Women's Studies ideology. The irony is that while the power of the U.S. government is not, in fact, a good example of "hegemony" as described by Foucault, many Women's Studies programs are: on the surface, there's plenty of pretty rhetoric about women's mutual support and nurturing and openness to diversity; the underlying reality, however, is one of hardcore ideological indoctrination and enforcement. As one Women's Studies professor told Patai and Koertge,

> "feminist process" in the classroom winds up being...a push toward conformism and toward silencing dissent. It's all done under the rubric of being nice and open, and not being an authoritarian, old-fashioned type of teacher. But this winds up being tremendously more coercive. Because with authoritarian teachers you *know* they're being authoritarian, and you can resist. You know who's doing what to you. But the other way is manipulation, which is far worse than straight coercion, because students are being led someplace without any clarity as to whose accountable for what and who's leading them there.

You could hardly come up with a more nearly perfect description of Foucault-style hegemony.

It's striking how many of the NWSA session titles seem unrelated to feminism. Just take some of the queer-related topics, which include "Pushing the Limits of LGBT [Lesbian, Gay, Bisexual, and Transgender] Equality and Queer Theory," "Queer Meditations on Race and the Nation," "Queering the Middle Eastern Cyberscapes," "Queering Pop Culture," "Complicating Visibility: Recognizing Diverse Queer Identities," "Troubling Queer of Color Critiques," "Queer Performance and Spectatorship," "Fat and Queer Perspectives," "What Counts as Queer?," "Queering Queer Visibility," and "The Paradox of Queer in (De)Colonial Orientations." To understand exactly what Women's Studies is today, I will certainly have to dip my toe into those waters. But since I want to start off with something *echt* feminist, I choose to attend a panel titled "Beijing +15: Difficult Dialogues at the 54th Commission on the Status of Women." It's a roundtable of women, most of them quite young, who attended a recent United Nations "practicum in advocacy" that took place fifteen years after the Fourth World Conference on Women was held in Beijing. In all, there are seven participants, including the moderator, Sandra L. Spencer, an older woman who teaches at the University of North Texas.

The session turns out to be, in large part, a meditation on the state of feminism in the world today. Spencer introduces the proceedings with a few words in favor of "transnational solidarity" among women, but the first speaker, Minjon Tholen, a dark-skinned young Dutch graduate student at the University of Wisconsin at Madison, insists that the term is "problematic." Case in point: at the UN practicum, she charges, two Muslim women were "silenced" by "white Western hegemony." She further asserts that "the lifestyles of many women in the West are made possible by the exploitation of women" in the non-Western world—that, in other words, "the privilege of some women relies on the lack of privilege of other women"—and that this fact is "not easily reconciled with" the idea of "feminist solidarity." (She doesn't need to explain to the audience, for it is implicitly understood that when she refers to the exploitation of non-Western women, she does not mean by their fathers and husbands, but by the West.)

Two other young panelists, Sara Alicia Cooley of the University of California, Santa Barbara, and Deneil Hill of the State University of New York at Binghamton, have different issues on their minds: Cooley is concerned that there is still a widespread belief that "all women are mothers, want to be mothers, or ought to be mothers"; Hill maintains that "all [academic] departments need to offer courses that address women's issues" and predicts that "women's studies will play a major role" in eliminating "gender prejudice" from American universities. Both Cooley's and Hill's "arguments" are Women's Studies cliches, reflecting the fact that it's safer in these parts to march in lockstep than to step out of line and risk being branded an apostate. (Thus the odd combination, in these young women's presentations, of texts that are assertive to the point of stridency with body language and styles of delivery that convey a palpable fear of straying so much as a millimeter from orthodoxy.)

Cooley and Hill are followed by the oldest panelist, Christine Marie Willingham of Barry University in Miami Shores, Florida—who, to my surprise, actually challenges certain aspects of Women's Studies dogma. Specifically, she rejects the rote linkage of men with an "ethic of justice" and "individual rights" and of women with an "ethic of care" and collective thinking. "Perhaps both women and men are capable of a wider range of behaviors," she says—a commonsensical statement that, as we shall see, is well-nigh heretical in these realms. Willingham is the first of what will prove to be several middle-aged to elderly women at the NWSA convention who dare to dissent from the current Women's Studies orthodoxy as articulated so reliably by the younger likes of Cooley and Hill. To be sure, Willingham is no Luther in this Vatican: when it comes down to it, she, too, seems to buy into most of the gender stereotypes that are a cornerstone of the discipline, referring to women's supposedly innate "reluctance to enter into debate" and asking (as if no one had ever asked it before) a question that has been posed thousands upon thousands of times in the decades since Women's Studies came into being: "As women navigate masculine institutions, should they copy men's behavior or try to introduce more female atmospheres?"

The heresies of the panel's elder states woman are followed by a plea on behalf of the rising generation of Women's Studies practitioners. Jasmine Winter of Mary Baldwin College in Staunton, Virginia, who identifies herself as a "young feminist," bemoans that "feminism…is faltering in my generation" and that the "gender divide between older and younger feminists" is at a critical point. Young women feel they're "not being heard" and can't find "mentors." How to "pass feminism from one generation to the other" under such dreadful circumstances? Some young women out there, she says (meaning in the real world), feel that the "war has already been won"; they "don't want to be identified as feminists" and "don't know what the fight is for." Jasmine wonders—and worries: has feminism become a "strictly academic" phenomenon? Young feminists such as herself, she urges, need older women "to teach feminist history so we can have a feminist future" and "make room for new goals." Winter's presentation, even more than those by Cooley and Hill, is a farrago of familiar Women's Studies formulations; the utter absence of any sign of original reflection is, in its own way, awe-inspiring.

As if in response to Winter's plea, the final speaker, Kristin Marie Alder, describes herself as a teacher of "young feminists" from "diverse" backgrounds and says she deplores "traditional notions of pedagogy" that oblige her to "speak for [the] experiences" of others. When she stood at the front of her first Women's Studies classroom, she confides, she saw in the students' "gaze" that because she was white and middle-class, she was, in their view, "the authority on the subject of women's lives"—a result, she laments, of the influence upon them of those "traditional notions of pedagogy." She's learned, she tells us, to ask herself: "How does what I do in this classroom... inform the actual practice of feminism?" She's also learned that she and other Women's Studies teachers "must critically examine *our* constructions" and how we "introduce unequal power relations." Sighing that "we make so many women feel alienated from feminism," she warns against "hegemonic feminism" and "colonial feminism." She recalls a black student who "felt there was no home for her in feminism simply because she is black" and declares her sympathy for "hijab-wearing" students who don't feel completely included.

Alder's brief reference to the hijab speaks volumes. Instead of frankly addressing the symbolism of the hijab, which, of course, betokens female subordination to Muslim male patriarchy, Alder has chosen to put a safe twist on reality and to view the hijab as an innocuous form of attire the sight of which causes many Western women—presumably out of some objectionable racist or Orientalist impulse—to look down upon and (in effect) oppress the women who wear it. In 1970, Women's Lib preached universal sisterhood and resistance to "patriarchy" anywhere and in any form; today, Women's Studies, like contemporary establishment feminism generally, is meekly multicultural, treating non-Western social practices with deference even when they involve the brutal subjection of females. For an illustration of the changes that the movement has undergone, one need only look at the shifting self-description of the National Organization for Women: according to its original Statement of Purpose, written in 1966, its goal was "to bring women into full participation in the mainstream of American society now, exercising all privileges and responsibilities thereof in truly equal partnership with men"; today, however, NOW describes itself as a "multi-issue progressive" group that "stands against all oppression, recognizing that racism, sexism and homophobia are interrelated, that other forms of oppression such as classism and ableism work together with these three to keep power and privilege concentrated in the hands of a few." This view of things can be fairly described as the current Women's Studies orthodoxy. "Who are we leaving out of the narrative?" Alder asks plaintively. "Who are we privileging?" Her point is that her heart bleeds for Muslim and other women whom Western feminists like herself unthinkingly exclude. Yet by whitewashing the hijab she is herself effectively complicit in the oppression of Muslim women by Muslim men—and is therefore, in the name of multicultural sensitivity and opposition to racism, engaged in the very "privileging" of Western women, and exclusion from the feminist tent of non-Western women, that she professes to deplore.

During the Q&A, in an unconscious echo of Greer's reply to Trilling on that long-ago evening at Town Hall, a member of the audience complains that "women abuse each other, and women destroy each other"—explaining that in addition to the terrible blight of "white privilege," there are conflicts between older and younger women, between mothers and nonmothers, and so on. "It's a question," she says, "that any oppressed group has to deal with." In response to this hand-wringing, Alder returns to the topic of Islam, lamenting that her students are "preoccupied with female genital cutting, hijab, and honor killing," but that they fail to "see connections" between these phenomena and "problems in the West." In other words, her students don't realize that it's politically incorrect to concern themselves overmuch with the violent oppression and abuse of women in non-Western cultures, and that if one does pay attention to such matters, it's obligatory to find some way to blame them on Western colonialism (*never* on the non-Western cultures themselves) or to play moral-equivalency games (pretending, that is, that men in the West are every bit as oppressive, in their own hegemonic way, as men in the Islamic world), or both. Minjon jumps in, fervently agreeing with Alder and asserting that her own students' interest in female genital mutilation makes it clear that they don't grasp the "larger framework," the "comprehensive framework." Another audience member nods, complaining that her students, too, simply "don't understand why they should be criticizing the culture they live in" instead of poking their noses into other cultures' business. This, she avers, is "a huge problem." Returning to the subject of women abusing women, Tholen notes that at the UN practicum she attended "there was competition" between different groups of women and that "we need to try to let go of competition." (*Competition*, as we shall see, is a dirty word in Women's Studies nowadays.) In a reference to the alleged "silencing" of those Muslim women at the practicum—they were, she says, actually booed—Tholen charges that too many feminists demand that everyone agree with them about everything. Since nobody has spelled out the details of that "silencing," I speak up from the audience. "Exactly what were the Muslim women saying," I ask Tholen, "that led them to be booed?" She replies that the Muslim women "didn't share our Western preoccupation with hijab" and other such matters but wanted to focus instead on issues like water supplies and shelter. Alder adds that "Islamic feminists" reject the "Western feminist ideal." It's interesting how tolerant these young feminists can be of dissent from the otherwise sacrosanct "Western feminist ideal" so long as the dissenters are women in hijab. (One difference between the feminism of Friedan's and Greer's era and that of today's Women's Studies establishment is that now, thanks to multiculturalism, many Western feminists readily accept that a woman dressed in a garment symbolizing her inferiority to men can be legitimately considered a feminist.)

But not everyone, it turns out, agrees with Tholen and Alder. Willingham, the older feminist, breaks in, saying she feels compelled to explain that those Muslim women at the UN practicum, which she also attended, "hogged the mike" and that she found them "aggressive." There were eight thousand women present, she says, and this handful of Muslims tried to hijack the entire event—their motive apparently being to shift the focus away from women's rights. In short (though this is not Willingham but me saying this), those "Islamic feminists" would appear not to have been authentic feminists but, rather, stooges for Muslim men and apologists for sharia. Far from being "silenced," they were themselves trying to stifle discussion of the plight of women in the Islamic world. It's no coincidence that Willingham—the older feminist, closer in age than the others to the movement pioneers of the 1960s and '70s—is the only woman in the room who seems willing to at least partially acknowledge the eagerness of some Muslim women to defend their own oppression.

*   *   *

The feminism that was on display at Town Hall on that boisterous evening way back in 1971 is now known as second-wave feminism; its current intersectional, multicultural incarnation, as represented by the young women on the "Beijing +15" panel, is third-wave feminism. The first wave, which flourished mainly in England and America and focused largely on suffrage, may be said to have begun in 1792, when Mary Wollstonecraft, the wife of anarchist William Godwin and mother of the author of *Frankenstein*, Mary Shelley, published *A Vindication of the Rights of Woman*. Wollstonecraft made the then-revolutionary argument that women are by nature every bit as gifted as men, that what may seem their inferiority is a result of their subordination, and that if they enjoyed equal rights they would boast equal accomplishments. The first major work by an important male writer in support of this proposition was *The Subjection of Women* (1869), in which John Stuart Mill argued that women might not be as good as men at everything, but that if women's rights were expanded, it would soon be clear what exactly women *were* good at that had been denied to them, and that permitting them to engage in these activities as full and active members of society would be to everyone's benefit.

Meanwhile, in the United States, feminist pioneers like Susan B. Anthony, Elizabeth Cady Stanton, and Lucy Stone were making the case for women's suffrage, which a now-legendary 1848 convention in Seneca Falls, New York, put on the national agenda. In most Western countries, however, women would not win the right to vote until around the time of World War I—in Britain, 1918; in America, 1920. Following this triumph, the women's movement went into abeyance; as Kate Millett would later put it, "when the ballot was won, the feminist movement collapsed in what can only be described as exhaustion." The 1920s—the "Jazz Age"—transformed female lives: only yesterday, in the Victorian and Edwardian eras, women and girls had been protected, patronized, and put on pedestals; now young ladies were smoking, dating, dancing, bobbing their hair, and gulping cocktails at speakeasies. The Depression (and the repeal of Prohibition) put an end to all that, and though World War II saw millions of women taking up traditionally male jobs freed up by men who were off at war, when the soldiers came back the women married, followed their husbands to newly built suburbs, and began lives as homemakers (then called housewives) and as mothers to the baby boom.

Those postwar years were a quiet time for feminism. One blip was the 1949 publication of Simone de Beauvoir's *The Second Sex*—though the book, now regarded as a founding document of modern feminism, was not very widely read in the United States until its resurrection in the late 1960s. Beauvoir's *chef d'oeuvre* covers a lot of territory—it seeks to provide an exhaustive, definitive account of women's status throughout human history, the stages of female growth and self-awareness from infancy onward, the depiction of women in literature, and much else. The nature of Beauvoir's particular blindness—one she shared with other icons of second-wave feminism—is summed up in a single sentence, written when Stalinism was in full flower: "It is in Soviet Russia that the feminist movement has made the most sweeping advances." In 1971 Beauvoir famously put her name to the feminist "Manifesto of the 343," whose signatories (all celebrated Frenchwomen) claimed to have had abortions; less well known is her signing in 1940 of another document, in which she affirmed to France's Nazi occupiers that she wasn't Jewish. (In her book *La Force de l'âge*, Beauvoir claimed that she "thought it repugnant to sign" the paper, but then again, she reasoned, everyone else at the lycée where she taught had signed it, too: "for most of my colleagues, as for myself, there was no way of doing otherwise.")

Then along came Betty Friedan. A Marxist and self-described "bad-tempered bitch" who had written for women's magazines as well as trade union journals, Friedan inaugurated the second wave in 1963 with her jeremiad *The Feminine Mystique*. If the first wave had been about equal rights, the second was about "liberation"—Women's Lib. The book begins at Smith, the "Seven Sisters" college whose student body (especially back then) was overwhelmingly composed of the daughters of privilege. Friedan was a Smith girl, and in 1957, fifteen years after her graduation, she sent her classmates a questionnaire, asking how satisfied they were with their lives. The answers, she wrote in the preface to *The Feminine Mystique*,

> simply did not fit the image of the modern American woman as she was written about in women's magazines, studied and analyzed in classrooms and clinics, praised and damned in a ceaseless barrage of words ever since the end of World War II. There was a strange discrepancy between the reality of our lives as women and the image to which we were trying to conform, the image that I came to call the feminine mystique.

What Friedan discovered was that these women—white, upper-middle-class, most of them now suburban wives and mothers—felt a secret discontent with their lives as homemakers, that they felt guilty about it, that they thought they were alone in their dissatisfaction, and that they believed this meant there was something wrong with *them*. Which brings us to the opening paragraph of the book proper—a ringing, dramatic statement about what Friedan portentously called "the problem that has no name":

> The problem lay buried, unspoken, for many years in the minds of American women. It was a strange stirring, a sense of dissatisfaction, a yearning that women suffered in the middle of the twentieth century in the United States. Each suburban wife struggled with it alone. As she made the beds, shopped for groceries, matched slipcover material, ate peanut butter sandwiches with her children, chauffeured Cub Scouts and Brownies, lay beside her husband at night—she was afraid to ask even of herself the silent question—"Is this all?"

Those three words—"Is this all?"—would ignite a revolution. Friedan's point was simple: women had been stifled by a narrow image of their sex. They'd been told they were more delicate and sensitive than men, and thus less suited to careers than to homemaking. This, Friedan argued, was a betrayal of everything that Wollstonecraft, Stanton, and others had worked for, and it betrayed the example set by the innumerable women who, in the 1920s, had rejected traditional roles and opted to shape their own lives. She invoked Nora in Ibsen's *A Doll's House*, who leaves her husband and children, dismissing his argument that she is primarily a wife and mother and insisting, rather, that above all she is "a reasonable human being." What, Friedan asked, had sapped the life and guts out of the would-be Noras of mid-century? The culprit, she answered, was the feminine mystique—a mentality according to which "the highest value and the only commitment for women is the fulfillment of their own femininity." The feminine mystique told women that they shouldn't try to be like men but should "accep [t] their own nature." As Friedan saw it, Smith undergraduates were now so thoroughly brainwashed by the feminine mystique that they had no interest in their coursework or in pursuing careers. As an example of the grim fate in store for them, Friedan told the story of a friend of hers, "an able writer turned full-time housewife, [who] had her suburban dream house designed by an architect to her own specifications.... The house...was almost literally one big kitchen...there wasn't any place where she could get out of the kitchen, away from her children.... The gorgeous mahogany and stainless steel of her custom-built kitchen cabinets and electric appliances were indeed a dream, but when I saw that house, I wondered where, if she ever wanted to write again, she would put her typewriter."

Friedan described the feminine mystique as having "bur[ied] millions of American women alive." "[T]he time is at hand," she prophesied, "when the voices of the feminine mystique can no longer drown out the inner voice that is driving women on to become complete." As evidence for her assertions, Friedan presented the table of contents of a typical 1960 issue of *McCall's* magazine, which she savaged for its insufficient attention to "the world beyond the home"—as if women couldn't subscribe, if they wished, to *Time* or *Scientific American* (and as if the men's magazines of the era weren't, in their own way, just as narrow and inane). Friedan devoted several chapters to the contents of women's magazines, as if they provided a complete picture of the reality of women's lives in the 1950s and '60s.

(Her preoccupation with these magazines may be explained, at least in part, by her professional connections to them, which perhaps gave her an excessive sense of their importance—this, plus the fact that she had plainly grown sick of writing about homemaking.)

Though Friedan had a few harsh words for the husbands who, in her view, had helped install their wives in gilded cages, she was considerably nastier about gay men, who, in her view, were "spreading like a murky smog over the American scene." Describing them as "Peter Pans, forever childlike, afraid of age," she attributed their homosexuality to (what else?) the feminine mystique: "The mother whose son becomes homosexual is usually not the 'emancipated' woman who competes with men in the world, but the very paradigm of the feminine mystique—a woman who lives through her son, whose femininity is used in virtual seduction of her son, who attaches her son to her with such dependence that he can never mature to love a woman, nor can he, often, cope as an adult with life on his own." For all her passion about the liberation of suburban housewives, Friedan had little sympathy for gay rights. Unsurprisingly, her hatred for lesbians has (to put it mildly) complicated her legacy in the eyes of today's heavily lesbian Women's Studies establishment.

Underneath the hyperbole, to be sure, Friedan had a valid point: because of the (often internalized) expectations of others, limited options (or unawareness of available opportunities), and/or their own narrow view of their capabilities (a view often inculcated in them by parents or teachers), many American women in the mid-twentieth century did indeed end up leading lives that made them miserable, or at least bored and restless. The rigid gender roles of the day *could* be stifling—not only for women, but for men as well. In the same way that many women who would have thrived in careers ended up stagnating in their kitchens, so more than a few men who would have loved to stay at home with the kids spent their lives in jobs they hated and were ill-suited for. How many couples would have been far happier if only they had exchanged places? But such thoughts were unthinkable. Add to this the fact that women who did pursue careers were used to being paid less than men, used to being passed up for promotions, and used to being viewed as less serious about their careers than men were. If they were married, they were seen as wives first, professionals second; if they weren't married, they were viewed as being on the prowl for a man and likely to exchange their careers for wedding rings. Then, of course, there were the double standards that, for example, identified promiscuous men as studs and promiscuous women as sluts, and that treated unwed mothers as objects of shame even as the fathers of those women's children suffered no stigma at all. And let's not forget the hypocrisy of secret abortions, arranged on the sly by doctors who would never have lent public support to the cause of legalized abortion.

Still and all, Friedan's rhetoric was over-the-top. She described some of the most fortunate individuals in human history as downtrodden and subjugated—and did so at a time when millions of people, in countries ruled by an ideology to which Friedan subscribed, really *were* downtrodden and subjugated. In a chapter of *The Feminine Mystique* subtitled "The Comfortable Concentration Camp," she actually opined that "[i]n a sense…the women…who grow up wanting to be 'just a housewife,' are in as much danger as the millions who walked to their own death in the concentration camps."

After Friedan came the deluge. In 1970, there was Kate Millett's bestselling *Sexual Politics*, which drew heavily on *The Second Sex*: like Beauvoir, Millett peered at women through the lenses of history, biology, anthropology, psychology, literature, and politics. (Like Beauvoir, too, curiously enough, she wrote about the sexually puerile Henry Miller and D. H. Lawrence as if they were representative males.) "[O]ur society…is a patriarchy," diagnosed Millett, who pronounced that "[t]he chief weakness of the movement's concentration on suffrage" during its first wave "lay in its failure to challenge patriarchal ideology at a sufficiently deep and radical level to break the conditioning processes of status, temperament and role." *Patriarchy*: no word more neatly summed up the second-wave sensibility.

Like Friedan, Millett admired Marxism: she endorsed Engels's proposal that the state, not the mother, should be a child's primary caregiver, and praised Lenin for seeking "to terminate patriarchy and restructure its most basic institution—the family." Though Lenin's effort to "restructure" the family was, of course, part of the larger Soviet project to crush all institutions that threatened the absolute power of the totalitarian communist state, Millett described it as having represented a promise of an advance for women's freedom; apropos of Lenin's failure to pull off the "restructuring," Millett lamented that "[a] population so recently freed did not know how to use its freedom." This was no slip of the pen: Millett referred repeatedly to the "new freedoms" and "new liberties" purportedly introduced by the Bolsheviks in Russia. (Millett was also impressed by Mao's China, which, she wrote, "is said to be the only country in the world which has no prostitution.")

The year 1970 also saw the publication of Greer's *The Female Eunuch*, in which the author—who over the years has identified herself variously as an anarchist, Marxist, and communist—described women as masochistically collaborating in their own oppression and encouraged them to practice "delinquency" by rejecting the nuclear family. While urging women to stop seeing themselves as erotic objects, Greer was not above using her own considerable sex appeal to maximum effect: she equated libertinism with liberation and made no secret of the fact that she regarded many of her fellow feminists as anti-sex, or as sexually repressed, and therefore not authentically liberated. At least in part for these reasons, *The Female Eunuch*, though perhaps the single biggest sensation of the second wave, is today, as her biographer Christine Wallace has observed, "essentially invisible on reading lists for women's studies courses."

Friedan, Millett, and Green: these were among second-wave feminism's leading lights. To read their books in the context of their Marxist sympathies is to recognize that second-wave feminism was, to no small degree, rooted in its leaders' ideological identification with America's Cold War adversaries. After all, to attack the suburban comforts that capitalism made possible—comforts beyond even the dreams of most Soviet subjects—was to attack capitalism itself. (When Mailer said it was all "just old socialism," in short, he wasn't entirely wrong.) As second-wave pioneer Phyllis Chesler acknowledged years later, second-wave feminism was a "cult" whose members all shared the same views about "capitalism, colonialism, imperialism," and so forth. They had a motto: "The personal is political." There were, however, two small problems with the linkage of Marxism and women's liberation: first, the "subordination" of women could hardly be attributed to capitalism, since the former predated the latter; and second, Marx's theories had absolutely nothing to do with liberating women from that "subordination."

Still, despite their missteps, misunderstandings, and excesses, the leading figures of second-wave feminism merit a degree of respect. They may have gone astray in many ways, but so do all pioneers when feeling their way into uncharted territory. At least Friedan and company were the real thing. Far from being careerists mouthing slogans to get ahead, they took serious personal and professional risks to speak their minds. And they could write.

Besides, in the larger feminist picture, they were moderates. Just compare them with, for example, the Boston College theologian Mary Daly, who, in the soberly written *The Church and the Second Sex* (1968) and *Beyond God the Father* (1973), made reasonable (and now very familiar) criticisms of Catholicism's misogyny and Christianity's "[e]xclusively masculine symbolism for God," but who later developed into a radical feminist, inviting other women, in *Gyn/Ecology: The Metaethics of Radical Feminism* (1978), to join her on a "Metapatriarchal Journey of Exorcism and Ecstasy," and concluding *Pure Lust* (1984), a paean to the carnal and spiritual delights of lesbianism, as follows:

> Aroused by the Touch of our Wonder-filled Woman-Lust, Wonderers fly with the Grace of Be-Witching, unfolding our spiritual powers. Like flowers, like serpents, like dragons, like angels, we Spiral in rhythms of Weirdward creation. Leaping with Wander-lust, Weaving new Wonders, we intend to be Fore-Crones of Gnostic Nag-Nations. As Dreamers we glimpse our sidereal cities that gleam in the heavens like Stars of the Sea. They call us all ways, now, to Be.

After Daly's death in 2010, Sara Corbett noted in a posthumous *New York Times* profile that she had "prided herself on being problematic, disagreeable, defiant" and "coached other women to do the same." Daly also made it clear that her brand of radical second-wave feminism had nothing whatsoever to do with equality and mutual respect between the sexes, but rather with rage and retribution: she denied male students permission to take her classes and, at lectures, refused to take questions from men (she said, wrote Corbett, that "it was important for them to understand what it feels like to be voiceless and ignored"). Aptly, she was forced into retirement in 1998 by charges of sexism. Yet none of Daly's offenses against equal rights have prevented her from becoming a Women's Studies idol. Among the hundreds of sessions I missed at the 2010 NWSA convention was "Feminism and Religion—a Panel in Honor of the Early Work of Mary Daly." At another session, "Queering Feminism, Feministing Queer," a male participant, concerned that Daly, "one of the most highly esteemed feminist philosophers," has been branded "transmisogynistic" (that is, hostile to male-to-female transsexuals), sought "to reclaim Daly for transfeminism."

Then there was Robin Morgan, who, after breaking from the antiwar movement over its purported sexism, helped found such groups as New York Radical Women, W.I.T.C.H. (Women's International Terrorist Conspiracy from Hell), the Sisterhood Is Global Institute, and the Women's Media Center. "White males," Morgan wrote in 1970, "are most responsible for the destruction of human life and environment on the planet today.... [A] legitimate revolution must be led by, made by those who have been most oppressed: black, brown, and white women." Morgan described "man-hating" as "an honorable and viable political act" because "the oppressed have a right to class-hatred against the class that is oppressing them." Despite this incendiary rhetoric, Morgan has always been a thoroughly mainstream presence—published by Random House and Simon & Schuster, invited to speak at major American colleges, awarded NEA and Ford Foundation grants, and accorded the honor of having her papers archived at Duke.

An influential subset of feminism that sprang up during the second wave's heyday was the rape-crisis movement. Rape, its leaders preached, was far more widespread than had previously been thought—an argument helped along by the sensational results of a famous *Ms.* magazine study. (The researcher who conducted it later admitted that the overwhelming majority of the women she had counted as rape victims did not, in fact, regard themselves as having been raped.) Previously, rape had been viewed as an infrequent crime committed by a tiny minority of disturbed individuals; now rape-crisis feminists depicted it as an expression of masculine power that reflected universal male attitudes. (In her 1975 bestseller *Against Our Will: Men, Women and Rape*, Susan Brownmiller described rape as "a conscious process of intimidation by which *all men* keep *all women* in a state of fear.") The movement also broadened the definition of rape to include any heterosexual act in which the woman feels violated—even if she doesn't feel violated until, say, the next morning.

Among the rape-crisis movement's stars were Catharine MacKinnon and Andrea Dworkin, who, often in league with right-wing leaders like Jesse Helms, mounted campaigns to ban pornography, arguing that it encouraged men to commit sexual violence. ("Pornography is the theory," wrote Morgan in 1974, "and rape is the practice.") MacKinnon and Dworkin were the perfect tag team—the former an attractive Smith graduate and law professor who strove to make her extreme positions sound sensible, the latter a shrill, morbidly obese, and exceedingly unkempt activist who felt no need to hide her violent hatred for men. "Pornography," Dworkin harangued a New York state commission on pornography in 1986, "is used in rape—to plan it, to execute it, to choreograph it, to engender the excitement to commit the act." In her 1987 book *Intercourse*, Dworkin went beyond criticizing pornography and condemned heterosexual intercourse *en tout*, arguing that women who sleep with men in a patriarchal society are debasing themselves and contributing to their own oppression. ("Intercourse," she memorably wrote, "is the pure, sterile, formal expression of men's contempt for women.")

MacKinnon's and Dworkin's efforts led to a number of ordinances prohibiting the sale of pornography in various U.S. jurisdictions, although many of these laws, faced with opposition by civil libertarians, were later declared unconstitutional. One of MacKinnon and Dworkin's major achievements was a 1992 Canadian Supreme Court decision permitting the confiscation of materials deemed (under a broad definition) to be pornographic. Among those who rejected MacKinnon and Dworkin's brand of feminism were Friedan and Greer, who, whatever their failings, stood, when it came to such matters, for freedom, not for constraints on freedom, and who found MacKinnon's and Dworkin's hostility to men and to sex over-the-top; they recognized rape-crisis feminism as nothing more than puritanism under a new name, a return to a 1950s-style concept of women as helpless creatures in need of protection.

But Friedan and Greer's movement had passed them by: rape hysteria became fully integrated into mainstream feminism, resulting in such events as the so-called Take Back the Night rallies at colleges around America, which are premised on the idea that when darkness falls over the quad, male students metamorphose, werewolf-like, into potential rapists. Typical of the inflated rhetoric that currently surrounds sexual violence on campus is the following, which appeared on the website of the Women's Resource Center at the University of Houston in 2010: "October is Domestic Violence Awareness Month.... Did you know that almost one-third of college students report dating violence by a previous partner and almost one-fourth report violence by a current partner? Dating violence can include coercion, stalking, jealousy, isolation, victim blaming, and emotional, sexual, and physical abuse." Even "jealousy" and "emotional...abuse" (which, of course, can mean almost anything), then, are now considered "violence."

The influence of second-wave feminism on Western culture was profound. A range of phenomena viewed as scandalous when Friedan wrote her book—including abortion, single motherhood, and stay-at-home dads—are now considered thoroughly unremarkable. In the 1950s, Western popular culture communicated the idea that Father knew best and that Mother belonged in the kitchen; now we've had at least a generation of TV series, commercials, and the like in which Dad is an idiot and Mom is a sage. Today, from kindergarten onward, children are taught *not* to think in terms of stereotypical gender roles—even though it's widely acknowledged (except in Women's Studies) that certain gender-distinct interests are, in fact, innate. On such matters, feminism has been self-contradictory, one minute fiercely denying any natural biological tendency for boys and girls to have different interests or strengths, the next celebrating women's supposedly distinct—and, of course, always superior—"ways of knowing." Meanwhile, there has been increasing concern about boys raised in a feminist society. Christina Hoff Sommers speaks of the "war against boys," who grow up being told by teachers and textbooks that they are intrinsically violent and that in a world without men there would be no war.

The great irony here is that even as feminists continue to paint men as oppressors, women are now, as Hanna Rosin noted in the *Atlantic* in 2010, "the majority of the workforce." Far more women than men get college degrees. We are living in a world-historic moment: "Man has been the dominant sex since, well, the dawn of mankind. But for the first time in human history, that is changing—and with shocking speed." Even in places like India, China, and Southeast Asia, male domination is crumbling. (The major exception, of course, is the Muslim world.) In explaining this revolution, Rosin invokes gender essentialism: we live at "the end of the manufacturing era," and "[t]he attributes that are most valuable today—social intelligence, open communication, the ability to sit still and focus—are, at a minimum, not predominantly male.... [S]chools, like the economy, now value the self-control, focus, and verbal aptitude that seem to come more easily to young girls." These passages illustrate the double standard feminism has implanted in Western society: while it's perfectly acceptable to say that men are worse than women at certain things, to suggest the inverse is to reap the whirlwind. (Just ask Lawrence Summers, who lost his job as president of Harvard because he suggested that men might be more predisposed than women to success in science.)

The success of a movement can be measured by the degree to which it withers away as its goals are achieved. Hence, as feminist attitudes became absorbed into mainstream American culture, the movement itself steadily waned. The National Organization for Women, once a powerhouse, declined in profile and influence. Though more and more young women attended college, pursued careers, and led independent lives—embodying the foremost ideals of second-wave feminism—more and more of them, as noted at that Beijing +15 panel, rejected the label *feminist*—which, in their minds, conjured up images not of worthy activism on behalf of social and legal equality but of shrill man-hatred.

Yet even as feminist ideas became mainstream ideas, and feminist self-identification and explicit feminist activism faded away in American society at large, feminism became an increasingly visible presence at colleges and universities. While the movement itself shriveled, in short, Women's Studies grew apace. It began with isolated courses in English or social science departments; then interdisciplinary programs (drawing on faculty members from a variety of humanities and social science disciplines) began to spring up; then full-fledged Women's Studies departments were formed, some of which at first offered only minors; over the years, more and more of these departments offered majors, then master's degrees, then Ph.D.s.

It was the founding of Black Studies that first opened second-wave feminists' eyes. If the oppression of blacks justified the establishment of a new academic field, what about women? Weren't women oppressed, too? Sheila Tobias, who taught the first Women's Studies course at Cornell, recalls that "[t]he Cornell community was educated and inspired (if sometimes terrorized) by its African American community," members of whom "'took over' the student union" in 1968, an act that led to "the establishment...of a significant black studies program under an African American director—a program that would serve as a model for women's studies." Similar stories underlie the conception of many of the earliest Women's Studies courses—and, in 1970, the first two Women's Studies programs, at San Diego State College and the State University of New York at Buffalo.

From the beginning, Women's Studies has been less about education in any traditional sense than about political indoctrination. In an anthology of articles from *Feminist Teacher*, the journal's editors declare that they're a "collective" whose motto is "*politics and teaching do mix*" (italics in original). Significantly, the founders of Women's Studies were not celebrated thinkers like Friedan and Millett but ideologues with backgrounds in civil rights and New Left activism. What distinguished these "socialists, communists, and careerists," as Phyllis Chesler puts it, was that they knew how to "tak[e] over institutions." "The best of us," she recalls, speaking of the women who defined second-wave feminism, "were anarchic, eccentric, and highly independent nonconformists" who "spoke truth clearly, not in postmodern academic voices." Women's Studies, by contrast, was the creation of "grassroots feminist nonauthors"—Chesler labels them "the sisterhood"—who were neither original nor courageous.

In the introduction to *The Politics of Women's Studies: Testimony from Thirty Founding Mothers* (2000), an anthology about the origins of the field, Mari Jo Buhle acknowledges that many of the first teachers of Women's Studies believed in "alternative styles of learning" (aka "politicized learning") that were "[i]nspired by Paulo Freire's *Pedagogy of the Oppressed*." The women who established SUNY Buffalo's program, for example, declared that "[t]his education will not be an academic exercise; it will be an ongoing process to change the ways in which women think and behave. It must be part of the struggle to build a new and more complete society." According to Buhle, "race, class, and sexual orientation" were "central" to Women's Studies from the beginning; Josephine Donovan, one of the book's contributors, recalls that "all we thought about" in those early days were "racism, colonialism, and imperialism. Feminism added gender to the mix."

Another contributor to *The Politics of Women's Studies* is Nancy Hoffman, who started out in the 1960s as a self-defined "radical student activist" at Berkeley, where she served time as an organizer and antiwar protester. "Our goal," she remembers, "was to open up the university to scrutiny, to challenge institutional power, and to take some for our own purpose.... We saw the youth on campus as ripe for radicalizing and organizing." After "living in Paris during *les années soixante*, participating in political rallies from Copenhagen to Milan," she got a job at the University of California, Santa Barbara, where "my department chair gave his permission" for her to teach a course on women and literature. (She mentions in passing that she and her students viewed "revolutionary women in North Vietnam" as role models.) From there she went to Portland State University, where, after being hired by the English Department "with little more than a casual interview," she cofounded one of the first Women's Studies programs. "For me," she recalls, "the women's studies classroom became the place…where you could teach in the radical style set out in Paulo Freire's *Pedagogy of the Oppressed*" Hoffman "applied community-organizing skills to the student community" and made sure that "[c]ollectivist practices character-ized women's studies at PSU." Similarly, Sheila Tobias emphasizes that the first Women's Studies course she taught at Cornell was "forged by a *collective*" and proffered a "radical feminist program." (The importance of the conceit that Women's Studies is a collec-tive enterprise cannot be overstated: as Tobias puts it, "[p]atriarchy, according to feminist theory, involved hierarchy; women's work need not.") Only two years after that first course, Cornell had a full-fledged Women's Studies program.

Women's Studies was, and is, the "academic wing of femi-nism," devoted to "consciousness-raising" and to helping young women liberate themselves and their sisters. In retrospect, it's remarkable how quickly and easily Women's Studies became a firmly rooted presence in American higher education. This growth, notes Buhle, "seem[ed] to happen overnight." By 1974, more than a thousand institutions had Women's Studies courses, and eighty had Women's Studies programs. By 1976, there were already "270 programs and 15,000 courses spread across the campuses of 1500 institutions" with 850 teachers. And by 1981, "the number of women's studies programs had increased to 350." Meanwhile organizations and journals sprang up: the Feminist Press and the journals *Feminist Studies* and *Women's Studies* were founded in 1972, the journal *Signs* in 1975, the NWSA in 1977, and the journal *Feminist Teacher* in 1985. If in 1930, notes Buhle, "one in seven Ph.D. s was granted to a woman" and by 1960 "the proportion had dropped to approximately one in ten," by 1976 the figure had jumped impressively, with women forming "45 percent of the undergraduate population." Between 1978 and 1985, more than 13,000 students wrote dissertations in Women's Studies. As of 2000, according to Buhle, there were about 615 Women's Studies programs in the United States, and about 12 percent of Amer-ican undergraduates were enrolled in Women's Studies courses, meaning that more American students were taking Women's

Studies than were taking courses in any other "disciplinary field." Today about 600 American institutions of higher education offer Women's Studies in some form. In 2009, 408 institutions and 2,011 individuals held NWSA membership; at this writing, the NWSA database contains the names of 661 institutions with undergraduate programs, 43 that award master's degrees in Women's Studies, and 15 that grant Ph.D.s.

One fact emerges clearly from *The Politics of Women's Studies*: although the founders of Women's Studies are routinely portrayed as brave pioneers who struggled valiantly against the patriarchy to carve out a space for themselves in the male-dominated academy, they would in fact never have gotten so far, so fast, if not for the readiness of liberal male administrators and faculty to approve and fund Women's Studies. Indeed, the very rise of Women's Studies belies its own rhetoric about the ruthless hegemonic power of the patriarchy. As Daphne Patai and Noretta Koertge point out, not one of the testimonies in *The Politics of Women's Studies* mentions any "concerted male resistance" to the rise of the discipline. On the contrary, as the testimonies themselves document, Women's Studies received extremely generous support, at a very early stage, from governments, universities, and foundations—especially the Ford Foundation, which seems to have played a larger role than any other single funder in helping to launch the new discipline. (In addition to funding individual programs and departments, the Ford Foundation provided the money that jump-started the NWSA and the Feminist Press.) As Jean Walton testifies in *The Politics of Women's Studies*, the deans, trustees, and faculty at the Claremont Colleges were highly supportive of efforts to create a joint Women's Studies program there; and Nancy Topping Bazin, who was the first coordinator of Women's Studies at Rutgers, recalls that while "some male professors expressed skepticism" about the program, "they approved it without delay." Even though such accounts, as Patai and Koertge point out, "implicitly reveal the presence of [a] favorable climate" in regard to Women's Studies at universities, a number of "the contributors show little recognition" of this fact, and indeed "seek to convey struggle and effort— on a grand scale and against formidable and entrenched forces."

Impressive though the statistics about the growth of Women's Studies are, moreover, they don't come close to reflecting the discipline's real influence. Women's Studies approaches have, after all, become commonplace throughout the humanities and social sciences, and are finding their way into more and more secondary and even primary school classrooms. Women's centers have become fixtures on campuses, where they tend to be closely aligned with the Women's Studies department or program itself; their purported objective may be gleaned from this official description of the Center for Women at Emory: "We advocate for gender equity throughout the University; provide resources and skill-building opportunities; and bring faculty, students, practitioners, activists, and other learners together to examine gender issues and work toward ethical solutions." At many universities, furthermore, there are other women-specific groups that collaborate regularly with Women's Studies. At Northeastern University, for example, the Women's, Gender and Sexuality Studies Program "works closely with the independent, student-run Feminist Student Organization to sponsor programs for Women's History Month and other events of special concern to women and LGBT students"; at Clark University, the Women's Studies Program "is part of the Worcester Consortium in Women's Studies, comprised of seven institutions of higher education, each with their [sic] own faculty active in women's studies research and teaching." At some universities, it can be hard to keep track of all the organized feminism: at the University of Minnesota, for instance, as Christina Hoff Sommers has noted, there is not only a Women's Studies Department and Women's Center, but also the Center for Advanced Feminist Studies, the Center for Women in International Development, the Young Women's Association, the Center for Continuing Education for Women, the Humphrey Center on Women and Public Policy, and the offices of not one but two feminist journals, *Signs* (the leading periodical in the field) and *Hurricane Alice*.

In many cases, moreover, Women's Studies has metamorphosed into, or been fused with, something called Gender Studies, which the NWSA website describes as "an evolution from the women's studies programs founded in the 1960's and after. In recent years some campuses have changed the name of their women's studies program to 'gender studies,' while others who [*sic*] have not previously had a women's Studies program have begun a new program using the name gender studies. Additionally many programs combine the names and are called 'women and gender Studies,' or the 'study of women and gender.' In some settings, gender studies may reflect additional attention to masculinities or sexuality studies." The Gender Studies Department at Indiana University, Bloomington, offers this rather exhaustive explanation:

> Gender Studies addresses such issues as femininity and masculinity; gender and the body; gender and culture; gender and knowledge; current and historical inquiries into the relationships between the *sexes*; gender and aesthetics; gender as an organizing factor on social, political, and familial institutions and policy; gender role development and institutionalization; feminist theory; sexual orientation; sexual identity politics and history, queer theory, and lesbian cultural criticism and other interdisciplinary inquiries related to sex, gender, sexuality, reproduction, and feminist theory. It examines ideas of femininity and masculinity across cultures and historical periods and how these concepts are represented within cultures (e.g., literature, popular culture, the arts, science, and medicine).

What all this comes down to is that in addition to "studying" female experience and female sexuality, students of Gender Studies also explore male experience and male sexuality—almost invariably, however, from a feminist perspective. With few exceptions, in short, Gender Studies "interprets" men's lives in light of the doctrine that men are by definition oppressors, warmongers, potential rapists, and the beneficiaries of patriarchal social structures, and that the only proper way to comprehend sexual identity and sexual relations is by viewing them through a feminist lens.

Women's Studies is old enough now that faculties that once consisted of women trained in "real" fields of study—so that there was at least the possibility that a Women's Studies department might offer some hint of traditional liberal education—now consist largely of women whose only real training is in Women's Studies itself (sometimes, to be sure, in combination with one or more other identity studies). The increasing replacement of interdisciplinary Women's Studies programs with standalone departments also tends to ensure students' insulation from materials and approaches identified with other fields with longer histories.

I have mentioned that the 2010 NWSA conference in Denver was dubbed "Difficult Dialogues." Yet if any of the "dialogues" were "difficult," it was because even the slightest deviation from absolute orthodoxy (such as Willingham's frank account of those Muslim women's aggressiveness at the UN practicum) is regarded in these circles as thorny, awkward, discomfiting. Though Women's Studies was supposed to give a voice to "silenced" women, all too many women who dissent from its orthodoxy have themselves felt silenced by intolerant professors—and students, too. Indeed, while some (generally tenured) older professors like Willingham do dare to challenge Women's Studies dogma, younger initiates, whether students or greenhorn instructors, often act as fierce enforcers of dogma, reiterating it (as did Tholen and Alder at the Beijing +15 session) with all the zeal of fresh converts to a fundamentalist faith and bristling at any violation of Holy Writ. Patai and Koertge quote professors who complain about students being "zombified" by Women's Studies, turned into "ideologically inflamed Stepford Wives" who "utter... stock phrases" and are plainly "terrified of a thought because if they ever had a serious thought, they might start reflecting on this stuff they're taught to repeat."

Indeed, though in its early days the discipline tended to treat Friedan, Millett, Greer, and company as honored prophets, by the mid-1980s, says Chesler, their books had dropped off the reading lists because, in a field increasingly preoccupied with intersectionality, social constructionism, and other postmodern ideas, they had come to be seen as guilty of ideological impurity. Nowadays, it's not unusual to hear some of those iconic second-wave pioneers denounced as unorthodox. In 1995, conservative columnist Mona Charen interviewed Friedan and was surprised by how much they agreed on: "The author of *The Feminine Mystique*," wrote Charen, "is a bit out of place these days. Never persuaded by the 'gender' feminists that date rape and sexual harassment were the most serious problems facing women, she admits that when she teaches now, she is not comfortable in 'women's studies' departments. 'I got into too many arguments,' she sighs." Friedan died in 2006.

When I was a graduate student, two women named Sandra Gilbert and Susan Gubar were the stars of feminist literary criticism and the makers of the new feminist literary canon. They cowrote a foundational second-wave text, *The Madwoman in the Attic: The Woman Writer and the Nineteenth-Century Literary Imagination* (1979), and have co-edited several editions of the *Norton Anthology of Literature by Women* (the first of which appeared in 1985). Yet as Kwame Anthony Appiah notes, Gubar ended up being attacked by Women's Studies colleagues "as a troglodyte" because, in their view, she was insufficiently theoretical and hadn't included enough writing by lesbians and women of color in her new canon. Then there's Michèle Barrett, who ventured to suggest, in her introduction to the first (1980) edition of *Women's Oppression Today*, that the word *patriarchy* was not entirely useful because, as she quite sensibly put it, "How useful is it to collapse widow-burning in India with 'the coercion of privacy' in Western Europe, into a concept of such generality?" Yet in the book's second (1988) edition, having been lambasted for this heresy, Barrett crawled back to orthodoxy and proffered a cringing *mea culpa*; "Many feminists suggested to me that it was completely wrong to suggest the abandonment of such an eloquent and resonant concept.... What is at stake here, which I later came to see, was the symbolic status of using the concept of 'patriarchy' as a marker of a position that in general terms I was in fact taking—that we recognize the independent character of women's oppression and avoid explanations that reduced it to other factors."

The 1990s brought a widespread backlash against this rigid feminist orthodoxy. For many, it was personified by Camille Paglia, a professor at an obscure university in Philadelphia, who, in her

1990 book, *Sexual Personae: Art and Decadence from Nefertiti to Emily Dickinson*, as well as in scores of essays and interviews, dismissed women's contribution to Western civilization ("There are no female Mozarts") and mocked the "weepy, whiny, white-middle-class ideology" of the "Stalinist" women's movement under Gloria Steinem, which Paglia reviled for its intellectual vacuity, sexual puritanism, and hostility to men—not to mention its obsessive victim mentality, which, in her view, only served to reinforce Victorian sexual stereotypes. For Paglia, women, far from being the weaker sex, were gifted by nature with an innate power over men—the power of sex.

The backlash continued with *The Morning After: Sex, Fear and Feminism on Campus* (1994), in which Princeton grad student Katie Roiphe reported on feminism in the academy. She focused particularly on rape-crisis feminism, which preached to female college students that they weren't responsible for their own actions, and could thus legitimately claim to have been raped if they decided the next day that they'd made a foolish personal choice. Roiphe also mocked feminist literary criticism, recalling a male fellow student who had described Edith Wharton's characters as "antifeminist because within the hegemonic male discourse, it is impossible for the female voice to be empowered" and a female fellow student who cared little for literature but was passionate about postmodern literary criticism: "Her conversation is peppered with words like inscription, appropriation, hegemonic, and transgress. In her world, things don't just exist, they are 'constructed.'"

The same year saw the publication of *Who Stole Feminism? How Women Have Betrayed Women*, in which Christina Hoff Sommers criticized contemporary Western feminists for their "self-preoccupation," their tendency to "speak of their personal plight" in words more appropriate "to the tragic plight of many American women of a bygone day and of millions of contemporary, truly oppressed women in other countries." Apropos of Women's Studies, she observed that "equipping students to 'transform the world' is not quite the same as equipping them with the knowledge they need for getting on in the world." Sommers noted that art courses were now focusing more on "female" arts such as quilting and less on painting and sculpture in order to "even out" the curriculum and that great male writers were being replaced on the syllabi of literature courses with female mediocrities. "What motivates the revisionist efforts to rewrite History or to revise the standards of 'greatness' in a manner calculated to give to women victories and triumphs they never had the opportunities to win?" asked Sommers. "We *now have* those opportunities. Why can't we move on to the future and stop wasting energy on resenting (and 'rewriting') the past?"

These reactions to an increasingly rigid and institutionalized feminism had a major impact on mainstream American society, and help explain why so many ambitious, intelligent, and independent-minded young women today choose not to identify as feminists. The feminist establishment, however, chose not to learn from but to vilify Paglia and company. And Women's Studies, unable to answer them, all but ignored them. On my way to Denver for the NWSA conference, I wondered whether members of the organization would be staring at me, wondering what a man was doing in their midst. As it turned out, there were more men at the convention than I expected. Not many, but some. There are, in fact, males who major in Women's Studies and males who teach it; at the conference, three or four of the presentations at the sessions I attended were given by men. Since these men's devotion to Women's Studies presumably betokens rejection of the patriarchy, one might expect that their female colleagues would welcome their involvement with unalloyed delight; but in fact more than a few women continue to view such men as accomplices (however unwilling) in the patriarchy—for whether the men like it or not, their sex, in the eyes of Women's Studies, confers privilege and power.

Outside the academy, the man-hatred that was a feature of second-wave radical feminism has dissipated. But it hasn't disappeared, and there are still plenty of feminists today, in and outside of universities, who prefer not to mix with men. I'm provided with a vivid reminder of this fact at the Cultural Studies conference at Berkeley, where, at a session sponsored by the Critical Feminist Studies Division, Amy Barber of the University of Wisconsin at Madison discusses women's music festivals as "alternative spaces to heteropatriarchy." Perky, skinny, and boyish, Barber looks as if she's leapt out of the pages of *Dykes to Watch Out For*, Alison Bechdel's popular comic strip about hip young lesbians. Barber's talk, based on her dissertation, is about the annual, weeklong Michigan Womyn's Music Festival in rural northwest Michigan, which draws thousands of women annually, is isolated from the outside world, and, Barber exults, provides "one of the few opportunities to live in a woman-only space." (She quotes a friend's enthusiastic description of it as a "completely female-worshipping environment.") "Women rearrange their lives and careers," Barber notes, to spend a week walking around bare-chested in a "*community* by and for women" where "women build everything." (When a platform needs to be constructed or a tent erected, the organizers go out of their way not to hire men.) If under "rare circumstances, men must enter the land"—for example, to "clean the port-o-janes"—the man in question is "always escorted" and everyone is warned beforehand so that naked or half-naked women can cover up and those who don't want to see a man can escape into the woods until he disappears. Some women, to be sure, decide not to run away or cover up: "I'm not putting my shirt on for any man," they'll say. "This is *our* space." (Barber's paper, by the way, is titled "I'm Not Putting My Shirt on for Any Man': Body Politics at the Michigan Womyn's Festival.")

Which brings us to Barber's point: for a week every year, these women can "feel good in their own bodies," free of "patriarchal expectations of how female bodies should look." They're encouraged to develop positive relationships with their own and other women's bodies. Most of the attendees are lesbians, but the festival isn't about sex—it's about the "right to be naked without being objectified." If "heteropatriarchal culture" makes women feel "uncomfortable in their own bodies," so that their bodies "serve as a source of oppression in everyday life," at the festival women are freed from the "threat of the male gaze." Not that "the male gaze" alone is threatening: women's gazes, too, Barber admits, can also be "judging" and "objectifying." After all, there's "lots of flirting, lots of sex" at the festival. "But I'm not going to keep down that path," Barber says. (Why not? Because it might lead to heresy?) The important thing, she insists, in a seeming contradiction, is that the Womyn's Music Festival "is a space where I *can't* be objectified." Whatever. The bottom line is this:

the festival is about much more than music. There are workshops in which women can "explore their feelings about their bodies" and ponder the question: "Are we oppressed and in what ways?" There's "fat activism and fat pride"—though not as much, Barber says, as there was back in the 1980s. (This decline seems curious, given that one of the fastest-growing new "identity studies" in recent years, as we shall see, has been something called Fat Studies.) Barber cites T-shirt slogans that are popular at the festival: "Fat Is Beautiful." "The Goddess Is Fat." "Your Diet Soda Oppresses Me." She notes that the festival is a "sex-positive place" where "public sex is acceptable," and that some of the workshops are "hands-on" affairs at which you can learn "how to find your g-spot" and find out about "sex toys" and "female ejaculation."

There have, however, been controversies. Sadomasochism, for example, has occasioned disagreements as to the appropriateness of "women policing what other women do with their bodies." Another source of contention, since 1991, has been the question of whether transgendered women should be admitted to the festival. The long-standing policy that "the festival is only for women *born* women" is protested annually, Barber says, and, she adds, is "definitionally problematic," given that "many transgender women feel they *were* born women." But other women reject this claim, pointing out that "transgender women have never had to worry about pregnancy or periods." Quoting a statement by Judith Butler—the postmodernist colossus whom we will meet again in the chapter on Queer Studies—to the effect that a fixed definition of the word *woman* can inhibit feminism, Barber asks what it means to have a woman's body, given that "biology itself can be ambiguous." (This seems a classic case of feminists tossing out social constructionism and embracing biology when it suits their purposes—about which more later.) One proposal floated at the festival has been a "no penises" policy. This might be a positive measure, Barber suggests, because if it were implemented then "no one would ever have to see a penis." But there are two problems with this idea, one of them being that it's "classist" because of "the cost of transitioning" (rich transsexuals can afford to have their penises sliced off, while poor transsexuals can't) and the other being that "there are women who identify as trans women" for whom surgery would, for one reason or another, be too dangerous.

Barber sums up her portrait of the festival by saying that it's about "women feeling safe"—because men, after all, are by nature violent. But she acknowledges that black women can also feel threatened by white women, fat women by thin, and so forth. The problems, in short, never cease; the dream of a space in which one can be certain of feeling entirely unthreatened, entirely comfortable in one's own body, remains elusive. She notes that women used to be allowed to bring their sons, as long as they were under seven years old, because the organizers figured that a seven-year-old boy was "presumably not old enough to oppress women." Then a seven-year-old boy "harassed" a little girl (Barber provides no details), so the age limit was lowered to five. To be sure, there's an "independent camp" where mothers can stow their male children aged five and up; there's also an area reserved for women with disabilities and, rather incredibly, "a woman-of-color-only space." By the end of Barber's talk, this event she's celebrating sounds like a product of the imagination of some master of speculative fiction like Philip K. Dick or Ray Bradbury—a mad dystopia in which feminist dreams have led to a forest full of separate clearings in which more and more women keep to smaller and smaller groups for fear of encountering difference.

In any event, to say that Women's Studies is intrinsically hostile to men is not an exaggeration but an understatement. For the field is antagonistic not just toward men themselves, but also toward a wide range of traditional academic phenomena that are considered "masculinist" or "patriarchal" or "phallocentric." Among the elements of academic life that are widely reviled as relics of outdated, male-identified ways of thinking are the bestowing of grades, the setting of deadlines, the presentation of logical arguments, the enforcement of prescriptive language rules, and regard for the scientific method. Some women in the field are uncomfortable with the power they wield as professors, because the very idea of being in positions of authority seems to them uncomfortably masculinist, and for this reason they refuse to make up syllabi or reading lists, to lecture, to take a leadership role in the classroom, or to admit to being more knowledgeable about anything than their students; instead, their classrooms become settings for undirected discussion about ones feelings. More generally, the widespread antagonism toward male-identified traditions results in a slovenly approach to the whole business of teaching: a lack of preparedness, sloppily written syllabi, and the like. Some Women's Studies practitioners actually profess to reject the entire edifice of civilization out of hand as a product of male culture (not that they disdain, in practice, any of the products of civilization, from indoor plumbing to Power-Point). If Friedan and Greer encouraged women to charge boldly onto formerly male-dominated playing fields and to strive for excellence in competition with men, in Women's Studies today the very concept of merit, whether aesthetic or intellectual, is often viewed with suspicion as offensively masculinist and as a threat to communal harmony and universal self-esteem.

Then there's "the math problem." Many female students have trouble with math and science—and while teachers of these subjects may encourage them to work harder, Women's Studies professors are likely to inform them that the problem lies not in their own short-comings but in the fields themselves. Math and science, they're told, are of limited value because these subjects are based on "male" ways of knowing—on, that is, rationality, a male social construction that ignores "female" (that is to say, emotionally rather than intellectually centered) ways of experiencing and understanding the world. Indeed, many Women's Studies students are taught to be suspicious of strictly intellectual endeavors—of endeavors, in other words, that don't involve or prioritize feelings. (Typical of this perspective is Andrea Nye's statement in *Words of Power: A Feminist Reading of the History of Logic* that logic is a tool of male oppression and "in its final perfection is insane.") Christina Hoff Sommers quotes one professor's complaint about "students who have been trained to take the feminist perspective": "For them *reason* itself is patriarchal, linear, and oppressive." In other words, Women's Studies agrees with the Victorians that women *are* the less intellectual sex; the difference is that in the view of Women's Studies this doesn't make them inferior but superior.

There is, to be sure, a countervailing tendency in Women's Studies. Michèle Le Doeuff, author of *The Sex of Knowing*, rejects the idea that women are less rational beings than men. And some women working in more rigorous academic disciplines openly resent professional feminists' disparagement of the scientific method. In *Manifesto of a Passionate Moderate* (1998), philosopher Susan Haack writes that she was unsettled to hear "feminists or multiculturalists" saying "that thinking about evidence and inquiry as I did revealed complicity with sexism or racism." Then there are some feminists who seek to make the sciences more "woman-friendly" by reducing or eliminating the rational component and introducing "empathy" and other supposedly female qualities. Complaining in *Feminism and Geography* that "geography has historically been dominated by men" and "concentrates on the spaces, places and landscapes that it *sees* as men's," Gillian Rose proposes a more female-friendly geography focusing on "women's spaces" and taking a "women's perspective." In a recent course on "Geography and Gender" at the University of Aberdeen, students could learn that "[geography's 'founding fathers'...viewed the world from a position of masculinist reason," that the study of geography traditionally involves undesirable "masculinist codes of...academic rigor," and that geographers display a lamentable "[m]asculine rationality" that reflects their (apparently misguided) view that "they can separate themselves from their body, emotions, values, past etc. so that their thoughts are context-free and objective." (The extent of such thinking about geography is testified to by the existence of a scholarly periodical titled *Gender, Place and Culture: A Journal of Feminist Geography*.)

A key text for third-wave feminism is Carol Gilligan's *In a Different Voice: Psychological Theory and Women's Development* (1982). At its most extreme, Gilligan's book is profoundly separatist, arguing that in a society suffused with patriarchy, women are better off withdrawing into a safe, women-only setting—Gilligan's island, one might call it (though Gilligan herself is heterosexual and has been married to a man for decades). Gilligan, who is a psychologist and ethicist, argues that there are "two ways of speaking about moral problems, two modes of describing the relationship between other and self," each of which is associated with one of the two *sexes*; and although "this association is not absolute," there is, she argues, a significant correlation, and our society, being patriarchal, operates according to, and gives preference to, the male mode while disdaining the female. The result is "a limitation in the conception of [the] human condition, an omission of certain truths about life," for theories once "considered to be sexually neutral in their scientific objectivity" turn out instead "to reflect a consistent observational and evaluative bias."

Gilligan quotes with approval the claim by sociologist and psychologist Nancy J. Chodorow that the differences between male and female mentalities are not biologically based but are, rather, manifestations of the fact that children are raised primarily by their mothers. Hence, writes Gilligan, "female identity formation takes place in a context of ongoing relation" with a person of the same sex, while identity formation in boys involves a distancing from their mothers—the result being that "masculinity is defined through separation while femininity is defined through attachment, male gender identity is threatened by intimacy while female gender identity is threatened by separation. Thus males tend to have difficulty with relationships, while females tend to have problems with individuation."

Gilligan attributes to women a greater gift for empathy, a greater "[s]ensitivity to the needs of others," and "an overriding concern with relationships and responsibilities." (Chodorow puts it this way: boys learn to relate to others in terms of power; girls don't.) While men are concerned with "the primacy and universality of individual rights," she maintains, women have more of a sense of being part of a community and of having responsibility to others. While women define identity "in a context of relationship" and judge it "by a standard of responsibility and care," and view morality "as arising from the experience of connection," for men "identity is different, clearer, more direct, more distinct and sharp-edged." But whereas "we have listened for centuries to the voices of men and the theories of development that their experience informs," women have lived mostly in silence and, when they do speak, have not been listened to. Another influential book that makes related points is *Women's Ways of Knowing: The Development of Self, Voice, and Mind* (1986) by Mary Field Belenky, Blythe McVicker Clinchy, Nancy Rule Goldberger, and Jill Mattuck Tarule. The authors exalt what they call women's "connected knowing," which, they argue, is based on a "commonality of experience" and on shared emotions, and reject men's "separate knowing," which is rooted in a dispassionate "mastery of relevant knowledge and methodology" and involves rigorous critical thinking and logical proofs. Educators, they conclude,

> can help women develop their own authentic voices if they emphasize connection over separation, understanding and acceptance over assessment, and collaboration over debate; if they accord respect to and allow time for the knowledge that emerges from firsthand experience; if instead of imposing their own expectations and arbitrary requirements, they encourage students to evolve their own patterns of work based on the problems they are pursuing. These are the lessons we have learned in listening to women's voices.

And then there's Peggy McIntosh, associate director of the Wellesley Centers for Women and author of a famous 1988 essay, "White Privilege and Male Privilege: A Personal Account of Coming to See Correspondences through Work in Women's Studies." McIntosh introduces race into the equation, identifying white men as "vertical thinkers," out to master topics and achieve excellence, and describing white women and people of color as "lateral thinkers" who are "relational" and "inclusive."

Although Haack complains wryly that "new-fangled feminist ideas of 'women's ways of knowing'" are nothing but the same old "sexist stereotypes that old-fashioned feminists used to deplore," one of those old-fashioned feminists, Phyllis Chesler, accepts that there are deep-seated differences between men and women. Yet in Chesler's reckoning, women don't always come out on the positive side of the ledger: "While men kill openly and directly and know how to enforce party lines, they also know how to give other men (but not necessarily women) some serious personal and ideological breathing room. Men do not take their differences *personally*, women usually do." In Chester's view, women fear conflict and prize conformity; many of them "self-censor as a way of belonging." (Certainly the dynamics of Women's Studies would seem to confirm this view.) What's more, "women's overwhelming need for intimacy...leads to passivity, conservatism, and a refusal to take responsibility for injustice." Gilligan, to be sure, speaks of the "tyranny of niceness," the need to be seen as polite and virtuous that can keep women from asserting themselves; but Chesler complains that Gilligan is "so invested in presenting girls and women...as...morally 'different' and superior to men" that she ignores the distinguishing moral failures of females—what Chesler calls "false niceness," conformism, and a tendency "to censor unpopular or original thinking."

One cannot discuss "women's ways of knowing" without mentioning *écriture feminine*, a French school of language theory whose name was coined by Hélène Cixous. Dating back to the early 1970s, it counts among its other leading lights Luce Irigaray, Julia Kristeva, and Monique Wittig, who argue that language is by nature masculinist, and that women, when they use it, are wielding an instrument that is foreign to them and that was invented as a means of suppressing them. Therefore it's the task of women to place their own stamp on language, an act that the "French feminists," as they're commonly called, associate with the female body. (Cixous, for example, compares "the desire to write" to "the gestation drive.") It's fair to say that these women's ideas don't easily translate into clear French, let alone clear English.

Even Peace Studies, of all things, is too "masculinist" for some Women's Studies stalwarts. I learn this at an NWSA convention session in which four white women discuss "outsider feminisms." (The session's title is "Bodies in Question: Outsider Feminisms, Oppositional Knowledges, and Common Struggles.") Anya Stanger of Syracuse University says that she started out as a student of Peace Studies, because she wanted to learn "how to contest violence in all forms." But she found that Peace Theory could cause, rather than resolve, conflicts. It was Women's Studies that taught her what the problem was: Peace Studies is too masculinist; it views identity as fixed, says that "violence is not natural," maintains that the key to teaching soldiers is "dehumanization" and "distanciation [*sic*] between people," and preaches that the converse of dehumanization is "humanization." But all these claims, says Stanger, are wrong, for violence and so-called dehumanization are a natural part of male behavior. Therefore Peace Studies needs to be corrected by "transnational feminist theory," which understands the importance of challenging "hegemonic Western masculine constructions of knowledge." Stanger now views Peace Studies through a Women's Studies lens, for she recognizes that "ignoring feminist insights" in peace work can result in "replicatingviolence."

What goes on in a Women's Studies classroom? A group of blogs kept by the professor and students in an introductory Women's Studies course at a state university that shall be nameless offers a rare look not only at what happens behind the closed classroom doors but also at what happens in the students' minds. On her blog, the professor, whom I shall call Ms. Channing, explained that in the course, which was taught in the spring of 2009, gender would be understood

> by examining ways in which power is deployed over and through bodies for use of the nation-state and elites. We will critique feminist histories, knowledges, and production in the face of imperialism, colonialism, environmental development-destruction & the negative consequences of violences deployed against poor, subordinated, and indigenous peoples. Tools and methods are provided to respond to expressions of anticolonial resistances to Western development logics.

Note that this was not listed as a course in imperialism or colonialism or international relations—it was a course designed to introduce students to Women's Studies. Its emphasis on matters that the pioneers of second-wave feminism never would have considered particularly relevant to the women's movement is typical. So is the teacher's prose style. (Why settle for knowledge, violence, and resistance when you can have "knowledges," "violences," and "resistances"?) The course reading list was also unsurprising, including such books as Gwyn Kirk and Margo Okazawa-Rey's *Women's Lives: Multicultural Perspectives* (2009), Barbara H. Chasin's *Inequality and Violence in the United States: Casualties of Capitalism* (2004), and Stephen Burman's *The State of the American Empire: How the USA Shapes the World* (2007), plus various online materials about rape, race, patriarchy, white privilege, heterosexual privilege, the rights of indigenous people, the feminization of poverty, and the military-industrial complex.

Channing explained that on the midterm, students would be expected to "give form and definition to the theories, methods and practices which inform your current understanding of gender and power in historical and contemporary contexts," to "move from untethered supposition and opinion to intentional, articulated, informed, engaged and specific footholds which speak to your understanding of the ways in which gender, and power relationships, are articulated as gender intersects race, class, hierarchy, patriarchy, religion, militarism, capitalism, global systems, work, labor, citizenship, and nation," and to "engage deeply in a critical analysis practice regarding the literatures and methods examined in class thus far and to articulate more concretely an appreciation for and understanding of systemic, institutional, and structural components in social relationships." Simply put, they would be expected to abandon their own views and start parroting Women's Studies rhetoric about social constructionism, intersectionality, and so forth. Channing called on her students to "[p]rovide an analysis that is engaged and using critical tools which you have had access to thus far in this course. Here is an [*sic*] model which you can build upon, and/or develop your own model. However, your model must have this level of complexity in terms of you are [*sic*] doing intersectional analysis: the INTERSECTION of gender, power, race, class, history, labor, migration, immigration, etc."

Channing introduced her students to the concept of patriarchy by having them read a portion of Allan G. Johnson's book *The Gender Knot: Unraveling Our Patriarchal Legacy* that was excerpted in *Women's Lives*, "I've never come across the word 'patriarchy' before," wrote H. (a biochemistry major from

Hawaii who listed her interests as "Music, Piano, Make-up, Arts & Crafts, Beach, Baking, anything and everything & just having fun"), "so I found this article in *Women's Lives* quite interesting.... I never knew it before, but we live in a patriarchal culture that creates inequalities between men and women." Her classmate A. commented on H.'s posting: "Like you, before this course I had not heard the term patriarchy in this context." But now "I notice power dynamics within my relationships with both men and women." And here's R., a journalism major:

> White, middle to upper class, males have surrounded me my whole life. My family is ran [*sic*] by them, my neighbor [*sic*] is full of them, my government is dominated by them, and they have mostly been the authority figures in my life.... I am sometimes in a bind between wanting to be extremely independent and also wanting to be taken care of.

> I must embarrassingly admit that often my room-mate and I will lie in bed at night and talk about how we want to fall in love.... why do I sometimes so strongly desire this? Is it because our society has embedded into my brain the ideals and wants a women [*sic*] should look for in a man?... As a society we promote behaviors of male dominance, and breed a misogynic [*sic*] culture.... This male dominance is everywhere.

Note that the students seem not to have been *taught*, in any objective way, about the radical-feminist concept of patriarchy, and were certainly not presented with a range of views about it; no, they were plainly inculcated with the concept and were put to work "dissecting patriarchy in our society." They were so wet behind the ears that they didn't even realize that they weren't being educated but indoctrinated; they were so malleable, so easily manipulated intellectually, that it didn't even occur to them that if they hadn't ever heard of or thought about patriarchy and its role in their lives, perhaps it was because the concept didn't have any great relevance to the way they lived in America in the twenty-first century. Another student, B., wrote that Johnson's "strongest message to me was that by doing nothing we contribute to this evil that allows for men to be on top and have superiority." She mentioned "the game monoply [*sic*]," which "not only teaches us to put ourselves on top, by giving us rules it allows us to have an excuse to act in a way that puts others below you." B. professed to share Johnson's concern that "when a man is accused of rapping [raping] a child, we very quickly blame him...rather then [*sic*] examining the society that allows violence towards women in video games and movies. Its [*sic*] about looking at the roots." One suspects that B. is entirely unaware of the disastrous consequences of Great Society programs founded on a let's-blame-society-and-get-to-the-roots philosophy; her comment here provided a fine example of what happens when you push ideology on young people who are almost completely innocent of history.

Women's Lives contains a substantial section on violence against women, including readings about rape. Here's what C. learned:

> [W]omen everywhere live under the threat of rape, the greatest risk often in their own homes! Rape is a highly unreported crime because people think that rape is only having sex. However, this is not true and rape constitutes any violence inhibited [she means committed] to assert male power and control. The article stated that estimates suggest that the actual incidence of rape may be up to 50 times the numbers reported. Where did things go wrong in American society to make living in America so dangerous?... It is apparent that rape, as well as many other types of sexual violence, has become a HUGE problem when a woman isn't even safe in her own home.... Now that women have gained more rights in all sorts of aspects in society, I feel that men are lashing out by inhibiting

acts of violence because it is the only means they
can think of to get back at them....

In addition to regurgitating the exaggerations about rape served
up in *Women's Lives* (and throughout Women's Studies), C. recorded
her response to a film about male violence that was screened for the
class: "Being that men are more likely to inhibit [again, she means
commit] murder and assault, as a women [*sic*] I need to be aware of
not only this, but also of the cultural influences and emphasism/pres-
sure [*sic*] for men to be this way. I need to become more aware of the
environment/people around me, as well as an understanding of the
pressures media places over men." A classmate, J., commented on C. s
remarks: "I wonder if men also commit acts of violence because they
are given no other examples of how to deal with complex emotions.
The entertainment industry (movies, music, etc) links violence with
toughness and masculinity, and the news media ignores the fact that
men are commiting [*sic*] the vast majority of crimes...."

In one exercise, Channing asked her students to comment
on a series of print advertisements plainly chosen because they
lent themselves to feminist interpretations. One ad, for Dolce &
Gabbana, showed four beautiful, bare-chested young men, one
of them holding a beautiful young woman in a sexy clinch on
the floor. Erotic stuff, but C. wasn't turned on: "This image...
displays a gender powered [*sic*] and is focused on white, wealthy
males as their audience. It looks like the man is about to beat the
woman with the other men intently watching.... This is representative to American society and the abuse that men inhibit on
women [curiously, while Channing often commented on student
blogs, she seems never to have explained to C. the meaning of the
word *inhibit*].... I feel that men inhibiting violence upon women
has become such a common topic that people are immune to the
effects it has." K. agreed: "When I look at this ad, I see this group
of men as trying to establish their dominance over this woman.
The fact that her back is extended and her legs are strained implies
that she is struggling to get out of the grasp of the muscular man
hovering over her." (What about the fact that her facial expression
clearly conveys not fear but arousal?)

Channing also assigned Judith Lorber's essay "The Social Construction of Gender." After reading it, R. pondered whether, if men and women stopped playing socially constructed roles (that is, if men baked cookies and women competed in NASCAR), men might no longer be "faster, stronger"—an idea that would, of course, be considered foolish anywhere outside of the academy, but that, in Women's Studies, represents a respected version of social constructionism. H., too, entirely accepted the idea of gender as a social construction, admitting that she herself was "prone to gendering" (she buys blue gifts for baby boys and pink gifts for girls) and quoting a Marge Piercy poem titled "Barbie Doll." The poem inspired Channing to post a comment on H.'s blog:

> There is quite alot [sic] of debate about "Barbie"-ing of femininity in U.S. culture, and the diminuization [sic] of female social, economic and political power as a backlash against females in general—in U.S. culture. Although there is a mass consumption idea that females have "gained" "power", I wonder... [ellipsis in original] to what degree? Is there a corollary between increasing violent crime rates targetting [sic] females (from infants to elderly women) in general, in U.S. culture, and a general sense of apathy and resistance of patriarchal leaders (political, religious, economic) against women's (Black, Native American, Mexican-American/Latina, Asian, White, poor, working class, immigrant) progress (i.e. healthcare, education, economic stability, reproductive choices....)????

One of H.'s classmates, T., agreed that "[g]endering really is part of society" and so did another, S.: "as a woman you are gendered to act a certain way." They had all swallowed the social-constructionist dogma, in short, without even realizing that it *is* dogma. And why shouldn't they? They had obviously been presented with social constructionism as if it were a scientifically demonstrated and universally accepted concept, like the Second Law of Thermodynamics.

Anti-Americanism figured significantly in Channing's course. To H.'s credit, after reading a chapter in the Burman book titled "How the World Sees America & How America Sees the World," she said she felt "like he is bashing the United States of America.... I don't think America is *that* bad.... Is it just me or is there a lot of negativity in this text?" Neatly complementing readings on the evils of America were readings on the evils of capitalism. "The United States of America," wrote B., "survives on capitalism, we live off of production and time is constantly on our minds.... I have always been told since I was a child that we had to work hard so we could get a good job. Whenever I said things like, I don't want money or don't need money I was shot down." L. had this to say: "It's sickening to me that people actually have an incentive to continue inequality.... Again, it seems to go back to these white men in corporations and all they want is to make money without regard to whom they hurt." L.: "This reading really opened my eyes to the power big corporations really have over the individual lifestyles we lead and the inequalities prevalent in our society today." C., for her part, suggested that violence in America is due "to American's strong desires of being the best. The competition in America is outrageous.... There is such a large emphasis on getting a good education, making a lot of money, and buying all of these material objects that make us look good to the public eye." How mischievous to implant such hostility to capitalism in students who know virtually nothing about the history of either capitalism or socialism.

Channing's course paid special attention to the supposed role of capitalist greed in military spending—and again, the students dutifully parroted what they were told. C.: "The amount of money and focus that goes into the military is excessive.... It is a conspiracy as to how the big business corporations team up with the government to improve their personal profits and maintaining the status of having the newest weapons etc." K.:

> This selection emphasized how sneaky and seductive U.S. militarization can be in our society....
> It doesn't help that since September 11th, not showing support of the military has been seen as

unpatriotic and disloyal. In fact, it is this increased militarization of our culture that largely allowed George W. Bush to go to war in the first place. This cultural militarization has made war seem patriotic, romantic, and has even inspired a sense of security in our society.... In high schools all over the nation, ROTC, Marines, Air Force, and Navy representatives are allowed to station booths in lunch rooms in order to advertise the benefits of joining to young, impressionable teens.

That wasn't all K. had to say. "The amount that the U.S. spends on its military and on militaristic operations," she wrote in another posting, "is absolutely staggering. A lot of this has to do with the agendas of personal investors in big businesses.... If there is no reason to go to war with another country, then we shouldn't! If they have a resource we want, we should negotiate with them! Didn't we learn in pre-school that it's nice to share?" This is the level at which college students are being taught to "think" about national defense. (Talk about taking advantage of "young, impressionable teens"!)

Now, if you're going to turn young people against America, it's important to convince them that Americans are uniquely racist. One of K.'s postings addressed a chapter in the Chasin book that "focused on crime committed by white individuals against black individuals." Her comment: "as I read through this, I was wondering whether our society has become less violent towards other races over time." (There is no need to ask, of course, whether the chapter contained statistics comparing the frequency of white-on-black violence with that of black-on-white violence.) Then there was the essay in *Women's Lives* titled "Media Representations and the Criminalization of Arab Americans and Muslim Americans." K.'s take:

This article discusses how Muslim and Arab women are typified [she means depicted] as weak, battered women due to their culture and the stereotypes placed on Arab men. I think that as a people in the U.S., we tend to see Arab and

Islamic men as embodying the terrorist ideals; it's only natural therefore that we feel compassion for the women that these terrorists live with. Since we typecast them as such horrendous people, we shudder at the disposition [*sic*] of the wives and young girls that get abused by them. When a terrorist activity or a crime is committed, we tend to label them as "Islamic/Arab/Muslim fundamentalists or extremists." By including the word "Islam" as their primary identity, we start identifying Islamic with crime and evil. In actuality, the Islamic religion is a very peaceable one that believes in the equality and support of women. In fact, in one of the Prophet Muhammad's last speeches, he illustrates: "Treat your women well and be kind to them, for they are your partners and committed helpers."... There is nothing wrong with the Islamic religion; it preaches equality for both men and women.... The Islamic culture is a very rich and beautiful one; we shouldn't blame it for being the cause of these extremist groups.

In this posting, K. perfectly summed up the standard Women's Studies position on Islam and women—namely, that Westerners shouldn't describe Muslim women as oppressed, because if we do so we're saying that they're weak and that their men are tyrants, and this is culturally insensitive (even though it's acceptable to say that all Western men are potential rapists). Nor should it ever be suggested that the acts of violence committed by Muslim terrorists have anything to do with Islam. Second-wave pioneers like Friedan, Millett, and Greer would have recognized solidarity with subjugated Muslim women as a vital feminist cause; today's Women's Studies refuses to take a clear, firm stand on the rights of the most downtrodden women on the planet.

Channing had her students read the Declaration of Independence, Constitution, and Bill of Rights. Their blog postings made it clear that they understood what was expected of them. Calling the Declaration "incredibly biased and slanted," R. wrote that "when you scan the document all you see is 'He.'... Immediately I think 'Great, my founding fathers did not want me to be apart [*sic*] of this nation.'" (R. appeared not to notice that the reason why the word *he* recurs so frequently in the Declaration is that the document consists largely of a litany of charges against King George III, whom it refers to as "he.") "All people were not created equal when the Declaration of Independence was written," R. lamented. H. seconded the condemnation: "The Declaration of Independence & the Bill of Rights…were written by a group of white, Christian, heterosexual males." C. was on board, too: "Before this was pointed out in the class discussion, I had never noticed the complication that can be derived from the U.S. Declaration of Independence when considering who 'we the people' is referring to." (Of course, the words "we the people" don't appear in the Declaration but in the preamble to the Constitution.)

Clearly, Channing had not taught her young charges that the Declaration and Constitution, while two of the noblest documents in the history of humankind, were also, naturally, products of their time that reflected the limitations of their time (which, needless to say, is why the Constitution has been amended so many times since its ratification); no, she had taught them to revile the founding fathers—men whose vision, courage, and sacrifice made possible the freedom these students have known (and taken for granted) all their lives. These young women were incapable of grasping that the very criteria by which they presumed to judge the authors of the Declaration and Constitution would not be available to them if not for those men's efforts. To say this, of course, is not to blame these students for their ignorance, but to underscore just how profoundly ill-served they are by courses of this sort.

On her blog, apparently addressing nonstudents, Channing acknowledged that her students "come into the class with very little critical preparation of historical processes and movements of the 20th century, much less U.S. history, or the history of U.S. foreign policy"—all of which, naturally, made them perfect subjects for indoctrination in Women's Studies dogma. Indeed, Channing, far from trying to rectify her students' nearly total ignorance about history, focused instead on instilling in them the "fundamental theories and literatures of 'gender and power,' through the matrix of race, class, sexuality, labor, migration, militarism, family, religion, and empire." To be sure, though Channing, on her blog, gave (as she put it) "prominance [*sic*] to the standpoints and differentiation which is [*sic*] occuring [*sic*] as students give voice to self and community identifications"—in other words, she posted some of the views they'd expressed—she lamented that they'd exhibited "resistances to applying critical theories required of the course syllabus, which are general applications in the fields of Social Sciences, Gender Studies, Critical Race, etc.," and had instead proffered "opinion." In other words, the students did too much independent thinking. Channing outlined the ideological approaches (or "tools") that she'd pressed upon her students, actually equating social constructionism and other ideologies that they had been too slow to parrot with "microscopes, petri dishes, beakers," and "the stuff of 'evidentiary scientific laws'"— her point being that while students don't question the laws of hard science "in the context of a 'science lab,'" they dared to question social constructionism, multiculturalism, and so on. This lack of readiness to become perfectly obedient feminist soldiers had led Channing to decide that, in future classes, she would challenge students to "confront critically the personal and group resistances to the sciences, methods and theories of gender, race, sexuality, systems, and histories of oppressed communities and polities"—in other words, she'd push them even harder to exchange their own views for Women's Studies orthodoxy. While Channing's students, then, were by any traditional academic measure disturbingly pliant, they weren't pliant enough for Channing. How strange to recall that second-wave feminism was born out of an urgently felt longing for a generation of women who would think for themselves!

To be sure, Women's Studies isn't only about lockstep ideology. After all, in feminism today, intellect is subordinate to emotion, and the movement's foundation lies in women's experiences, not their ideas. Consequently, many Women's Studies courses involve something very much resembling therapy. An essay included in *The Feminist Teacher Anthology* describes one such innovation: the "NO circle." When overcome by "wrenching pain" in reaction to some brutal act against a woman, students form a circle and call out the names of things they say "no" to: "Rape! beatings! harassment! racism!" "For empowerment to occur," explains the author, Martha E. Thompson, "we must act collectively to challenge violence against women." Note that she is not talking about engaging in actual *activism*—no, the classroom therapy is itself the "act," the "challenge."

One familiar justification for study-as-therapy is that it's not enough for a professor simply to pump young women full of the proper precepts; they must also have enough drive, motivation, and self-esteem to be able to act properly upon those precepts. And many female students (or so goes the theory) simply don't have the requisite self-esteem because they've grown up in a society run by men who've labored to keep females' self-esteem down, so that they might remain subservient. (So, at least, goes the theory. In reality, what often happens is that young female students in Women's Studies classes tend to be treated with such kid gloves, as if they were tender saplings, that they *become* tender saplings—they learn, in short, to see themselves as precisely the kind of fragile flowers that Friedan and Greer strove to convince women they weren't.) Another reason to put emphasis on subjective feeling and not objective fact is that, as we have seen, many Women's Studies practitioners view objectivity as a false concept—a masculinist concept—and consider personal experience the one true thing.

All of which helps explain the existence of a 2010 NWSA session titled "Writing Our Feminist Selves: Uses of Memoir in Feminist Pedagogy and Action." The four panelists are drawn from a group of about thirty Oregon State University students who took part in a memoir-writing project. One of them, a pretty white girl in a stylish green-and-white outfit and a chic hairdo (and with a disconcerting beauty contestant smile), speaks of the project as "transformative feminist pedagogy" and describes memoir writing as an act of "identity building" and "feminist knowledge production" that "disrupt[s] hegemonic ideologies" (which is "especially important in terms of race and ethnicity"). The point of writing the memoirs, she says, was "to convey how we were situated in oppressive circumstances": indeed, by writing the memoirs, students "came to a new understanding of how we participated in these systems of oppression" and learned how to "engage" those systems. While students from privileged backgrounds were "forced to confront" how their lives "oppress others," underprivileged students learned to recognize and resist their oppression. All in all, she enthuses, the project showed how "the feminist classroom is an outlet for creating social change," gave "our feelings and emotions...a place in the classroom," and reflected the fact that Women's Studies offers "more than just a focus on the mind"—it "builds empathy." (She does acknowledge one problem with the memoir project: namely, some students "are unwilling to be liberated.")

The next speaker celebrates the cathartic aspect of memoir writing: it purges, "brings traumatic events to the surface," allows one to "process emotions." And, of course, "empowers." "We want [students'] *eyes* to be open," she says, "to social constructions" that have affected them. She tells us (as several speakers at this conference have done) that "the personal is political and the political is personal." Writing memoirs "gives women time and permission to process" their emotions, "sets [them] free to express [their] stories in personally meaningful ways," and allows them to "take ownership of the interpretation" of their experiences and to have those experiences "validated" by their classmates. Describing the project as "cathartic pedagogy," the student acknowledges "the value of being heard": "validation is a very important need for human beings," she says, and "we found that validation among our sister classmates." She points out that when the memoir-writing group touched upon violence against women, students were told that if the material hit too close to home they could leave the classroom at any time, and were given the phone numbers of people who could help them get through the trauma of having heard these things discussed. The speaker adds that students who had been abused or raped were told (in line with rape-feminism orthodoxy) that their trauma wasn't the work of an individual but was "orchestrated by a larger system that *depends* on the terrorization of women and other marginal groups."

The third participant celebrates memoir writing as a boon for "traditionally marginalized students" because it can create "counter-narratives that challenge racist and heterosexist" positions. She confesses that when the project began, she wondered: "Who would want to hear the story of a Latina multiracial queer woman?"—meaning herself (though, like all the other panelists, she looks white). But then she realized that she had internalized the prejudices of a "racist, heterosexist society." Now she views memoir writing as "radical pedagogy" and "liberatory education" that challenges "traditional" practices, "offers alternatives" to the "hegemonic," and "interrogat[es] biases in curricula." Once she "felt invisible"; now she and the other memoir writers are "hearing one another's voices and recognizing one another's presence." She says she doesn't like the word *memoir* because it's a Western word for "a decidedly Western construct." The word, she tells us, "comes from the French—I think—I have no French." She looks around to see if anyone else on the panel knows any French. Nope. Another panelist ventures: "It *sounds* French." (This brief exchange about whether or not *memoir* sounds French underscores just how far removed all this activity is from actual education.) In any case, panelist number three explains that because the word *memoir* carries so much Western baggage, she "use[s] 'life writing' exchangeably [she means *interchangeably*] with the word *memoir!*'

Only one of the panelists has any reservations about memoir writing. Nancy Barbour, who (like Willingham at the Beijing +15 session) is older than the others, views feminist memoirs as evidence of the "narcissistic tendency of third wave feminism" and, on a larger scale, as representative of the "confessional mode of society today." Lamenting the recent "mainstreaming of personal memoir" that, she says, can be attributed at least partly to Oprah Winfrey and that "turn[s] victimhood and oppression into a performance," Barbour asks: how can we make feminist memoirs politically meaningful, and not just acts of narcissistic display? She worries: will the writing of memoirs "fragment the group of women"? Will there be "competitive suffering"? Will non-oppressed women feel left out or compelled to invent? Instead of producing "self-congratulatory, feel-good" journals, she insists, we need to "engage...systems of oppression"—for too many memoirs are individually oriented and thus "aren't condu-cive to activism." Barbour calls on younger women to "analyze your own experiences within systems of oppression" in accordance with "second-wave methods of consciousness-raising," and concludes, in a tone of urgency, that "the personal memoir should be voluntary," lest students be pressured into situations that will only enhance their narcissism or cause them emotional damage. A pattern is starting to emerge at the NWSA: though the dominant voice is that of the delicate-flower, navel-gazing sorority sisters of the third wave, with their multicultural fears, hesitations, and equivocations, sprinkled among them are a few second-wave dinosaurs, like Willingham and Barbour, who still believe in universal sisterhood and in resistance to *all* patriarchal oppression.

I've heard so much about the Women's Studies classroom as a site for touchy-feely personal exchanges that I feel compelled to attend a Friday morning session titled "'I'm not your mother, your mentor, your big sister, or your best friend. I'm your women's studies professor.'" Four of the women on the panel are black; two are white. The moderator is Frances Smith Foster of Emory University, a stout, vivacious, good-humored older black woman in an African-looking multicolored jacket; her singsong, syrupy, accented voice, punctilious pronunciation, and combination of down-home charm and self-as-sured authority vaguely recall Maya Angelou. Foster kicks off this very well-attended session by noting that it's common in Women's Studies to experience a "conflict of expectations between a student and professor, or between students" and to encounter pedagogically challenging situations in which "relationships are not always harmo-nious." Professors, she underscores, "are not teachers. Our jobs, our contracts, require that we do more than teach." And she enjoins the audience to consider her and her fellow panelists "provocateurs, not speakers." The panelists, she says, will offer brief statements just "to get the conversation started," and then we can all "talk about things we haven't had the opportunity to talk about, or haven't felt comfort-able talking about." It soon becomes clear that the therapeutic aspect of Women's Studies has taken a major psychological toll on the professoriate, to the extent that even good soldiers are now willing to carp about it and—amazingly—to invoke traditional "masculinist" notions of professional distance. Jennifer Lynn Freeman Marshall of Purdue, who is also black, laments that Women's Studies students "expect to form relationships with their professors that cross professional boundaries"; they "equate the Women's Studies perspective with kindness" and mistake it for "ethical weakness," and are thus "surprised" to "get the grade they deserve." She says firmly that she doesn't "mentor"—she "models." Jamie Madden, a slim, bespectacled, businesslike young white woman from Virginia College in Texas, explains coolly that she employs a "customer service" model in her classroom. But Susan Cummings, a blond, fortyish professor from Georgia State, dissents. She says she *is* a mother and all those other things to her students: "We're not teaching course content. We're teaching human beings.... I am the first person who's ever provided them with a space" where they can talk about sexual violence. "I keep Kleenex by my desk."

Still, Valerie L. Ruffin of Emory, a black woman in a Mary Tyler Moore hairdo and gray turtleneck, wonders: how do you "maintain authority" if you're "jovial, outgoing, fun, congenial"? And Stanlee James, an older black woman with long cornrows who is the director of African American Studies at the University of Wisconsin at Madison, tells a story. Once she assigned the students in her course on "Gender, Race and Class" to write a paper about another person. A white lesbian student announced her intention to write about another white lesbian. James insisted she write instead about an African American woman. The student put up fierce resistance. Shortly afterward, the black lesbian poet Audre Lorde came to campus, and at a "reception for women of color" that was held in her honor, James told Lorde about the student's request and asked: "Am I being homophobic?" No, Lorde said. Lorde visited James's class and the white lesbian student actually told Lorde what James had done—and James had the satisfaction of hearing Lorde support James's decision. James's conclusion: "Racism in the gay and lesbian movement needs to be addressed!"

When it's time for Q&A, the audience members join in passionately—making it clear that the issue of where to draw the line between the personal and the professional resonates widely. "There's an orthodoxy about what these classrooms should look like," one black woman says, "and our students try to discipline us!" She cites one tragic case: "an African American grad student committed suicide, and some students said it was because African American professors hadn't given her enough support." Two audience members discuss how much to open up about their own lives: "It's a weird balance." A young black woman says that in the course she teaches on black feminism, "I *am* my content.... For me it's a sisterhood.... This is me and my sisters.... This is our experiences. I embrace that in the classroom, being a sister.... I don't know how to divorce it.... Maybe my youth has an influence. Maybe I'm still being naïve." A somewhat older woman who teaches courses on gender wonders "how to be human but maintain my authenticity as a professor"; her decision has been to talk not about her family but about her "intellectual journey," about "how these disciplines saved my life."

A black woman testifies to having "had some crazy experiences" regarding the obligation of African American professors to African American students. She describes this as a "dilemma": "I have these expectations...and if a student doesn't meet these expectations" and she grades them accordingly, "they don't understand why I as a black woman am not 'down.'" They don't understand why she "can't validate" their mediocrity—and she can't figure out "how to negotiate that sense of betrayal." Another black woman replies by insisting that her black students have a responsibility to *her*: she says she's told them that when they slouch and talk in the back of the classroom, they're being disrespectful to *her*—after all, they know all about "institutional racism" and should therefore "have my back." A Latina woman agrees, saying that she makes a point of giving her Latina students "a kick in the butt," assuring them that, far from giving them a free ride, she expects them to be the best.

A young white undergraduate contributes a lament: one of her professors says that "the personal is political" but has also, confusingly, ordered that there will be "no sharing, no caring" in the classroom. The student wants to know: how can she, a member of a generation that wasn't around when the women's movement began, forge a personal connection to it *without* sharing and caring? Another student agrees: "I do have these expectations" of Women's Studies professors that "it's [their] social responsibility to—I don't know—extend office hours." Marshall says that when she weighs whether or not to share personal material with a class, she first asks herself: "Is it useful or am I just sharing? If it's not useful, then it's none of their business." Though this whole session could be described as therapy about therapy, I must confess to being impressed that so many Women's Studies professors are willing to acknowledge their frustration in these matters. Then again, they seem blind to the culpability of the discipline itself, which encourages a blurring of the private and the professional. These women knew as much when they took this career path. They were, presumably, happy enough to receive academic credit, during their own student years, for contemplating their navels; it's only now, when their own students expect them to listen in while they contemplate *their* navels, that these professors recognize how little all this has to do with actual education.

On that long-ago night at Town Hall, as noted, there wasn't a black person in sight. Women's Studies today is a different world. Certainly, for feminism to be taken seriously, it had to look beyond the often frivolous-seeming complaints of upper-middle-class white women and recognize the grievances of millions of poor black women. When the movement began to take into account the lives of women of color, moreover, second-wave feminist dogma about rape required adjustment. "Whereas the official feminist analysis held that there is a very strong presumption that any female who alleges rape is telling the truth," note Patai and Koertge, "black women remembered too many cases in which black men had been lynched as rapists simply on the say-so of a white woman." All these years later, race is firmly privileged over everything else—gender included. The scale of this transformation can hardly be overstated. White men may still be attacked with impunity as patriarchal oppressors, but a white woman cannot level charges of oppression against a man of color. Indeed, many black women in Women's Studies describe themselves not as "feminists" but (employing a term popularized by the novelist Alice Walker) as "womanists," indicating that they're at least as concerned about racial oppression as about sexual oppression. Black women in Women's Studies, though more than fairly represented in the field, nonetheless often describe themselves as living under the thumb of not only male power but also white female power. One way of looking at all this is that the Friedans and Greers ended up being hoisted by their own petard: the charges of oppression that privileged white women once leveled indiscriminately at men ended up being turned back on them by women of color. Then there are the lesbians. Friedan famously loathed their presence in the movement, worrying that they would drive heterosexual women away from it and discredit it in the *eyes* of men. Over the decades, lesbians have had their revenge, and then some: to a remarkable extent, they now dominate the discipline. Many of them treat straight women as second-class members of the sisterhood—after all, the latter are "sleeping with the enemy," a fact that throws into question their loyalty to their fellow women. Some lesbians in Women's Studies, following Adrienne Rich, have argued that heterosexual women are by definition unevolved creatures who are still bound by male-created social conventions and whose intimacy with men makes them enablers of male oppression. Sexuality, after all, is socially constructed—if you're truly serious about your devotion to your fellow women, you can and will make the switch from straight to gay. (Proudly progressive lesbians in Women's Studies, then, take the same line about "choice" when addressing their straight colleagues that ignorant right-wing bigots take when addressing gays: you can change if you really want to.) French lesbian Monique Wittig rejected the very concept of "woman" because "what makes a woman is a specific social relation to a man, a relation that we have previously called servitude"; yet lesbians, she argued, comparing them to "the American runaway slaves," escape this servile relationship "by refusing to become or to stay heterosexual." Women, insisted Wittig, can become truly free only through "the destruction of heterosexuality as a social system."

By far the most admirable aspect of second-wave feminism was the very real, even passionate concern that many Western feminists displayed for women who experienced subjection and abuse in cultures and subcultures far removed from the privileges of the

Western middle class. Yet as feminism fell increasingly under the influence of multiculturalism and postcolonialism, it became politically incorrect to criticize Third World men for oppressing Third World women, or even to call that oppression by its true name—for the relationship between men and women in non-Western cultures was an intrinsic aspect of those cultures, and therefore off-limits for Western critics. Thus was female solidarity trumped by "respect for other cultures." In 1978, the otherwise flaky Mary Daly devoted an entire chapter of *Gyn/Ecology* to thoroughly legitimate criticism of female genital mutilation in Africa; two or three decades later, any white American Women's Studies professor mounting such a critique would be excoriated as neocolonialist, imperialist, and racist.

A couple of sessions at the 2010 NWSA convention exemplify Women's Studies' betrayal of the world's truly exploited women. One of them features three white female panelists and bears the tongue-twisting title "Situated Feminisms, Production of Knowledges & Transnational Feminist Challenges to U.S. Rescue Narratives of Women." The "rescue narratives" in question involve women in non-Western countries who have been pressed into working as prostitutes and saved from this misfortune by Americans participating in what's called the "anti-trafficking movement." These acts of liberation sound admirable, but not to Carrie Baker, a young white woman from Berry College in Mount Berry, Georgia, who explains that they're driven by execrable religious, imperialist, nationalist, and patriarchal motives, and that the alleged rescuers, far from saving the women in question, are disempowering them. Baker complains that much of the "rescue narrative" rhetoric represents trafficked girls as perhaps not even recognizing their own victimhood until the rescuers illuminate them on this score. An odd complaint, perhaps, given that feminism seeks to raise women's awareness of their own supposed victimhood—but this consciousness-raising isn't kosher, obviously, when the women in question are dark-skinned non-Westerners and the consciousness-raisers are white Western men. Baker complains that the anti-trafficking movement is riddled with a disgusting "rhetoric of imperialist salvation," not to mention "chivalrous masculinity." The audience laughs merrily along with

Baker at the "hyper-masculine images of men" and the representation of white men as "defenders" on movement websites. ("Even
the font" at defendersusa.com, Baker nags, "is masculine!")

Baker goes on to accuse the anti-trafficking movement of
using "the imagery of the sex industry to recruit men into
opposing the sex industry": the movement's promotional materials, she says, depict "disempowered young women" who are
"often sexualized," as well as older women—"faded beauties"—
with long, frizzy hair. Baker even sneers about the use of the word
defender, because, she insists, this word is usually used to refer
to the defense of animals. When she tells us that *New York Times*
columnist Nicholas Kristof bought two girls from Cambodia
out of sex slavery and that one of them went back, resulting in a
column in which he observed that it would be good if slaves always
wanted to be freed from slavery, the audience bursts into scornful
laughter at the patriarchal audacity with which Kristof, like other
"privileged white Western men," presumed to decide what was
best for Cambodian girls. These self-styled "saviors," rages Baker
(who is on fire about all this), are only out to "reinstate traditional sex roles" and to "reproduce traditional gender ideologies."

And they do so, she emphasizes, by representing women as
"sexually vulnerable"—something she plainly considers unac-
ceptable, even though (again) it's precisely the notion of women
as sexually vulnerable that's at the root of feminist rape rhetoric.
Baker laments that even some "feminist discourses" represent
non-Western sex slaves as "helpless victims" and their native
cultures as "primitive and barbaric"—thereby "reinscrib[ing]
patriarchal" patterns of power. But *good* feminist discourses, she
instructs us, reject "victimization rhetoric" that "denies" female
sex slaves the "opportunity for self-definition" by portraying them
as "victims of their backward cultures." What's needed, Baker
tells us, are more "multilayered" accounts that eschew "Orientalist" images of the cultures in which these women live—for, she
complains, the rescue narratives "deploy stock colonialist tropes"
and "frame the problem in individualist terms," thus ignoring
underlying "systematic problems" and supporting "the neoliberal
economic interests of corporations." The exploiters of these sex

slaves, she further charges, are always portrayed in the "rescue narratives" as brown men. (Never mind that they almost always *are* brown men.)

Baker calls for accounts of sex slavery that don't "deprive women of agency"—as if it were Western accounts of slavery and not slavery itself that "deprive" Asian slaves of "agency"! One cannot help recalling a passage from Chester's book *The Death of Feminism* in which she notes that "[p]ostmodernist ways of thinking" have "led feminists to believe that confronting narratives on the academic page is as important and world-shattering as confronting jihadists in the flesh and rescuing living beings from captivity." Chesler cites the claim by the Palestinian American writer Suha Sabbagh that Western feminists, simply by writing about Muslim women, exert "a greater degree of domination" over those women "than that actually exercised by men over women within Muslim culture." A brown woman in (say) some Pakistani village, then, is actually more oppressed by some white woman tapping away at a computer at some American university she's never heard of than by the man who's beating and raping her in her home. For white Western women like Baker to actually think they wield such power, of course, is a species of hubris—a sign of narcissism and disconnection from reality. So what is Baker's solution to all this? She turns out not to have much to offer—just a few feeble sentences about the need to address structural problems and globalization, to "foreground…the agency of women," to take a "transnational feminist perspective," and so forth. "We need to be attentive to how we frame the issue," she concludes, "so we don't disempower women." As if the words of some professor giving a paper at a conference in a luxurious Denver hotel could contribute to the disempowerment of some teenage girl held in bondage in Cambodia.

Autumn Marie Reed of the University of Maryland is another young white woman who professes to be worried about Western rhetoric that "disempowers" non-Western women. Her topic: honor killing in Pakistan. She explains that when she watched TV news coverage of "honor-based violence" in the United States (she says she prefers that term to "honor killing," but doesn't explain why), she was troubled by the networks' "Orientalist" discourse. On the one hand, "as an activist I felt coverage would help," but "the more critically I watched…and thought about Orientalism and postcolonial feminist theory…the more uncomfortable I felt." Why? Because while honor-based violence is, well, violent, the manner in which honor-based violence is discussed in the West "is also violent"—it involves "demonization of Muslim men"; it construes Third World women as "homogeneous and powerless"; and it implies, unforgivably, that the United States is "superior" to countries like Pakistan. Western rhetoric about honor killing is about "saving the brown woman from the brown man" and is used as a "way to demonstrate Muslim inferiority." Reed's reference to "saving the brown woman from the brown man" isn't original; it originated with Gayatri Chakravorty Spivak as a way of scorning Western feminist solidarity with non-Western women who suffer abuse at the hands of their fathers, husbands, and sons. Instead of celebrating that solidarity, Spivak has characterized it as racist, colonialist, and imperialist. The phrase has since been echoed by countless Women's Studies figures who are eager to show that they're *not* racist, colonialist, and imperialist.

As Reed makes her comment about "saving the brown women," she emits—incongruously—a condescending little laugh. She's not alone. Throughout her presentation, the women in the audience laugh merrily in sympathy with her sardonic comments. The laughter is disturbing. Reed is talking, after all, about girls and women being beheaded by their fathers and husbands—but she transforms this horrific reality into numbingly familiar abstract rhetoric about imperialism, American supremacism, and so on. Reed maintains that while the media insist on associating honor killing with Islam, it takes place in "all religions" (an assertion that neatly skirts the fact that its frequency among Muslims is sky-high, while its incidence in other faiths, especially outside Arab and Muslim-dominated countries, is minimal). She talks about 9/11, the Times Square bomber, and other Muslim terrorist acts—but her focus is not on these acts themselves but on their representation by such media figures as Bill O'Reilly, who, she charges, present offensive images of "savage Muslim men infiltrating an orderly and morally superior U.S."

As she builds her case, flippantly tossing off references to murderous atrocities, Reed keeps emitting that superior little chuckle. She's so brainwashed that she can't even see what the real story is here. And the same goes for the women in the audience, who are full of lofty, gleeful disdain for the U.S. media. The woman sitting beside me snorts contemptuously over the news reports quoted by Reed, which have the audacity to suggest links between the beheading of women and the Muslim religion and which, in Reed's view, depict Muslim men as uniformly, monolithically dangerous. "This discourse degrades the Muslim community," Reed charges, and is used to justify U.S. violence (that is, war) in and exploitation of the Muslim world. She asks: "Is there an alternate feminist method" of addressing honor-based violence? In a tone dripping with venom, she mentions Chesler, whose principled attention to honor killing in recent years has made her a pariah among the multicultural-minded feminist mainstream. "She positions herself as such a feminist," Reed sneers, but Chesler's work, in her view, only goes to show that any concern for the victims of honor killing "needs to be positioned within a transnational postcolonial feminist perspective" rather than within "white Western hegemonic feminist positions." What we need, Reed argues, is "coalitions between women" in the West and those living under honor codes. She adds that we must also recognize that violence is everywhere and be sensitive to the "damage of racism and Islamophobia."

As I walk numbly out of the room, I reflect that unlike Chesler—whose righteous rage about the subjection and abuse of women under Islam is rooted in her own harrowing experiences as the young bride of a Muslim man in Afghanistan and has flowered into decades of hands-on, productive activism on behalf of women in similar circumstances—these privileged white American girls are floating on clouds of theory; in some sense, the terrible things they're pontificating about aren't real to them at all. Women's Studies has not taught them to bravely and usefully address the problems of real women in the real world; it's taught them a lot of jargon that pretends to be about those people and their problems but that's only about itself.

*   *   *

While second-wave feminism's leaders were household names across America, third-wave feminism's "stars" have tended to be far more famous in the academy than outside of it. Two exceptions are Jennifer Baumgardner and Amy Richards—a pair of nonacademics who, in 2000, sought to define third-wave feminism in a book called *Manifesta*. My sojourn at the 2010 NWSA convention ends with session number 354, a Sunday afternoon workshop featuring these two writers. Pretty, blond, and energetic, they recall how, back in the late 1990s, having grown up with feminism, they envied their elders' experience—sixties activism, bra burning. Unlike the second-wavers, "we didn't have our epiphany moment as a generation"; instead of becoming activists, third-wavers chose to express their feminism "in more mainstream places," making feminism "more dispersed than it ever was." Today, in place of a few celebrated national leaders like Gloria Steinem, there are leaders all over; NOW is losing power, but feminists are taking their places "where the power is." Whereas the second-wavers broke down barriers and kicked open doors, "we're in the room—and that's a more complicated negotiation." Theirs is the generation of male feminists and of dramatic shake-ups in the American family. When their book came out, Baumgardner and Richards were "single women living in New York City"; now they're mothers with "a greater openness to what feminism is." They no longer feel that women need to call themselves feminists—"you can accomplish something" even if you don't embrace the label. They say that some women ask them, "Do I have a right to be conflicted" about abortion? Their answer: yes.

After several days at this convention, I find the simple candor of this session almost mind-blowing. Baumgardner and Richards aren't junior professors or grad students mindlessly mouthing Women's Studies platitudes; they're two women who are living their lives out in the real world and who have spent much of the last decade holding workshops with groups of ordinary women around the United States. (It occurs to me that they've probably never heard of "intersectionality.") They're not anxious about getting tenure or alienating faculty colleagues, and therefore don't hesitate to say things that NWSA officers would consider heretical.

Today, Baumgardner and Richards suggest there are "more and more hints of a fourth wave of feminism" on the rise. What defines fourth-wavers? They're "dualists." Third-wavers "were escorted to clinics" for abortions; "dualism" involves *all* options, including the arrangement of adoptions for the infant children of women who don't want abortions. What's fresh here, they say, is the recognition that there are *three* options in the case of pregnancy, which they call "a profound way of looking" at the abortion controversy—a way of defusing it. This certainly sounds promising (even though I can't help wondering: exactly when was adoption *not* an option?). But then a young woman in the audience stands up to talk about date rape. Praising the Take Back the Night events for helping young women to recognize that they've been raped, she speaks as if in the voice of such a young woman: "Oh, I really didn't think that was rape, but now I realize it was." She suggests that a person in such a situation might wish to write a letter to the man who assaulted her and tell him: "I know you may have a different view of what happened between us, but this is my view...."

And with that, any hope I might have had for this discipline goes out the window. For while Baumgardner and Richards are the voices of the mainstream American women of their generation, that young woman in the audience is the voice—and, I'm afraid, the future—of Women's Studies.

CHAPTER 3
The Ebony Tower: Black Studies

Every time I attend a conference of white writers, I have a method for finding out if my colleagues are racist. It consists of uttering stupidities and maintaining absurd theses. If they listen respectfully and, at the end, overwhelm me with applause, there isn't the slightest doubt: they are filthy racists.

—James Baldwin, *Professing Feminism*

"I was one of those who were in on the founding of Black Studies programs," Shelby Steele tells me. His tone, touched with rue, is almost that of a repentant sinner in a confessional booth.

But we're not in the confessional. It's a gorgeous spring day in 2010, and we're having lunch at a sprawling restaurant near his home in Monterey, California. Outside the ultrahigh windows, the blue Pacific stretches to the horizon; inside, across the table from me, the courtly, gregarious Steele, whose 1991 book, *The Content of Our Character: A New Vision of Race in America*, won the National Book Critics Circle Award, and who is now a fellow at the Hoover Institution at Stanford University, smiles good-humoredly. "I graduated from college in 1968," he says, "in the middle of the whole Black Power movement." He went on to grad school at the University of Utah—and at the same time entered the world of "Great Society programs in education." First he worked as a teacher with Upward Bound in East St. Louis. That federal program was connected to another one, an "experiment with higher education" that sought to help inner-city youth make it through junior college. "The people who ran it hired me almost immediately to help design the first Black Studies programs in the country. So I was one of the people who helped come up with them." He chuckles. "I was a twenty-two-year-old kid just out of undergraduate school, and I was designing higher education." Now in his mid-sixties, he laughs at the absurdity of it all. "That'll give you some idea of the intellectual heft that went into it!" He describes his role in that strange parturition: he flew around the country to places ranging from Long Beach State on the West Coast to City College of New York (CCNY) in the East. "We'd talk to the administrators, and talk them into having Black Studies programs." This kept him busy "all the way through grad school." And—he chuckles again—"there was so much white guilt that you could just go into these places and they'd give you everything you wanted," even though the whole thing was "ill-conceived" from the start.

Steele recalls that back in those days (his "far-left liberal days," as he calls them), he and other founders of identity studies programs, "whether it was blacks or women or Chicanos or whatever," debated whether they should be arguing for "an independent, free-standing academic department" or, more modestly, "an interdisciplinary collection of courses from within different disciplines…that people could take as a minor." Steele believed in going all the way: "I was one of those who invented the idea. It was about Black Power. We wanted parity. We wanted our own separate departments, we wanted to grant degrees, we wanted our own curriculum, and so forth."

But the scales soon fell from his eyes. "It didn't take me long to realize that we completely lacked the wherewithal to have independent, free-standing academic departments. No one knew what Black Studies was, no one had any sort of clear intellectual handle on it. The fundamental problem is that we were trying to present ourselves as an academic discipline, but we had no methodology. In psychology there's a methodology; obviously in the sciences there's a methodology; even in literature there's a methodology. We had no such thing at all, nothing to give coherence or meaning to anything." In the final analysis, he perceived, the departments he and his colleagues were putting together had nothing to do with education: "It was just a joke from the very beginning." He also began to notice—and this was no small detail—that Black Studies wasn't attracting real educators but "obvious hustlers. Crooks." He mentions a colleague in East St. Louis "who came to work one day in a brand-new Mercedes-Benz."

Not only were they hustlers; they were dummies. "The guy I worked for was so illiterate!" Steele recalls. And he wasn't alone: "Very few of the people I was working with were much more than minimally literate. I was the one who could actually write a grant [proposal]. And that was where I was useful." Thinking back to those days, when "I was still so naïve and innocent," he shakes his head in wonder at the way things worked. "You could say we want fifty thou to set up a library, and get it! You'd get the money! So I learned what white guilt was. But very quickly I came to see that we had no future that way. That we had no respect, we had no methodology, we had no discipline. Black Studies could just be *anything*. And so I thought the way to go was to go to already established academic departments, like history and sociology, and find scholars who were interested in working in our area and have them design classes that they would offer within their departments, under the imprimatur of their departments, and we would put together a collection of those courses that students could take. I thought—I *knew*—that that was the best way to go, because then you could have some seriousness, some academic stature, some gravitas, some credibility."

He tried to make the case. "At Utah I said, 'We don't have a methodology; we haven't yet conceived an academic discipline. We're relying on other genuine academic disciplines. So we just ought to put together a collection of courses and offer that as an emphasis to students.' I thought that was the respectable way to go." This was the thinking at some other schools as well, where "you could find people in the literature department, for example, who were quite willing to offer a very serious class in African American literature. And I think African American literature is a full, rich subject—it's almost the equivalent of a national literature. And so that was a place where you had real legitimacy. But it had to be taught under the auspices of an English department, where the formal conventions of criticism were applied vigorously. We had to be able to say why, for example, Ralph Ellison was a better writer than LeRoi Jones or somebody."

The same approach was taken in other subjects. "You go to sociology and get somebody there to talk about inner cities. You study people like William Julius Wilson," the distinguished black sociologist. While illiterate hustlers were setting up Black Studies departments at some universities, then, at others there *were* people who were "doing absolutely first-rate, legitimate academic work on the black American situation." Hence Steele came to feel that "if you want to put together a bunch of classes doing that, then that's great—nobody will have any problems and the people who teach these classes will have been vetted by their own disciplines. You could have serious study." But the people Steele was working with didn't agree. They weren't concerned about seriousness; they wanted power. They were "street guys who came to hustle." And their numbers, if not legion, were considerable. Steele brings up Leonard Jeffries, who despite a long record of venomously anti-white and anti-Semitic statements, including his famous distinction between brutal, violent "ice people" (whites) and gentle, warmhearted "sun people" (blacks), served for more than two decades as chairman of the Black Studies Department at CCNY—where he remains a professor to this day. Jeffries, says Steele, was an "out-and-out hustler. And he got away with it." Steele also mentions Edward Crosby, who "went to Kent State and started the Black Studies program there. He was just hustling the university, which felt no obligation to look at what they were teaching" under the rubric of Black Studies.

And so it went: at one university after another, these sharp characters hustled their way into lucrative careers while administrators more or less looked the other way. What did these new Black Studies curricula consist of? It seemed not to matter: "No authority had ever even seriously looked at what they were teaching. They had no idea. And it was just slipshod, and jerry-built, and then you looked up by the mid-seventies or late seventies and there were four or five hundred Black Studies programs. I came to see very quickly that this was an avenue for minorities to gain the economic security of the university professorship. They had no real credentials, so their argument became 'You have to hire me to do this because I'm black.' So your blackness itself became your primary credential." And how did Steele feel about this at the time? "I was still very left-wing and into Black Power, but I began to feel I was facilitating a corruption." Looking at the Black Studies departments he'd had a hand in creating, he realized he didn't want to see minority students wasting their time majoring or even minoring in the subject.

So it was that "as time went on, there came to be two kinds of black professors"—indeed, two kinds of black and Chicano and women professors. Some were "mediocrities and hustlers, who wanted independent departments precisely so they would *not* be under the purview of serious academic standards, so they could hide out there and enjoy all the perks of tenure and so forth" without ever having to be judged according to any standards of achievement. These people created departments that "became a haven for corruption and mediocrity." At the same time "there were always black, Hispanic, and women scholars who were first-rate and serious people." Steele notes that today "you can be invited to be appointed to the Black Studies program at Harvard [the W. E. B. Du Bois Institute for African and African American Research] by Skip Gates," the institutes director, more formally known as Henry Louis Gates Jr., "but every single one of those people" who receive such invitations "demand an appointment in the discipline of their origin. 'Okay, Skip, I'll teach a class for you, but my professional credibility requires that I be appointed to the English Department or the Sociology Department or whatever.' And there are many blacks who say, 'I don't want anything to do with you.'"

Then again, "Harvard is a special case. If you're teaching at a state university in the California system and you're the black and you're a natural appointment in Black Studies, there's no worse thing to be. You have no credibility at all. You're sort of a charity case. When I went to San Jose State [to become a professor of English in 1974], for example, they had a Black Studies program, and I said,

'I'll have nothing to do with it. I will teach whatever I please and your students can take whatever classes of mine they want, but I don't want to be associated with you in any way.' And I think that's the way most serious minority academics really feel—even though they won't admit it and don't want to talk about it in public." Bottom line: "It's a shame." He has to admit now that one prediction he made back in the early days of Black Studies has proved spectacularly wrong. Surveying Black Studies' mediocrity and lack of seriousness "I thought: This will never go anywhere.' But no: it just got worse and worse and worse. And now they've taken over English departments. Now it's all about ethnicity and racism. And anytime you see that, you know that it's a hustle. It's part of the larger affirmative-action culture. Once you implant an idea like racial preferences in the culture, people are going to run with it—money, fame. My generation of minority people has been ruined by this. We've been freed to be hustlers. It's *made* us into hustlers. It's *demanded* that we become hustlers. That's how you move ahead: you keep trading on your race, and then you get good enough at doing that to trade on your race at a higher level, and then you get good enough at it to trade on your race at an even higher level, and then finally you become somebody like Skip Gates—an empty figure who could honestly now become the president of Harvard if he wanted to." He laughs at the preposturousness of that picture. "He's too lazy, but he could. They'd be proud to have him. Not that he's ever written anything of any real interest. But he's a talented inside trader in the culture of racial preference. He knows how to get money out of white people. He's really good. They line up to give him money."

It didn't have to be this way. In fact, there was a time when it wasn't. Not only does there exist, as Steele says, a rich canon of African American literature; there's also an impressive body of serious critical and scholarly writings about African American identity and culture that predates the Black Studies of the 1960s and afterward. In a 1973 book called *Black Studies: Threat or Challenge*, Nick Aaron Ford records that "Afro-American Studies…at [predominantly black] Atlanta

University…extends back to the 1890s," and he lists courses given at predominantly black Fisk University from the 1920s onward about "Problems of Negro Life," "The Negro in American History," "The Study of Negro Music and Composition," and the like.

A century ago the two most prominent black American intellectuals were a pair of deeply cultured and internationally respected educators named Booker T. Washington and W. E. B. Du Bois. Washington (1856–1915), the son of a slave woman in Virginia, worked for several years as a laborer, acquired an education, and from 1881 to his death served as head of the Tuskegee Institute, a teachers' college in Alabama; Du Bois (1868–1963), born in Massachusetts, was the first African American to be awarded a doctorate, and went on to become a celebrated educator, activist, and author, and a cofounder of the National Association for the Advancement of Colored People.

Though both men were fervently devoted to the advancement of black Americans, they had extremely different views as to how this goal might best be accomplished. Washington, like Gates, was gifted, to borrow Shelby Steele's words, at "get[ting] money out of white people"—among them John D. Rockefeller and Andrew Carnegie. These donations didn't go to anything remotely resembling today's identity studies; for the most part, they were spent to build and maintain primary and secondary schools at which young black people were able to learn what they needed in order to be able to support themselves and be responsible citizens. Washington, who placed his emphasis on vocational training for blacks, devised the so-called Atlanta Compromise of 1895, whereby he accepted segregation in the South in return for basic educational and employment opportunities for southern blacks.

Washington had many black critics, first among them Du Bois, who rejected both the Atlanta Compromise (his answer to it was the Niagara Movement, founded in 1905) and Washington's focus on vocational training. Du Bois believed that black Americans would achieve little progress unless they were granted equal rights and unless a significant number of them were able to receive a respectable higher education, including extensive exposure to the arts and humanities. He rested his hopes largely on the "best minds" of the black race—the "Talented Tenth," as he famously called them—

who, he argued, would, if properly educated, elevate the entire race through their contributions.

Du Bois is generally viewed as the seminal figure of Black Studies, and his 1903 book, *The Souls of Black Folk*, is usually listed as the most important text in the field. (The editors of *A Companion to African-American Studies*, Lewis R. Gordon and Jane Anna Gordon, note that "the undisputed, most influential intellectuals in the development of African-American studies are W. E. B. Du Bois and Frantz Fanon.") What's ironic, given the course of development Black Studies has followed, is that Du Bois, in *The Souls of Black Folk*, placed immense emphasis on the significance for both whites *and* blacks of a thorough grounding in Western history and culture. His constantly repeated point was that the heritage of the West was the heritage of all; as he explained, in eloquent homiletical cadences that foreshadowed the rhetoric of Martin Luther King Jr., he did not snub the glories of Western civilization, and they did not snub him, but were in fact his own possessions as much as they were anyone else's:

> I sit with Shakespeare and he winces not. Across the color line I move arm in arm with Balzac and Dumas, where smiling men and welcoming women glide in gilded halls. From out the caves of evening that swing between the strong-limbed earth and the tracery of the stars, I summon Aristotle and Aurelius and what soul I will, and they come all graciously with no scorn nor condescension. So, wed with Truth, I dwell above the Veil. Is this the life you grudge us, O knightly America? Is this the life you long to change into the dull red hideousness of Georgia? Are you so afraid lest peering from this high Pisgah, between Philistine and Amalekite, we sight the Promised Land?

To be sure, Du Bois maintained that while American blacks could indeed understand, profit from, and relate to the Western classics, they approached these works with a set of intellectual equipment different from white people's. They were equipped, as he put it, with "double consciousness," which he defined as "an anxious 'twoness'"—meaning that American blacks lived in, or shuttled between, two worlds. Du Bois's explanation of this concept is one of the most frequently quoted passages in African American letters: "[The Negro] ever feels his two-ness—an American, a Negro; two souls, two thoughts, two unreconciled strivings; two warring ideals in one dark body whose dogged strength alone keeps it from being torn asunder." This twoness was exemplified by Du Bois's own life. In his later years, increasingly involved in civil rights activism, he grew less interested in communing with Shakespeare, Balzac, and Aristotle than in encouraging the writing of black fiction and poetry that would serve as propaganda for the cause. Indeed, after decades of flirtation with radicalism—which landed him in hot water during the McCarthy era—Du Bois joined the Communist Party at age ninety-three, not long after receiving the Soviet Union's Lenin Peace Prize.

Still, the admirable and humane vision articulated in *The Souls of Black Folk* remained, serving as a powerful influence for a generation of scholars who, during the first half of the twentieth century, produced a number of pioneering studies of black American history and culture. For instance, Carter G. Woodson (1875–1950), known as the father of black history, founded the *Journal of Negro History* in 1916 and ten years later introduced "Negro History Week," the forerunner of today's Black History Month. Lorenzo Dow Turner (1890–1972), who pioneered the study of the Gullah language spoken along the Carolina coast, was head of the English departments at Howard and then Fisk universities, and founded an African Studies program at the latter institution as early as 1943.

One can imagine Black Studies, then, taking a very different course than it did, and building on the achievements of people like Du Bois, Woodson, and Turner to become a legitimate and serious field of academic study. But it was not to be: history intervened. First there was the civil rights movement. In 1954 the Supreme Court, in *Brown v. Board of Education*, declared segregation in schools unconstitutional; in 1955, the refusal of Rosa Parks to give up her bus seat to a white man led to the Montgomery Bus Boycott. Ten years later, riots erupted in the Watts neighborhood of Los Angeles and helped trigger disturbances in cities across the country. The Black Power movement was born. To quote Black Studies veteran Maulana Ron Karenga, author of *Introduction to Black Studies* (1979) and currently the director of the Kawaida Institute of Pan African Studies, this new movement "argued for a *relevant education*" focused "on *cultural groundings* studying and recovering African culture and extracting from it models of excellence and possibility."

In 2007, Fabio Rojas, a sociologist at Indiana University, wrote a history of Black Studies that has been widely embraced as definitive. The title and subtitle say it all: *From Black Power to Black Studies: How a Radical Social Movement Became an Academic Discipline.* By way of background, Rojas points out that as early as the 1700s, American schools had provided at least some coverage of African American history. Rojas also highlights court cases argued by Thurgood Marshall in the 1930s and '40s that helped open white colleges to black students and led to *Brown v. Board of Education.* Yet not all black intellectuals, Rojas emphasizes, prioritized integration: in the 1960s, the *Negro Digest* promoted "cultural nationalism," which would lead to "demands for black-controlled education and black studies." Meanwhile the NAACP's publication *The Crisis* supported integration and "liberal reform," running, for example, an article by a black judge, Francis Rivers, arguing that Black Studies would hinder students' development of critical skills and that "black identity was an inherently extracurricular concern."

Yet "cultural nationalism" was on the rise—a rise abetted by the founding of the Revolutionary Action Movement (RAM), a Black Power group, by students who'd been "[p]ersuaded by [Robert F.] Williams's analysis of black America as a colony inside the United States with much in common with Cuba, China, and other nations." While "the Nation of Islam provided a religious model of what a self-sustaining black community might look like" (and showed blacks "that nonviolence was not the only option"), RAM offered a secular model; Rojas calls its founding "a critical moment in black nationalism's organizational development."

RAM's Oakland chapter gave birth to the Black Panther Party, founded in 1966 by Bobby Seale and Huey P. Newton, whose violent revolutionary ideology was based largely on Mao's *Little Red Book* and Fanon's *The Wretched of the Earth.* By 1968 the Black Panthers had spread around the country and won thousands of members; by 1970, Panthers had killed over a dozen police officers and injured dozens more. Rojas notes that it was out of RAM, the Black Panthers, and other black nationalist organizations, such as Stokely Carmichael's Student Nonviolent Coordinating Committee (or SNCC, and which in 1969 replaced the word *nonviolent* in its name with *national*), that "[t]he black studies idea emerged."

Indeed, the founding of Black Studies, as Gordon and Gordon point out in *A Companion to African-American Studies,* was influenced by the Black Panthers' goal of "*decolonizing the minds of black people.*" Thus, they write, "African-American Studies is an *intrinsically* politicized unit of the academy" whose objective is to overcome the "false consciousness" (a Marxist term) created by "white supremacy"—or, to put it differently, to understand "what W.E.B. Du Bois called *double consciousness*" but which after the 1960s was understood more as a matter of "contested truth." (All italics in original.)

Black Studies' first beachhead would be San Francisco State College (now San Francisco State University). Rojas describes its targeting by black nationalists: over the course of two years "a handful of Black Panthers enrolled at San Francisco State College with the explicit goal of mobilizing black students to organize strikes." The most important of these activists was Jimmy Garrett, a member of both the Black Panthers and SNCC. Garrett led discussion groups at which, as he later explained, "we would talk about ourselves, seeking identity, and stuff like that. A lot of folks didn't even know they were black. A lot of people thought they were Americans." Garrett and his group, writes Rojas, "spent much time thinking about how the entire college might be racist." The college gave office space to the Black Panthers, who set up "tables with Maoist propaganda"—as did SFSC's Black Student Union (BSU). A crucial event in the backstory of Black Studies, Rojas explains, was the establishment at SFSC of something called the Experimental College, which "allowed students to teach their own courses" and even turned "informal 'rap sessions' into formal courses." Several of these courses were on black subjects, and at some point they were brought together "into a package called 'black studies.'"

But the real turning point was the so-called *Gater* incident. In November 1967, in response to violence by black students demanding "control of various student government organizations," SFSC's school newspaper, the *Daily Gater*, "ran editorials criticizing black students" and "accused the BSU of being racist." In response, "a group of about ten black students"—including "BSU member and Black Panther" George Murray, who worked in SFSC's Tutorial Center program—raided the newspaper's offices and beat up its editor. After two years of hearings and trials, Murray was not only permitted to remain a student and to keep his Tutorial Center job, but also "gained admission to the master's degree program in the Department of English," where he was assigned to teach classes. Meanwhile, in the summer of 1968, he "gave a fiery speech" in Cuba attacking American soldiers in Vietnam, and that fall delivered a talk at the college calling for students "to carry guns to protect themselves from 'racist administrators.'" Yet he went unpunished, for the mayor of San Francisco and the president of the college agreed that any disciplinary action "could lead to riots." When Murray finally was suspended on October 31, 1968, partly under pressure from California governor Ronald Reagan, the suspension set off what would become known as the Third World Strike.

The strike, engineered by the BSU, began on November 6 and climaxed with a clash between "hundreds of students and dozens of police." Among the BSU's demands was the establishment of a Black Studies department. (Such a department had, in fact, already been approved and a chairman hired, but the administration had been dragging its feet.) That day the campus was closed indefinitely—an act that Reagan decried as capitulation. There followed what Rojas calls a "guerrilla campaign" on the part of the BSU. Its strategy, he writes, "was fairly straightforward: disrupt the campus through a combination of physical intimidation, bombings, and publicity campaigns.... A common tactic was to have a dozen or more students stand behind white students while they were talking.... Throughout the strike, nine bombs were set and four detonated on the San Francisco campus." At one January 1969 rally, there were no fewer than 457 arrests.

S. I. Hayakawa, a professor of English and linguistics, became a symbol of resistance, calling the BSU campaign a "reign of terror" and rejecting the claim that its critics were all racists; when the college president, unable to stand the heat anymore, tendered his resignation, Hayakawa took his place. But for all Hayakawa's tough talk (which won him statewide popularity and eventually led to his election as a U.S. senator in 1976), he ended up giving in to the BSU's demands. SFSC's Black Studies program began offering classes in the fall of 1969. (Soon Hayakawa was one of Black Studies' leading champions, defending it the next year not only on the grounds that "studying the Negro's contribution" to American society was a "legitimate and necessary intellectual enterprise" but also on the grounds that black young people, cut off from their ancestors' culture and "deprived of a sense of...worth by the heritage of slavery," had a real need for Black Studies' "therapeutic" effects as a counter to the sense of "inferiority" into which they'd been "brainwashed.")

After SFSC fell, the domino effect took over. Black Studies, writes Rojas, became a nationwide phenomenon "overnight." As Karenga puts it, black students at other colleges "paid close attention to the struggle at San Francisco State and were impressed with the capacity of students to win concessions from the administration." Within a few months, student strikes at a wide range of colleges and universities—including Harvard, Yale, Cornell, Columbia, Howard, and Amherst—had coerced terrified administrators into establishing Black Studies there, too. As Rojas notes, "in the 1967–1968 school year, eleven of the eighteen California colleges experienced some form of black student activism," ranging from "mild" (uprooting trees, setting fires) to violent. By 1969, writes Karenga, most major American institutions of higher education had "some form of Black Studies"; according to Rojas, between 1969 and 1974, 120 degree-granting Black Studies programs and departments were formed at institutions around the country. Though historically black colleges and universities resisted this movement at first (their "bourgeois" curriculum of "negro history," as Karenga puts it, had little in common with the "liberationist" approach favored by Black Studies advocates), the rapid fall of Harvard and Yale to the Black Studies tsunami led these institutions, too, to institute Black Studies curricula.

In 1969, civil rights leader Bayard Rustin weighed in on Black Studies, encapsulating the major concerns about it in a handful of sharp questions: "Is Black Studies an educational program or a forum for ideological indoctrination? Is it designed to train qualified scholars in a significant field of intellectual inquiry, or is it hoped that its graduates will form political cadres prepared to organize the impoverished residents of the black ghetto? Is it a means to achieve psychological identity and strength, or is it intended to provide a false and sheltered sense of security, the fragility of which would be revealed by even the slightest exposure to reality? And finally, does it offer the possibility for better racial understanding, or is it a regression to racial separatism?"

For Karenga, Black Studies is a desperately needed corrective of "traditional white studies," which was and is "inadequate and injurious in its omission and/or distortion of the lives and culture of the majority of humankind, especially the fathers and mothers of humankind and human civilization, African people." It goes without saying, perhaps, that Karenga's account of the founding of the discipline in *Introduction to Black Studies* is free of any mention of "hustlers." In his view, given that "African people are the fathers and mothers of both humanity and human civilization," Black Studies (which in Karenga's definition includes "Black History; Black Religion; Black Social Organization; Black Politics; Black Economics; Black Creative Production...and Black Psychology") represents "a *vital contribution to the critique, resistance and reversal of the progressive Europeanization of human consciousness and culture*" and "an important contribution to humanity's understanding itself." (Italics in original.)

Houston A. Baker Jr., who teaches at Vanderbilt and has been a top name in Black Studies since the beginning, doesn't use the word *hustlers*, either. On the contrary, he describes in heroic terms the "[c]ourageous and brilliant...young black men" who started Black Studies at Yale. "The first covenant of what might be accomplished," he writes (and, yes, this is the prose of a distinguished professor of Black Studies), "was limned by the symposium on Black Studies organized by black undergraduates, in coalition with well-resourced and influential white allies. The symposium produced a volume titled *Black Studies in the University*."

The idea was that a committee—to which Baker, then age twenty-five and with "absolutely no Black Studies expertise or experience," was appointed—would create a Black Studies program based on the proposals continued in the symposium's book. Baker decided that the program had to be "autonomous" and generously endowed; must have full "departmental status" and grant Ph.D.s; must deal not only with black America but with "Africa, South America, and the Caribbean"; and must seek to transcend traditional notions of " 'legitimate' academic work" by making a connection with and having an impact on the black community at large. But when he presented these demands to the committee's white chairman, the other black committee members distanced themselves from him, and he ended up in hot water, "a 'revolutionary'...in the state-rooms of Ivy League whiteness." All these years later, he claims, the problem of white people planning the "study of 'blackness'" continues to haunt Black Studies. Yet his story is ultimately triumphant: Black Studies at Yale was the result of the efforts of "thousands and thousands of uncowardly men and women.... There were exploding bombs in downtown New Haven, a Yale chaplain who was not afraid to take religion into the fray, and the cry everywhere of: 'The ultimate solution is black revolution!'"

Charlotte Morgan-Cato, an associate professor emerita of Black Studies at Lehman College of the City University of New York, spent thirty years at Lehman, where the Black Studies program was—like Black Studies programs at other colleges—a result of student disruptions: "After more than a year of strikes, scuffles, demonstrations, shutdowns, and lock-ins, Black Studies and Puerto Rican Studies were approved as departments." This was in 1970. "[O]ne Sunday afternoon in Harlem more than 150 persons gathered in a dance hall to plan the successful strategy which forced university administrators to capitulate. On the chosen day, all involved Black and Hispanic students left their classes, exited the buildings, and chain-locked building entrances. The faculty were locked in a lecture hall where they were debating the establishment of Black Studies and Puerto Rican Studies. The programs were approved, and the departments were established within six months." Black students, Morgan-Cato notes approvingly, rejected "'objective' pedagogy," preferring classes that would "communicate the recognition, respect, even reverence for Black culture."

In addition to Black Studies, another fruit of the Black Power tree was the Black Arts Movement, founded in 1965 by the poet and playwright Amiri Baraka (born LeRoi Jones), a devotee of Karenga's Kawaida philosophy (about which more shortly). Black Arts, which is considered to have begun with Jones's establishment of the Black Arts Repertory Theatre/School (BARTS) in Harlem, and which Baraka conceived of as the artistic wing of the Black Power movement, represented a fusing of art and militancy; among its most prominent members were Nikki Giovanni, Gwendolyn Brooks, Maya Angelou, and Lorraine Hansberry. The movement's quick fade-out in the 1970s was triggered by Baraka's own ideological shift from Black Power and black nationalism to Marxism. Without Black Arts, novelist Ishmael Reed has said that "there would be no multiculturalism"; indeed, the Black Arts Movement may be described as the real beginning of the contemporary practice of according points to mediocre work by minority writers simply because they *are* minority writers and because their writing focuses on (or obsesses over) group identity, oppression, and enraged victimhood. Given the presence of major Black Arts figures in academic Black Studies programs, one cannot really separate Black Arts from Black Studies, any more than one can isolate Women's Studies from feminism.

Though other Black Arts figures have become more famous, it is Baraka who shaped the movement and who remains its public face; it is defined by him as modernist poetry was defined by Ezra Pound. I first became aware of Baraka in the 1970s, when I was an English major at Stony Brook University on Long Island and he was the crown jewel of the Africana Studies Department. Born LeRoi Jones in 1934 to a middle-class black Newark, New Jersey, family (he changed his name in 1967), Baraka was at first a communist, Castroite, and fringe Beat poet, then (after Malcolm X's murder) a black nationalist revolutionary, and later a Marxist (specifically, a Maoist) and Pan-Africanist. But throughout his career, whatever political label he has attached to himself, his writing has been racist, misogynistic, anti-Semitic—and violent. Some of it reads like a parody by Howard Stern or a young Eddie Murphy of mindless black radical hate: "Rape the white girls. Rape / their fathers. Cut the mothers' throats." In a single 1965 essay Baraka managed to be equally appalling about whites, gays, and women, writing that "[m]ost American white men are trained to be fags," that black men should want to rape white women as a way of taking from white men everything they have, and that white women know that only when they're raped by black men will they "get cleanly, viciously popped."

Baraka's long rap sheet includes arrests in the 1960s for possessing firearms and disturbing the peace, in the 1970s for domestic violence, in 1989 for assaulting a police officer, and in 1990 for inciting a riot. A post-9/11 poem containing the line "Who told 4000 Israeli workers at the Twin Towers / To stay home that day?" caused a public outcry that lost Baraka the title of New Jersey poet laureate. Because of the virulent hate expressed in his plays and poems, there has, over the years, been a degree of hand-wringing in literary, academic, and theatrical circles to the effect that his work is morally problematic. On the contrary, there's nothing problematic about it: he's repellent and his writing is mediocre. That he's considered a literary luminary and that such institutions as the American Academy of Arts and Letters, the Rockefeller and Guggenheim foundations, and the National Endowment for the Arts have showered him with awards and grants only affirms that being a fourth-rate black artist who oozes race hate is, in at least some cultural elite circles, not a minus but a plus.

For some years after its founding, Black Studies thrived—benefiting, as Rojas writes, from "the intense time after King's assassination and the ensuing urban riots." For professors and administrators, the discipline provided a way "to pursue novel intellectual agendas, diversify a college's faculty and course offerings, offer social support for black students, encourage discussions between blacks and whites, or mollify disruptive students." Priorities differed: for some, Black Studies was above all about "community education"; for others, it was about "research." While "students with a nationalist bent tended to view black studies as a service to the African American community," there were "other activists" for whom it was "comparable to area studies, such as Africa or China studies."

Of course, as longtime Black Studies professor Molefi Kete Asante points out, the discipline had, and has, a variety of names:

"Among the more popular...were 'Afro-American Studies' as in the UCLA Center for Afro-American Studies; 'Africana Studies' as in the Cornell University Department of Africana Studies; 'African-American Studies' as in the Temple University Department of African-American Studies; 'Africa World Studies' as in the Miami University Africa World Studies program; 'African Diaspora Studies' as in the PhD program at UC Berkeley; and 'Africology' as in the Department of Africology at the University of Wisconsin at Milwaukee." At American University, the department is called "African American and African Diaspora Studies." Rojas notes in passing the rise of the concept of "Inner-City Studies," and quotes a 1970 memo indicating that Black Studies at the University of Illinois at Chicago would be based not on race but on "one's relationship to the imperialist system." Karenga's coverage of post-1960s developments in Black Studies places emphasis on what he calls its "multidimensional thrust toward consolidation and expansion," as exemplified by the emergence of such subjects as Black Women's Studies, Multicultural Studies, and Classical African Studies. He notes the 1976 founding of the National Council for Black Studies, "the preeminent discipline organization." Black Studies and Black Power, in Karenga's view, were engaged in a "revolutionary struggle...to end racist oppression and change society and the world." They also rejected the goal of turning "[b]lack students into vulgar careerists with no sense of social commitment" or into "pathetic imitators of their [white] oppressors." Karenga quotes Nathan Hare, who ran the Black Studies program at SFSC and whom Karenga calls "one of the guiding theorists and founders of the Movement," as saying that "a Black education which is not revolutionary in the current day is both irrelevant and useless," and cites Fanon's statement that "each generation must...discover its mission, fulfill it or betray it." "For Fanon and the Black Studies advocates," Karenga writes, "this mission was the liberation of the people and building of a new world and a new people in and for the world." He quotes Hare's "statement which became a slogan" of the movement: "We must bring the campus to the community and the community to the campus."

Alas, "[b]y the mid-1970s," writes Rojas, "student protest had waned"—and without the activism, what *was* Black Studies? For a time, then, the discipline suffered from waning student interest. Morgan-Cato notes that after CUNY put an end to Open Admissions, made faculty cuts, and imposed a core curriculum, Black Studies at CUNY shrank (though "non-Black enrollment" in Black Studies did go up and core curriculum courses taught by Black Studies faculty served as "recruiting tools" for Black Studies). Morgan-Cato laments that in the 1980s "consumerism, careerism, and computer assisted instruction" led students "away from activist postures to the safety of the marketplace. They came to Black Studies asking not what they could do for their communities, but rather, what they could do to get a good job." Moreover, as "memories of the 1960s faded," "fewer students acknowledged the impact of racism." Sylvia Wynter, professor emerita of Black Studies and Spanish and Portuguese Studies at Stanford, shares Morgan-Cato's distress. Recalling that the black students who agitated for Black Studies were "galvanized by Stokely Carmichael's call…for a turning of the back on the earlier integrationist, 'We shall overcome' goal of the first phase of the Civil Rights Movement, and for the adoption, instead, of the new separatist goal of Black Power," she complains that over time the "original transgressive intensions" were "defused." As a result, Black Studies became simply one more "Ethnic Studies" discipline that "served to re-verify the very thesis of Liberal universalism" in opposition to which Black Studies was (in her view) founded.

But Black Studies' decline didn't go on forever. The turning point came in 1991, when Harvard hired Gates to run its department. He brought in "star" faculty, assembling a Black Studies "dream team" funded in part by the Ford Foundation and by corporations like Time Warner. Gates's achievement sparked a turnaround in the entire discipline—a turnaround aided (again) by the Ford Foundation, which spread around a lot of money and, according to Rojas, sought actively to steer the discipline away from politics, especially black nationalism.

Who is Henry Louis Gates Jr.? Raised in West Virginia, he went on to study history at Yale and English at Clare College, Cambridge. Though his oeuvre is, indeed, as Steele observes, less than spectacularly impressive, he has managed to convince a good many people in positions of power that he is a scholar, critic, and thinker of the highest order. He has been awarded no fewer than fifty-one honorary degrees (plus the National Humanities Medal), has been named a MacArthur Fellow, and has been elected to the American Academy of Arts and Letters. He is *the* public face of Black Studies. Part of the reason for his celebrity, one senses, is that he has struck exactly the right balance: he presents himself in such a way as to seem respectable to white cultural authorities seeking a Distinguished Black Intellectual to honor and reward, yet at the same time is sufficiently provocative to satisfy many (if not all) black activists and fellow Black Studies academics.

Gates himself is an illustration of "double consciousness": while citing in profusion the leading white purveyors of postmodern theory (Mikhail Bakhtin, Michel Foucault, Jacques Lacan, and Jacques Derrida) and acknowledging what some Black Studies professors would call the "white" canon, he always views literature, whether by blacks, whites, or others, through a black lens, writing, for example, that "critical signification," an academic variation on the traditional African American verbal practice known as "signifyin'" is "a useful concept in explaining…black-white relations," such as the "relation of Phillis Wheatley's poetry [Wheatley, of course, being the first published African American poet] to that of Milton and Pope." Cannily combining the highfalutin language of European and American postmodernist theory with more homely ideas and imagery drawn from black American folk culture and from African cultural history, Gates manages to seem, depending on one's vantage point, an establishment figure, an anti-establishment figure, or both at once. Consider this passage from his 1989 book *Figures in Black: Words, Signs, and the "Racial" Self*:

> [T]he challenge of the critic of Afro-American literature is to translate it into the black idiom, renaming principles of criticism where appropriate, but especially naming indigenous black principles of criticism and applying these to explicate our own texts. It is incumbent upon us to protect the integrity of our tradition by bringing to bear upon its criticism any tool of sensitivity to

> language that is appropriate…. [I]t is language, the black language of black texts, that expresses the distinctive quality of our literary tradition.

Note the deliberate signs of strain here, his effort to seem as if he is struggling to articulate a complex idea with absolute precision, even though the point he is making here is essentially a commonplace; note, too, his use of words like *principles, tradition, integrity*, and *sensitivity*, which manage to convey the impression that African American literature could not be in better, safer, and more sober hands than those of Henry Louis Gates Jr., who labors here to communicate the idea that he reveres that literature and has the soul of a caretaker. But note, too, that even as Gates stirringly affirms the importance of "translat[ing]" African American literature "into the black idiom," he is, in fact, speaking in what more than a few of his colleagues would call a "white idiom." It is, one must say, an elegant tightrope walk.

Gates's most celebrated work, and a cornerstone of Black Studies, is *The Signifying Monkey: A Theory of African-American Literary Criticism* (1988). He claims that the ideas developed in the book are based on the "critical practice" of Ralph Ellison—the towering black novelist and thinker whose 1952 novel *Invisible Man* is one of the great American classics, and who is in some ways too conservative for the taste of many Black Studies professors—as well as on the "revisionary techniques of parody and pastiche" pioneered by the more radical black novelist Ishmael Reed (*Mumbo Jumbo*). Holding up both Ellison and Reed as role models is itself something of a tightrope walk.

The Signifying Monkey, in Gates's words, "explores the relation of the black vernacular tradition to the Afro-American literary tradition" and "attempts to identify a theory of criticism that is inscribed within the black vernacular tradition and that in turn informs the shape of the Afro-American literary tradition." Gates leads the reader into a rather dense forest of "theory" based on "two signal trickster figures, Esu-Elegbara and the Signifying Monkey [the former a Yoruba figure, the latter Afro-American], in whose myths are registered certain principles of both formal language use and its interpretation" that he professes to find reflected in black literature. Among Gates's main points are that "[r]epetition and revision are fundamental to black artistic forms, from painting and sculpture to music and language use," that "black formal repetition always repeats with a difference, a black difference that manifests itself in specific language use," and that "[f]ree of the white person's gaze, black people created their own unique vernacular structures and relished in the double play that these forms bore to white forms." Gates notes—in yet another example of ingenious tightrope-walking—that the "notion of double-voiced discourse" that is central to the critical method he employs in the book is at once "related to Mikhail Bakhtin's theory of narrative" and "also indigenously African."

This is not valuable scholarship, in that it does not unearth new facts, and it is not valuable criticism, because it does not bring a fresh, illuminating perspective to the material at hand. What it is, is a brilliantly strategic bringing together of postmodern jargon and big postmodern names (such as Bakhtin) with previously established insights about African and African American literature. The point is not to bring new insight to these literatures but to suggest that there are important continuities between postmodern theory and African and African American literature. In other words, Gates isn't bringing anything of substance to the table here—he's just putting things together in such a way as to allow Black Studies practitioners to feel more intellectually formidable and au courant and to give postmodern "theorists" the ivory-tower equivalent of street cred. What he's doing in this book is an accomplishment more of academic politics than of scholarship or criticism—and it's ultimately more about Gates himself than about anything else. For Gates wants us to see that he, like Walt Whitman, contains multitudes—that he's intellectually and culturally capacious enough to build an edifice upon the foundations of both Ellison and Reed, both postmodernism and Black Studies. That edifice, of course, being Gates himself.

Shelby Steele isn't the only black intellectual who has criticized Gates—though most of the others have done it from the left.

In a 2006 book titled *A Companion to African-American Studies*, Hazel V. Carby, a professor of African American Studies and American Studies at Yale, cites Adam Begley's description of Gates, in a 1990 *New York Times Magazine* profile titled "Black Studies' New Star," as practicing an "entrepreneurial P. T. Barnumism." Carby, who shares the view that Gates is an attention-grabbing showman, disdains him for this, complaining that all the attention Gates has directed to himself keeps other Black Studies scholars from getting the notice they deserve. (She also argues that Gates's appearance in a *New Yorker* ad for the IBM ThinkPad "attests to the presence of capitalism as a universal world system.")

In the same book, Martin Kilson, an emeritus professor of government at Harvard and a faculty member there for four decades, recalls that when Black Studies first came to Harvard, he, like Steele, argued "that new faculty members teaching the Black Studies curricula should be selected out of established humanities and social science disciplines—literary studies, English, philosophy, history, political science, sociology, economics, etc." But Harvard's African and Afro-American Students Association disagreed: "They favored instead a faculty appointed solely to teach the Afro-American Studies curriculum." They won. Kilson, because he didn't like this setup, ended up being tagged as an opponent of Black Studies. Apparently in response to this, Kilson is eager to demonstrate his progressive credentials and to distinguish himself from Steele, dismissing as "bizarre" the objection by Steele and other "conservative Black intellectuals" to "Black-ethnic activist mobilization." Yet he shares Steele's view of Gates, calling him "a top-rank academic-entrepreneurial Black scholar" who "exhibits a keen grasp of the salience of what might be called the 'self-promotion ethos.'"

Kilson says, moreover, that Gates's claim that "Afro-American Studies [at Harvard] was dead" when Gates came on the scene in 1990 "is not only incorrect" but also an unfair put-down of those who were there before Gates: "It just so happened—a matter of serendipity—that with the new Neil Rudenstine Harvard administration in 1990 came a fundamentally new, assertively pro-Afro-American Studies outlook at the center of Harvard University." Kilson says that Gates's put-down of his predecessors "tells us something fundamental about the salience and character of the 'self-promotion ethos' in his academic-entrepreneur persona, I suggest." Having, in his view, been wrongly branded as an opponent of that revolutionary discipline, Black Studies, Kilson attempts here to flip things around, depicting himself as the "progressive" and Gates as a man with "establishmentarian" ties who has engaged in "tacky...self-promotion and pandering for conservative public favor." (In his comments on Gates, Kilson repeats the word *pander* or *pandering* several times.) He concludes: "As a leftist Black intellectual who embraces a keen belief in Black people's honor, I've always looked with dubious eyes on Gates's obsessive combining of the self-promotion ethos and establishmentarian linkages in the hope thereby to maximize benefits as a Black academic-entrepreneur intellectual."

Apropos of Gates's hustling, Steele sighs, "My whole generation has gone down that road." Expert hustlers like Gates, he says, are what his generation of black intellectuals has instead of substantial artists and thinkers like Ellison. "We don't have any Ralph Ellison in my generation. We don't even have any James Baldwin, whom I disagreed with in many ways but whose talent I have enormous respect for. We don't have that. We have bean counters." And it all happened because "identity studies seduced this generation."

If Gates is the indisputable top dog in contemporary Black Studies, number two is almost surely Cornel West. The differences between the two men are reflected in their appearance: Gates cultivates a distinguished look, with a neatly trimmed, professorial beard; West sports an Afro and a shaggy beard and mustache that bring to mind a 1960s Black Panther. Though he wears suits, they tend to be snazzy and close-fitting, making him look less like a member of an Ivy League faculty than like, say, a professional magician. And while Gates conducts himself like a serious man of letters, West sports a huge, goofy, gap-toothed grin and seeks to come off as an irreverent, street-savvy cutup. Gates writes scholarly tomes in dense academic prose; West bangs out chatty, shortish books aimed at the general reader. And while Gates largely confines himself to respectable scholarly activities, West has thrown himself into a range of pop-culture endeavors, such as appearing in the second and third *Matrix* movies and recording rap CDs. (On May 28, 2010, Bill Maher introduced West, a frequent guest on his TV program *Real Time*, as "author, actor, professor at Princeton University, and rapper.") Unlike Gates, West is not very likely to turn to either Ralph Ellison or Ishmael Reed as a touchstone of the best of African American culture. In his view, "there are two *organic* intellectual traditions in African American life: *the black Christian tradition of preaching* and *the black musical tradition of performance*"; no black writer or literary intellectual, he maintains, has ever equaled, say, Louis Armstrong. (The sole, majestic exception is Toni Morrison, whom West celebrates, along with other "black diasporan women," for having enabled "postmodern black intellectuals" to shape "a new cultural politics of difference.")

In 2000, while teaching at Harvard, West was famously called in by then university president Lawrence Summers, who questioned some of West's activities—among them his rapping, his involvement in Al Sharpton's presidential campaign, and his allegedly easy grading—and also brought up West's failure to produce any scholarly or critical work of substance. Given the number of unemployed Ph.D.s and adjunct professors around the United States who would give their eyeteeth for such a position, and whose gifts and accomplishments certainly merit such an appointment more than West's do, one can understand Summers's concern. Yet West was outraged and insulted, insisting that all his nonacademic activities constituted acts of teaching, for they were all means of reaching the general public with his "ideas." In 2002 he allowed himself to be wooed away to Princeton, where he had received his Ph.D.; he was given a joint appointment in religion and African American Studies, and the university president was reportedly very happy to have him. In 2011, it was announced that West would take up a position the next year at Union Theological Seminary. West's most celebrated books are *Race Matters* (1993) and *Keeping Faith: Philosophy and Race in America* (1994). In the latter, he favorably compares life in contemporary Ethiopia to America's "hedonistic culture and market-driven society"; talks about the disappointment of "black folk" with America (yet resolves to continue to "struggle for human dignity and existential democracy"); serves up a sizable helping of scare rhetoric about the "escalating xenophobias against people of color, Jews, women, gays, lesbians and the elderly" in today's "highly commercialized North Atlantic capitalist cultures"; attacks the "WASP" Arnoldian canon; and aligns himself with what he sees as criticisms of the "WASP establishment" mounted by a progressive coalition of "African Americans, Latino/a Americans, Asian Americans, Native Americans and American women" employing theories of "the Frankfurt school (Marcuse, Adorno, Horkheimer), French/Italian Marxisms (Sartre, Althusser, Lefebvre, Gramsci), structuralisms (Lévi-Strauss, Todorov) and poststructuralisms (Deleuze, Derrida, Foucault)" while revising American history "in light of the struggles of white male workers, women, African Americans, Native Americans, Latino/a Americans, gays and lesbians." (Reading this as a gay man, I feel as if I'm being herded into a square in Pyongyang to participate in a "spontaneous" pro-government demonstration in which I didn't ask to take part.)

West presents himself, then, as being at war with the Western cultural establishment and as rejecting "people of color" who embrace "the Booker T. Temptation" by involving themselves "with the mainstream and its legitimizing power." Which is not to say that he identifies with Booker T. Washington's antagonist, W. E. B. Du Bois, either, because he also condemns the Du Boisian "Talented Tenth Seduction, namely, a move toward arrogant group insularity." For good measure, he also washes his hands of individualism, which he describes as the "Go It Alone Option." The fourth option, and the one he identifies with, is that of being "a Critical Organic Catalyst. By this I mean a person who stays attuned to the best of what the mainstream has to offer...yet maintains a grounding in affirming and enabling subcultures of criticism." He has another way of putting this: he has chosen to be a practitioner of "demystification" or "prophetic criticism." In other words, he's a prophet. This approach, he suggests, is "appropriate for the new cultural politics of difference—because while it begins with social structural analyses it also makes explicit its moral and political aims." He cites Louis Armstrong, Martin Luther King Jr., and (rather confusingly, given West's rejection of his "Talented Tenth Seduction") Du Bois as forerunners of this approach, which he says is equally open to the creations of Beethoven and Stevie Wonder, Picasso and Spike Lee. Some might argue that the teaching of critical thinking involves making distinctions between, say, Beethoven and Spike Lee; but those who feel strongly about such matters would be best advised not to send their children to study under Cornel West.

He is frequently interviewed on TV about a variety of subjects—social problems, Obama's Nobel Prize—but whatever the question, his answers tend to be self-referential, drawing attention to his own role as a critical "prophet," and to employ the same handful of catch-phrases (America is divided into "vanilla suburbs and chocolate cities" and needs to be more "Socratic and prophetic"). The talks he gives at universities are sermons, delivered in energetic, black-church style, that begin with sweeping rhetoric, drawing on Plato and Shakespeare, about "the unexamined life" and "what it means to be human," and that then narrow in on the proper role of educated Americans in our time: we are obliged, he urges his audiences, to "think critically," to engage in "critical patriotism," to "question presuppositions [and] surrender prejudice," to "challenge conformism" and "contest dogmas" and bear "prophetic witness." Sounds good. But for all his talk of bold contrarianism, virtually everything he spouts is received academic opinion; for all his rhetoric about the importance of being challenged, none of his student audiences are challenged by anything he says—for he's giving them exactly what they want, reaffirming the very orthodoxies they've been fed from day one by their humanities professors. He calls on his listeners to "contest dogmas" but then adds that he means "dogmas like white supremacy, dogmas like male supremacy, dogmas like class privilege"—a list that is itself an affirmation of reigning academic dogma about race, gender, and class. West's incantatory style and his frequent collegial references to biblical prophets conceal the fact that pretty much everything he has to say is a contemporary academic cliche.

As an example of the common practice in Black Studies of celebrating blacks for actions and accomplishments that would be condemned if the people in question were white, West, in the preface to *Keeping Faith*, writes proudly of his mother-in-law's membership in "one of the great families of Ethiopia"—great because she is a descendant of the "leader of the Oromo people, who wedded the sister of Menelik II, the nineteenth-century creator of modern Ethiopia," and because she once "owned thousands of acres of land" before it was confiscated "under the communist regime." Interesting words from a man who is otherwise not in the habit of smiling on inherited fortunes, titles, and estates; but of course it all depends, apparently, on the color of the people who possess those fortunes, titles, and estates.

*   *   *

If Gates and West are among the leading figures in Black Studies, the leading textbook in the field, as noted, is *Introduction to Black Studies* by Karenga (born Ron Everett), the 1979 publication of which has been described by Asante as one of the "defining moments" in Black Studies. Karenga, who from 1989 to 2002 was the chairman of Afro Studies at California State University, is not shy about his book's importance, noting at the outset of the third edition (2002) that it has occupied "a preeminent position among introductory texts in the discipline...since it was first published." Karenga defines Black Studies as "an area of critical intellectual study and an instrument of social change in the interest of African and human good," and though he acknowledges that it originated in the 1960s, he is quick to add that "[s]ome scholars...argue that Black Studies began in ancient societies like ancient Egypt, Mali and Songhay[,] which clearly established an intellectual tradition of study of themselves."

Indeed, while most serious Egyptologists would deny that today's sub-Saharan Africans and black Americans are the descendants of ancient Egyptians—or would at the very least advise extreme prudence in asserting such a connection—Karenga throws all caution to the winds, presenting as indisputable Cheikh Anta Diop's notorious arguments in *Nations nègres et culture* (1954) and later works "for the African or Black character of Egypt" and citing Diop and others to the effect that ancient Egyptians originated in black Ethiopia. Karenga does not so much as hint at the nature of the rather strong case *against* these claims. Ancient Egypt's "real history," he insists, "reveals a debt to Africa that Eurocentric and racist thinking can neither concede nor accept"—in other words, those who dispute this dubious "history" are, quite simply, motivated by racism. Karenga is prone to making sweepingly grand statements not only about the significance of ancient Egyptian culture in the shaping of black culture right up to the present day but also about the supreme greatness of ancient Egyptian culture itself and its incomparable influence on all of human civilization (arguing, for example, for "the contribution of Egyptian to Greek philosophy"). For Karenga, in short, it is a well-nigh religiously held belief that today's blacks are the descendants of ancient Egyptians and that the culture of ancient Egypt is the earliest and by far the most important foundation for the cultures of sub-Saharan Africa and of the black diaspora—and the true origin of many of the Western ideas and values that are more traditionally viewed as having been bequeathed to us by the ancient Greeks. To put it bluntly, Karenga has put all his eggs in one basket: if Egypt *isn't* "black," then his entire conception of black heritage collapses utterly.

There's no disputing, of course, that ancient Egypt had one of the world's great civilizations. But for Karenga this isn't sufficient: he routinely inflates the facts, proffering a long list of items that make up "the legacy of Egypt" and "Egyptian values," many of them, at best, questionable or exaggerated. (For example, he states, untruthfully, that ancient Egyptians "were aware of blood circulation.") Though in many ways, furthermore, the ancient Egyptians were indeed more socially and culturally advanced than many other ancient civilizations, Karenga ascribes to them a profound social consciousness—and, in order to keep from complicating his rosy picture, soft-pedals the fact that they held slaves and utterly rejects the idea that those slaves built the pyramids.

Karenga claims for modern blacks not only the legacy of ancient Egypt but also that of Muhammad's Muslim empire. He embraces wholeheartedly the myth of *Andalus*—the fanciful notion that Spain, and all of Europe, reached a cultural and ethical zenith during the centuries when portions of Iberia were governed by Muslims. "The Moorish empire in Spain represents not only a golden age in Islamic civilization," Karenga writes, "but also a golden age of civilization for Africa, Europe and ultimately the world." There follow several pages of propaganda rehearsing the familiar line about the glories of Moorish Spain and its supposed "religious tolerance and multiculturalism"—a bit of nonsense that is not leavened by even the most fleeting mention of dhimmitude, the Moors' systematic and often brutal subordination of Christians and Jews. Karenga even respectfully cites Ivan Van Sertima's crackpot 1976 work *They Came before Columbus*, which argues that Africans traveled to America in ancient times and founded the Olmec civilization. Though Karenga at least acknowledges that there are historians who disagree with Van Sertima on legitimate (in other words, nonracist) grounds and begins his account of Van Sertima's theory by saying, with relative caution, that it "invites serious consideration," four pages later he states without qualification that Van Sertima "has clearly shown the African presence and legacy in ancient America." Hence, when Columbus went to America, "he found Blacks had already preceded him."

Karenga depicts the historical cultures of sub-Saharan Africa almost as glowingly as he does those of ancient Egypt and Moorish Spain. For example, he describes African societies of centuries ago as having pursued knowledge not just for its own sake but "for human sake" [*sic*]. As in the case of ancient Egypt, he is quick to dismiss any pesky factual details that might spoil his perfect picture: he deals with the central role of black Africans in the capture and sale of slaves to white Europeans and Americans—a well-established historical fact—by dismissing it out of hand. (Everything, in Karenga's world, has to be the fault of Europeans and capitalism.) To be sure, he admits that "Africans enslaved others before the coming and demands of the European." But this man who repeatedly hammers home the idea that black slavery in America was nothing less than a "Holocaust" essentially defends (indeed, all but praises) slavery in Africa, arguing that it was "in no way like European enslavement," that most slaves in Africa were taken in war or were being punished for crimes, and that their slavery was less like American-style slavery than like medieval serfdom. While Karenga represents the holding of black slaves by whites as the greatest crime in human history, then, he makes ample excuses for slaveholders who happened to be black.

Given Karenga's presentation of African civilizations of the past as highly developed, he feels obliged to account for the continent's current backward state. "Invariably," he admits, "students of Black

Studies raise the question of why did Africa with all its glory and achievement fall to the European advance." His answer: Western guns, Western ships, and Western capitalism. Africans were by nature peaceful, "communalistic," friendly to foreigners, "deeply spiritual and deferential to nature and concerned with living in harmony with it rather than conquering it"; Europeans, by contrast, were aggressive, bloodthirsty xenophobes bent on conquest. Repeatedly in this book, Karenga celebrates black "collectivity" as opposed to European individualism. Anyone with even rudimentary knowledge of the real history of Africa will recognize just how factually challenged Karenga's image of that continent's historic civilizations is.

Not surprisingly, Karenga supports the reparations movement, the call for white Americans to give money to black Americans in partial compensation for the crime of slavery. Karenga's logical inconsistency is especially manifest here: though he argues, apropos of black African participation in the slave trade, that "it is factually inaccurate and morally wrong and repulsive to indict a whole people for a Holocaust which was imposed on them and was aided by collaborators," he would in fact "indict" all American whites today for the actions of a small minority of American whites more than a hundred and fifty years ago. Never mind that slaveholders always made up a small percentage of the white population; never mind that many white Americans today descend from soldiers who fought and died to free slaves; never mind that most white Americans today descend from immigrants who came to America after the Civil War; and never mind that some whites are themselves the descendants of slaves while some blacks aren't. Karenga plainly doesn't wish to face the fact that the black African "collaborators" in slavery weren't just collaborationists, like the Dutch bureaucrats and French gendarmes who helped the Nazis—they were crucial figures in the slave trade without whom the whole business would've been impossible. As even Gates acknowledged in a *New York Times* op-ed in 2010, "90 percent of those shipped to the New World were enslaved by Africans and then sold to European traders. The sad truth is that without complex business partnerships between African elites and European traders and commercial agents, the slave trade to the New World would have been impossible, at least on the scale it occurred." Slavery was already a fact in Africa; it took commerce between black Africans and European and American whites to extend it to the West.

Karenga's umbrella term for the rise of Black Power and related developments is "the Reaffirmation of the 1960s"—a label he purports to find appropriate because blacks, during that decade, "reaffirmed... themselves as Africans" and at the same time reaffirmed a "social justice tradition" that reached "back to the ethical teachings of ancient Egypt." He can hardly avoid writing about Martin Luther King Jr. (though he does manage to entirely omit Bayard Rustin, Lyndon B. Johnson, and the Great Society), but his real enthusiasm is for people like Malcolm X and "the Honorable Elijah Muhammad," head of the Nation of Islam. Elijah Muhammad, in Karenga's view, "broke the monopoly whites had on good and God by revealing an alternative truth and reconstructing reality in Black images and interests." Karenga also praises the black Christian leader Albert Cleage, who "portrayed Jesus as a Black revolutionary," "argued God is Black," and considered blacks "God's Chosen People." He likewise celebrates the activist Imari Obadele, who demanded an independent black republic consisting of South Carolina, Georgia, Alabama, Louisiana, and Mississippi. (Karenga says that this "question is still a burning one and is not solved by non-believers dismissing it as Utopian.")

But Karenga's biggest hero is plainly himself. While Martin Luther King Jr. gets five lines in Karenga's index, Karenga himself (who, by the way, invented Kwanzaa and wrote the mission statement for Louis Farrakhan s 1995 Million Man March) gets nine, his Us (short for United Slaves) Organization (established in 1965 with the goal of waging "a cultural revolution") gets three, and his "Kawaida philosophy" (on which Us was founded) gets seven. What is "Kawaida philosophy"? It's basically a set of truisms about the need for Africans—and when Karenga uses the word, he is including African Americans—to "recover the best of their culture and use it to envision a new world and to support the struggle to bring that world into being." (Karenga's book contains pages and pages of such rhetoric.) For Karenga, power is all-important; he quotes himself as saying, "We must move on every level to get power. We must have an organization that thinks, acts, breathes and sleeps on the question of power." Perhaps the most important thing to know about the Us Organization is that, to quote J. Lawrence Scholer, it "was more radical than the Panthers, setting off quarrels between the two." Take, for example, the 1969 dispute over "the leadership of the new Afro-American Studies department at UCLA." The Panthers and Us supported different candidates; at a meeting held to discuss the standoff, "Panthers John Jerome Huggins and Alprentice Carter...verbally attack[ed] Karenga," and afterward, "[t]wo US members, George and Larry Stiner, confronted Huggins and Carter in a hallway...and shot and killed them." Scholer provides further biographical background:

> On September 17, 1971, Karenga was sentenced to one to ten years in prison. ...The charges stemmed from a May 9, 1970, incident in which Karenga and two others tortured two women who Karenga believed had tried to kill him by placing "crystals" in his food and water.
>
> A year later the *Los Angeles Times* described the events: "Deborah Jones...said she and Gail Davis were whipped with an electrical cord and beaten with a karate baton after being ordered to remove their clothes. She testified that a hot soldering iron was placed in Miss Davis' mouth and placed against Miss Davis' face and that one of her own big toes was tightened in a vise. Karenga...also put detergent and running hoses in their mouths, she said."
>
> ...Eight years later California State University at Long Beach made Karenga the head of its Black Studies Department.

According to Karenga, an important element of Kawaida is striving after "excellence"; he repeatedly asserts that Black Studies is "rigorous," "intellectual," "serious," and so on. Yet Karenga's book is notable for its frequent sloppiness and its often spectacularly terrible prose. It is awash in elementary agreement problems, misplaced commas, and mistakes such as "Queen, New York" for Queens. (And this is, note well, the third edition of a widely used textbook.) Sample sentences:

In addition to the stress on social justice as a core concern of politics, the emphasis on power as an indispensable element and focus is also made.

However, the question of for what purpose do we seek power remains.

Us has maintained since the Sixties concerning European cultural hegemony, one of the greatest powers in the world is to be able to define reality and make others accept it even when it's to their disadvantage.

It [slavery] also involves lifting Africans out of their own history making them a footnote and forgotten casualty in European history and thus limiting and denying their ability to speak their own special cultural truth to the world and make their own unique contribution to the forward flow of human history.

Throughout his book, Karenga waxes poetic (or tries to) about the glories of ancient Egypt and the "Holocaust" of slavery. Black history, he writes, "is a history of ancient wonder and achievement in the Nile Valley, awesome tragedy and destruction in the Holocaust of enslavement," and so on. "We must always be conscious," he counsels, "of our identity as the fathers and mothers of humanity and human civilization in the Nile Valley, the sons and daughters of the Holocaust of enslavement and the authors and heirs of the Reaffirmation of our African-ness and social justice tradition in the Sixties." And he informs his young black readers that "our culture has the most ancient of ethical traditions, the oldest ethical, spiritual and social justice texts," and that "[w]e introduced the concept of human dignity and divine image of the human person." Rarely has any book been so packed with vapid, repetitive platform rhetoric about "enhancing the human future," "meaningful interaction and mutually beneficial exchanges," and the like; continually, one finds oneself reflecting that it would be far more of a service to black American students, and to black American culture, to give them the kind of solid education that would enable at least some of them to help create a great culture than to soothe them *ad nauseam* with the lie that they are already great, by virtue of the supposedly monumental cultural legacy of their African forefathers and the demonstrably magnificent cultural legacy of their alleged ancestors who lived along the Nile many millennia ago. Yes, ancient Egypt, along with ancient Greece, Rome, and other civilizations of millennia ago have indeed bequeathed us a great heritage, but the things they have given us are, as Du Bois so stirringly argued, the common inheritance of all humankind, and are no reason for any of us to congratulate ourselves or relax on our laurels; on the contrary, they should be—for *all* of us—an object of devoted study and a source of inspiration.

Perhaps surprisingly, Karenga actually includes a few lines in his book about "black conservatives," though his take on them is hardly a surprise: for him, Shelby Steele and company are the despicable progeny of Booker T. Washington—blacks who seek rewards from white society for betraying their people.

Today, there are more than eight hundred tenured Black Studies professors in the United States, and nearly one in every ten universities grants degrees in the subject. Rojas sums up the Gates era—to coin a phrase—as "characterized by a focus on legitimacy." He feels that the field has oriented itself during these years toward more "traditional social sciences and humanities" and has thus acquired respect and stability. He also contends that "the dominant style of black studies is not overly associated with nationalism" like Karenga's— most programs, he says, do not encourage separatist or nationalist sentiments but rather appeal to students of all colors. In Rojas's view, Black Studies has transcended its revolutionary origins and achieved moderation, intellectual seriousness, and academic legitimacy. Yet what he seems to regard (and admire) as moderation is, by nonacademic American standards, anything but. Black Studies' leading lights, after all, are people like Gates and West; within its walls, the ideas of people like Shelby Steele are considered anathema, and are cited only for the purpose of mockery. There is, in short, a considerable distance between Black Studies—whether it's the Black Studies of Karenga or that of Rojas—and the black man and woman in the street. And nothing illuminates this state of affairs more vividly than the case of Bill Cosby.

*　　*　　*

While professors like Karenga are busy indoctrinating students in strident anticapitalism and racial supremacism, and other inhabitants of the Ebony Tower are preaching only somewhat less extreme versions of the same ideology, a very different message about race has been resonating with ordinary, hardworking black Americans. In recent years, the comedian and actor Bill Cosby has been speaking to audiences in black churches and other community centers, lamenting the prevalence among black Americans of unwed teenage mothers and absentee fathers, violent and misogynistic gangsta rap, and black-on-black crime. He has been calling on young black people to reject these self-destructive social pathologies and to embrace traditional American values of self-respect and personal responsibility.

In an *Atlantic* article about Cosby's crusade, Ta-Nehisi Coates maintains that Cosby's call for "hard work and moral reform" rather than "protests and government intervention" resonates with "conservative black Americans who are convinced that integration, and to some extent the entire liberal dream, robbed them of their natural defenses." Coates points out that in 2004, the *New York Times* found that black parents in Louisville, Kentucky, the site of a historic battle over school desegregation in 1975–76, were now "more interested in educational progress than in racial parity." Coates also cites a survey showing that 71 percent of American blacks consider rap "a bad influence." Coates quotes lines from one of Cosby's speeches in which the comedian assails some black Americans' uninformed image of themselves as Africans: "We are not Africans. Those people are not Africans. They don't know a damn thing about Africa—with names like Shaniqua, Shaliqua, Mohammed, and all that crap, and all of them are in jail."

Whatever one may make of Cosby's diagnoses and prescriptions, one thing is clear: he's no hustler. On the contrary, he's a very rich and respected cultural figure who, by wading into these waters, only risks alienating millions of people whose affection and admiration for his work have made his fortune. Yet he's taken this step because he recognizes that the black "leaders" of our era (Jesse Jackson, Al Sharpton) and the academic Black Studies establishment (Gates, West, Karenga) not only have failed to say things that need to be said, but have in many cases encouraged the kinds of pathologies Cosby is alarmed about.

Not surprisingly, a leading black academic, Michael Eric Dyson, has taken on Cosby in a very big way. Dyson, who has taught at DePaul, the University of North Carolina, Columbia, Brown, and the University of Pennsylvania, is now a professor of sociology at Georgetown University and can frequently be heard serving up commentary on NPR, CNN, and *Real Time with Bill Maker*. In addition, he is an ordained minister who, in 2010, at the upscale New York restaurant Cipriani, officiated at the wedding of a deejay named La La and a pro basketball player named Carmelo Anthony, who at the time were starring in a VH1 reality series. ("The 320 guests," according to Dyson's Wikipedia entry, "included Justin Timberlake, Kim Kardashian, Khloe Kardashian, Lamar Odom, Ciara, Spike Lee, Ludacris, Kelly Rowland, and LeBron James.") Dyson, it should be noted, is considered an academic star and is paid a salary in the high six figures. This means that he's several times more handsomely compensated than many of Americas most distinguished scholars in the humanities and social sciences—or, to look at it in another way, he takes home a bigger paycheck than any dozen or so adjunct professors put together, people who are far more gifted and accomplished than he is and carry much heavier course loads.

Over lunch in Philadelphia in 2010, Alan Charles Kors brings up the subject of Dyson, his former (and much younger) colleague at the University of Pennsylvania. "For years," says Kors, "Dyson was the highest-paid member of the Arts and Sciences faculty at Penn." This is an astonishing distinction for anyone as young as Dyson, no matter what his professional record. Dyson's *oeuvre*, which includes books with titles like *Reflecting Black*, *Making Malcolm*, *Race Rules*, *Between God and Gangsta Rap*, *Debating Race*, and *Know What I Mean? Reflections on Hip-Hop*, hardly explains his disproportionate level of compensation. "He's a huckster," says Kors bluntly. Kors explains that Dyson was hired by Penn's Department of Religious Studies "to teach a course on 'Great Religious Thinkers of the West.' Each time around it focuses on a different figure, and over the years they've done Augustine, Luther, Tillich, and so forth. Dyson taught it more than once." And whom did Dyson focus on when he taught it? Tupac Shakur. "As a *great religious thinker*," Kors adds drily. After he spent a few years of teaching this sort of thing, "Georgetown offered him a higher salary which Penn couldn't match, so he left." Noting the tiresome predictability with which Dyson flouts what Karenga calls "traditional white studies" and shamelessly follows the latest academic fashion, Kors wonders: "What would he say if you put him on truth serum? People tend to convince themselves of the positions that are most profitable to hold."

The dedication page of Dyson's 2005 book *Is Bill Cosby Right? Or Has the Black Middle Class Lost Its Mind?* consists of a long list of names, each followed by a cloying phrase plainly designed to shape a picture of the author as a virtuous, sensitive soul ("To...Who fed me and taught me the true meaning of ministry and manhood"; "To... Who fed me and first inspired a young pastor to pursue a Ph.D."). All this narcissism is prelude to a stunning nasty personal attack in which Dyson lambastes Cosby for his "overemphasis on personal responsibility" and supposed indifference to the "structural features" that underlie black poverty. (To which one might reply that Cosby's crusade is a reaction to a half century of preoccupation with "structural features" that has proved disastrous.) Dyson professes to be offended by Cosby's insistence that young black people learn to speak and write proper English—or, as Dyson puts it, in his own surprisingly shaky English: "Cosby also spies the critical deficiency of the black poor in the linguistic habits, displaying his ignorance about 'black English' and 'Ebonics.'" Dyson also accuses Cosby of "disregard for the hip-hop generation," claiming that the comic's "poisonous view of young folk who speak a language he can barely parse simmers with hostility and resentment"—even though Cosby's entire campaign is plainly motivated by a deep concern for those young people. Dyson even has the nerve to contrast Cosby to his own wonderful self, writing about his visit to a youth detention center where he and his wife "were touched, even moved to tears" by the young thieves and murderers there and quoting several pages of comments by the inmates about how much his visit meant to them.

Countering Cosby, Dyson maintains that "body piercing and baggy clothes express identity among black youth." Yes, but what *kind* of identity—an individual identity marked by self-respect or a group identity marked by mindless copycatting? As for hip-hop, Dyson considers Sean "P. Diddy" Combs and Russell Simmons good role models because they've "made millions from their clothing lines." And he claims that "[n]ames like Shaniqua and Taliqua," ridiculed by Cosby, "are meaningful cultural expressions of self-determination and allow relatively powerless blacks to fashion their identities outside the glare of white society." Yes, and keep them from finding jobs. "Cosby's comments," gripes Dyson, "bolster the belief that *less* money, political action and societal intervention—and more hard work and personal responsibility—are the key to black success." Cosby doesn't exactly argue this, but the dismal failure of Great Society programs only proves how right Cosby is when he argues that simply throwing government money at social problems won't solve them. After two or three generations of self-serving antics by increasingly appalling con artists like Jesse Jackson and Al Sharpton, the positive response by black Americans to Cosby's campaign reflects a widespread recognition that it *is* time for a leading black voice to emphasize personal responsibility. (Even Barack Obama, after all, has said many of the things that Cosby has said.)

Repeatedly, Dyson chastises Cosby for not having been more preoccupied during the course of his career with his "black identity." He repeats this term over and over for pages (noting, of course, in dutiful postmodern fashion, that "the focus on race... surely doesn't block the consideration of other equally compelling features of identity rooted in gender or sexual orientation or religion or class"). "For most of his career," Dyson complains, "Bill Cosby has avoided race with religious zeal." Or as he puts it elsewhere in his book, a bit less coherently: "Cosby has for the most part banished the galvanizing virtues of blackness to the realm of inference." Meaning what? Is every writer, artist, or performer who belongs to a minority group obliged, in his work, to constantly make a point of his membership in that group—especially when his membership in that group is written on his face? "Despite Cosby's brilliant work, race hasn't disappeared; it seems he might have as usefully led us *through* the battlefields of race instead of *around* them," Dyson complains. This is the most unfair kind of criticism: Dyson is, in effect, going after Cosby for not being Richard Pryor. In any case, it's untrue that Cosby has "avoided race": it was impossible, for example, to watch *The Cosby Show* without noting that the walls of the Huxtable family home were covered with African and African-influenced works of art and even featured an anti-apartheid poster (which, as it happens, Cosby kept in place over NBC's fierce objections). In reply to those who defend Cosby's criticisms of inner-city social pathologies by noting "his majestic philanthropy over the years," Dyson argues that defending Cosby on such grounds is "like saying that it's all right to rape a young lady because you've given a million dollars to a women's college." (The allusion here is to Cosby's munificence: his donation of $20 million to Spelman College was the single largest contribution ever made to any historically black college or university.)

For blacks, Cosby has been a trailblazer. Yet he's condemned by Dyson for not having been a grandstander. Dyson repeatedly accuses Cosby of lacking courage. "Cosby," Dyson claims, "is so obviously embarrassed by the masses of black folk that he has taken to insulting and, truly, intimidating them." But if Cosby were embarrassed by his fellow blacks, the last thing he'd want to do would be to run around the country talking to them about themselves. Dyson likens Cosby to the black "elites" of previous generations who criticized the black poor because they damaged the race's image, and depicts him as a member of a snooty black elite that looks down on working-class blacks; yet it's Dyson who belongs to a black elite, namely the black power establishment based in the academy and in various "activist" rackets. Far from lacking courage, Cosby has shown considerable bravery in taking on that establishment, which (as Dyson exemplifies) is not above answering cogent critiques with personal attacks.

Cosby can't win with Dyson: though on *I Spy* in 1965 Cosby "shattered television's race barrier as the first Negro to star in a network series" (unless you count CBS's *Amos 'n Andy* in 1951–53 and Nat

King Cole's 1956–57 variety show on NBC), his "race on the series was no big deal at all, a point that made him the darling of many white critics." Perhaps Dyson is too young to easily grasp that in 1965, the fact that the program didn't make a "big deal" out of Cosby's race *was* a "big deal." As for *The Cosby Show*, Dyson approvingly quotes a passage from Gates indicting that series for "reflecting the miniscule [sic] integration of blacks into the upper middle class" and thus "throw[ing] the blame for poverty back onto the impoverished." It is striking to see Cosby criticized by Gates and Dyson, professors at major universities who earn huge salaries, for portraying a black family at or near their and his own socioeconomic levels—thereby providing blacks at lower socioeconomic levels with an image of a life to strive for, as well as of responsible parenting and professionalism.

Dyson does acknowledge that in his comic routines, Cosby, "like a jazz artist," has "constructed narratives of sometimes haunting ethical beauty that offered insight into the human condition." But he also accuses Cosby of not being "practiced or articulate in matters of public negotiation with the subtleties, nuances and complexities of racial rhetoric." I would counter that there is absolutely no sign in Dyson's book of subtlety, nuance, or complexity—and I would also point out that one of the people whom he *does* celebrate for these virtues is Al Sharpton. Dyson has no respect for Cosby's comedy philosophy, which he quotes: "I don't think you can bring the races together by joking about the differences between them. I'd rather talk about the similarities, about what's universal in their experiences." This philosophy underlies the work of all great authors and artists, but it's not a philosophy that'll win you a tenure-track job in Black Studies.

Dyson sneers at Cosby's complaints about "[t]he poverty pimps and the victim pimps"—but Dyson refuses to acknowledge that there are such pimps, and that Jesse Jackson stands at the head of that pack. As it happens, Dyson contrasts Cosby unfavorably with Jackson, whom he praises for understanding "the dynamic relationship between personal and social responsibility" and calls "the most gifted social activist and public moralist of our times." (This is the same "public moralist" who called New York City "Hymietown.") Jackson, Dyson adds, "has also worked tirelessly to erase social injustice and the structural inequalities that prevent blacks and other poor people from enjoying the opportunity to exercise their full citizenship." Absent from this tribute is any mention of the damning revelations contained in the book *Shakedown: Exposing the Real Jesse Jackson*, in which Kenneth R. Timmerman demonstrates conclusively that Jackson is a world-class shakedown artist whose *specialité de la maison* is threatening to publicly attack companies as racist unless they grease his (or a crony's) palm. (In 2001, University of Colorado law professor Paul Campos recounted in the *Rocky Mountain News* Jackson's boycott of Anheuser-Busch, a company whose "warm feelings for the Jackson family overflowed to the point where the corporation gave Jackson's sons a beer distributorship." Asked Campos: "How can a man who at this point retains all the moral authority of a professional extortionist continue to hold himself out as one of America's political and spiritual leaders?")

Dyson would seem to be a perfect example of Steele's top-drawer hustler—the kind who's managed to hustle his way to the summit of the Black Studies pile. Certainly excellence has nothing to do with it: Dyson is neither a clear nor an original thinker, and is an absolutely terrible writer. "To a degree," he writes in a typical sentence, "the black elite acted out of necessity, but perhaps to a larger degree, their actions proved how they had unconsciously drank [*sic*] in the poisonous view of the black poor that whites forced on them." He is especially fond of painfully awkward metaphors: "Every time the black aristocratic finger pointed at poor black folk's pathology, four more fingers of white moral unease folded into its palm." And: "The aesthetic ecology in which they [black youth] are nurtured surely contains poisonous weeds and quicksand, glimpsed in sexist tirades on wax [?] and the hunger to make violence erotic." His illiteracy, moreover, is matched by his innumeracy: "In 1954," he writes, "the neonatal mortality rate for blacks per one thousand live births registered at 27 percent." This statement is followed by several others in which he similarly misuses the word "percent." (Plainly he means to say that the mortality rate was 2.7 percent.)

Ta-Nehisi Coates admits to having considered Cosby an elitist—but he notes that his own father, a member of the older black generation, respects the comedian as a voice for "black empowerment." It is for that reason, says Coates, that "Cosby's argument has resonated with the black mainstream." Yet although Coates—who suggests that Cosby is the ideological heir not only of Booker T. Washington, the "conservative" preacher of black self-reliance, but also of the radicals Marcus Garvey and Malcolm X, both of whom "fault[ed] blacks for failing to take charge of their destiny"—remains critical of much of Cosby's message, he treats Cosby with respect and implicitly rejects the effort by Black Studies figures like Karenga to sell young people on the myth of a noble and glorious Egyptian heritage. "Black people are not the descendants of kings," Coates asserts. "We are—and I say this with big pride—the progeny of slaves. If there's any majesty in our struggle, it lies not in fairy tales but in those humble origins and the great distance we've traveled since."

Bill Cosby isn't the only high-profile black American to ruffle the feathers of Black Studies. Steele, of course, is another. He has been a major contrarian black voice since the publication of *The Content of Our Character: A New Vision of Race in America* (1990), in which he argued that centuries of brutal discrimination against blacks did not justify "positive" discrimination in the form of affirmative action, which he considers condescending and destructive. He underscored the role of white guilt in the establishment of such counterproductive policies and noted the skill with which some blacks exploited that guilt to personal advantage—a pattern that Steele considered an ugly, unhealthy model of race relations. Steele also divided black public figures into two groups: while the "challengers," such as Malcolm X, Huey Newton, and Jesse Jackson, send whites the implicit message that "only by paying my race back for our suffering at your hands can you prove that you're not racist," the "bargainers," such as Martin Luther King Jr., Oprah Winfrey, Bill Cosby, and Barack Obama, send the implicit message that "I'll take it for granted that you're not racist, and you'll be so thankful that you'll like me, watch me, elect me."

Another heretic is the linguist John McWhorter, whose book *Losing the Race: Self Sabotage in Black America* (2001) asks a series of questions:

> Is school a "white" thing? If not, then why do African-American students from comfortable middle-class backgrounds perform so badly in the classroom? What is it that prevents so many black college students in the humanities and social sciences from studying anything other than black subjects? Why do young black people, born decades after the heyday of the Civil Rights movement, see victimhood as the defining element of their existence?

Quoting passages from books published in the 1990s in which "successful black men" bemoan their alleged victimization—some of them comparing themselves to slaves or victims of lynching—McWhorter points out that "most of us would be hard pressed to match these portraits with the lives of most of the black people we know." Rejecting the idea "that the Civil Rights revolution has had no notable effect upon black Americans' lives," he argues that cults of victimology, separatism, and anti-intellectualism have sent Black America off "on a tragic detour," pumping up support for affirmative action and Ebonics and keeping black Americans from "reach[ing] Martin Luther King's mountaintop." Setting things back on track, he argues, "will require some profound adjustments in black identity."

For one thing, blacks will need to face up publicly to things they have already faced up to in private: "In the black community today," McWhorter observes in *Authentically Black: Essays for the Black Silent Majority* (2004), "there is a tacit rule that black responsibility and self-empowerment are not to be discussed at any length where whites can hear." While many black people "sound like Shelby Steele among 'their own,'" in mixed-race groups they'll "carefully dredge up episodes of possible racism" and complain about the lack of "positive images of blacks in the media." He illustrates the self-destructive nature of the kind of thinking found among many blacks today by quoting a comment about *Losing the Race* posted on Amazon.com by a black women: "I insist on my right to be mediocre." McWhorter's reaction: "Du Bois would turn in his grave." He insists that " [w]e will not earn whites' admiration by blackmailing them into pretending to respect us," that "[a] race does not make its mark by how successful it has been at exacting charity, but by how much it achieves without charity," and that "the race that reaches the mountaintop is one that embraces with vigor its achievements, trumpets them to all who will listen, and teaches its children that doing so in the face of obstacles only makes the victory sweeter." Instead of teaching Tupac Shakur as a great religious thinker, McWhorter invites readers to "[i]magine an America where blacks do not bop their heads in warm assent when they hear Tupac Shakur shouting, 'Fuck the police! *Fuck* the police!'"

*   *   *

At the 2011 annual convention of the National Association of African American Studies, in Baton Rouge, Louisiana, I attend a panel on "Race in America: The Myth of the Post-Racial Era." The first speaker, Gregory L. Bosworth, who teaches history, government, and public policy at St. Augustine's College in North Carolina, cites Cornel West's book *Race Matters* and asks (in an almost impenetrable southern accent): "Does race still matter with the rise of President Obama?" Many observers, he says, claim that the "racial era" ended with Obama's election, but he begs to differ. On the very night Obama was elected, he says, two white men assaulted a black man in New York. (How many black men assaulted whites that night across the United States? Bosworth doesn't say.) He also notes an effort to make the Confederate flag the state flag of South Carolina. So much, in his view, for the "Post-Racial Era."

He passes the baton to Marcus P. Nevius, an attractive, earnest-seeming young man of about twenty-five, also from St. Augustine's College. Citing John Hope Franklin's *The Color Line* (1993), which argues that the rise of the conservative movement slowed the fading of the color line in American society, Nevius argues that "we [blacks] have to begin to look at ourselves as American first," just as German Americans, Korean Americans, and other Americans do. He suggests that with the election of Barack Obama, African Americans have "transcend[ed]" their niche identity and joined the mainstream. "As I move forward with my career," he says, "I try to position myself in the same way [as Obama]. I try to represent what Obama could bring to my classroom." He wants to be "someone who is American first, with an African American heritage," and seeks to help construct "a post-racial era that can be beneficial to young blacks." He also mentions his use in the classroom of the works of John McWhorter.

The response to Nevius's presentation can be summed up in two words: stunned silence. Finally the next speaker, Mary Scott-Brown, finds something to say. "I'm a bit struck by my young colleague," she tells us. "I'm of a different generation." (She's fiftyish.) This is a polite way of saying that the idea of being American first and black second goes against every fiber of her being. The next speaker, a very young woman named Jarenda E. Williams (she looks like a student but is, in fact, a faculty member), seems even more unsettled by Nevius's remarks. Its important, she says, to "claim [one's] African heritage" and recognize one's connection to "African people throughout the diaspora." She suggests that "until we know what it is to be African, we cannot take on the American part. We are not viewed as American anyway." She takes an excruciatingly long pause, not knowing what else to say. She finds a suitable, and safe, academic cliche: "We rely on corporations to tell us how we feel about ourselves." Another long pause. "President Obama," she says, rather inscrutably, "is a poster child for this." Yet another pause. A man in the audience says something about Obama's America being "transracial." Williams objects: "We have a different background than President Obama. He's not a descendant of slaves."

Next up is Jihan N. Gales, a young woman from North Carolina Central University and the only graduate student on the panel. She takes exception to Williams's Afrocentrism. "Although I love Africa," she says, "I believe there is a romanticism about Africa." She notes that while black Americans idealize Africa as a place of authentic blackness, in fact black Africans take their cultural cues increasingly from black America: young African men "idealize hip-hop culture" and young African women use "skin lighteners" and "fake hair" just like their black American counterparts. Young black people, she insists, need to understand themselves "in *current* perspectives": "we came here as slaves," but "there has been prog-ress" and "we need to think about the future." As for Obama, "if we see success" of the kind he represents, "we can use that" to achieve more success and transcend the past. Obama, she says, is a "role model," and role models are necessary because "they represent success for black America at the moment. When [people] look at the president, they see a black man."

When the time comes for Q&A, a man in the audience rips into Nevius for including a book by McWhorter on his reading list. McWhorter, the man charges, is a "poster child for the far right" who is "paid handsomely to denigrate a race of people." The man insists that "other groups have been afforded a greater chance of assimila-tion than we have" and that whites "don't see us as Americans." In response, Nevius assures the audience that he uses McWhorter only "to emphasize the American process.... I want to clarify not mini-mize ethnicity in this country." As he nervously strives to distance himself from McWhorter, I reflect that this exchange offers a good example of the way in which outliers in these identity-oriented, orthodoxy-fixated disciplines are gently but firmly nudged back into the herd. Nevius does stand firm on one point: "If students don't understand what it means to be American, they can't under-stand themselves and be successful as Americans." He also says that he leaves it to other colleagues to emphasize the African stuff; his job, as he sees it, is to emphasize "understanding the American process." Still, he feels a need to point out that while his students respond enthusiastically to Lerone Bennett's *The Shaping of Black America*, "they didn't like [McWhorter's] book at all." The audi-ence member who challenged him about McWhorter shouts back angrily: "Nor should they have!"

Though intersectionality, as I've noted, is a significant pres-ence throughout identity studies, it plays a less pronounced role in Black Studies than in any of the others. There's an element of feminism in Black Studies, but it generally takes the form of "womanism," a term coined (as noted) by the black novelist Alice

Walker. Womanism refuses to make an enemy of black men, whom it views, rather, as allies in the struggle against white racism and oppression; it also tends to contain a theological element. Large swaths of Black Studies, moreover, have resisted infiltration by "Queer Theory"; indeed, Black Studies tends to go out of its way to ignore or soft-pedal the gay identity of important black Americans such as poet Langston Hughes, author Countee Cullen, and civil rights leader Bayard Rustin. For all its revolutionary pretensions, one gathers that Black Studies, to a considerable extent, shares the black community's traditional discomfort with the subject of homosexuality.

To be sure, some Black Studies practitioners have challenged the discipline's resistance to intersectionality, to "theory" (queer and otherwise), and to the soup-to-nuts thematic preoccupations of Cultural Studies. These challengers' cause goes by the name of Critical Black Studies. At the 2010 annual conference of the Cultural Studies Association, I attend a session titled "New Conceptions of Racism" (which takes place, appropriately enough, at the Martin Luther King Student Center) and hear Jared Sexton, a light-skinned young African American from the University of California, Irvine, who seems smart and exudes energy, give a paper in which he talks at length about "higher levels of theoretical development" and the "analysis of power structures," praises Du Bois's extremely didactic-sounding 1928 novel *Dark Princess* for its "prophetic messianism," and tells us that American society is now divided not into whites and everyone else but into blacks and everyone else.

Sexton is followed by Maisha Wester, a black woman from Bowling Green State University whose paper is titled "Forgetting to Remember: 'Post-racial' Amnesia and Racial History." Wester sneers at the idea, which has gained currency since the election of Barack Obama, that "race matters less than it used to," pointing out that there were "racial incidents" immediately after Obama's inauguration in 2009. "I don't buy into the notion of 'post-racialism,'" she says flatly, explaining that she has come here to "interrogat[e] the idea of the 'post-racial.'" One damning aspect of "post-racialism," as she sees it, is the unnuanced representation of American history (from Colonial Williamsburg to accounts of the U.S. military's role in bringing down Nazism) as "heroic." Wester somehow appears not to have noticed that thanks to the efforts of Howard Zinn and company, American history courses, from primary school onward, now pay ample attention to U.S. atrocities and hardly ever dare portray Americans as heroes.

When the time comes for Q&A, a woman in the audience pours out a pure stream of jargon that I can't write fast enough to take down. Another woman observes that "[i]t seems as if the black body is the necessary host for the parasitic product of progressive discourse." The word *power* keeps cropping up: Jared condemns the "paranoid modality" of white Democrats who view the "struggle against power" by black civil rights activists as an "accumulation of power." And he accuses unspecified "elements of the left" of being "very resonant with far-right discourse." Labeling himself "polemical," Jared describes "settler colonialism" as a "genocidal project," tells us he's "intervening in a particular context," and assures us that he hates the "politics of inclusion." And he tells Wester that what he's offered in his paper is "a space-clearing gesture for the kind of discourse you're talking about." Wester, for her part, keeps quoting Toni Morrison, and says that she looks forward to a "pluralist" but not to a "universal" or "post-racial" culture. After listening to fifteen or twenty minutes of this material, I find myself thinking that all this rhetoric isn't about people and their lives; it's just about words: interrogating is good, pluralism is good, multiracialism is good—but post-racialism, color blindness, and a host of other things are just plain bad.

At one point Wester catches herself in the act of using the word *colorblind* in a positive way, and she laughs—and everyone seems to share her mirth. For an instant, the masks drop; it's as if everyone has shared a friendly wink, acknowledging that they're all just spouting jargon that has no real connection to their own lives and convictions (if any).

Acknowledging, that is, that it's all a game and that they're all playing it together—all hustling away.

CHAPTER 4
Visit to a Queer Planet:
Queer Studies

I'm at a Queer Studies conference at Humboldt University in Berlin, listening to a talk by Susan Stryker, a middle-aged American woman with a strapping male body and a deep male voice. After telling us she is here to offer some "provisional thoughts on a new line in my work," Stryker warns that her "argument is not entirely worked out even to my own satisfaction." She proceeds to serve up what seems like a grab bag of observations, from a brief history of the post-World War II American economy to reflections on the 1970s advent of punk rock as a form of "resistance to market-driven culture."

Eventually something resembling an argument comes into focus: now, as in the 1970s, an economic crisis is spawning a musical reaction. Back then it was punk; now, according to Stryker, it's "alternative country." She brings in the Tea Party movement, which she regards as a fascist, racist "upsurge of right-wing populism among non-elite white residents of the United States." Yet she's so hostile to the "neo-liberal" U.S. establishment that she sees the Tea Party as a promising development. She asks: Why do members of "the leftist intelligentsia" (of which she counts herself a member) who oppose the U.S. government respond with such reflexive negativity when right-wing nonacademics say *they* oppose it, too? The Tea Party movement, she insists, makes it clear that both the intellectual left and the populist right share a hostility to the "neoliberal middle," and raises hopes for an anticapitalist coalition between the two.

Listening to Stryker savage democratic capitalism (she takes it for granted, of course, that everyone in attendance shares her contempt for it) and talk blithely about forming an alliance with people she considers to be fascists, I look out the high windows at Unter den Linden. Here we are in what was once East Berlin, only a few minutes' walk from where the Berlin Wall once stood. This place was tyrannized by two succeeding sets of rebels against liberal democratic capitalism. There is a point crying out to be made, and it is made, if delicately, by Adrian de Silva, a graduate student at Humboldt, who has been appointed to provide a "commentary" on Stryker's paper. Though he praises parts of her presentation, he notes that "as a German" he is made uncomfortable by her sympathy for "right-wing populist racism." Her tone-deaf reply: she is desperate for "a politics of resistance" against capitalism, and she sees promise in the current success of the "right-wing fascism" of the anti-estab-lishment Tea Party. In short, this woman who has done so hand-somely under the American system (she commutes weekly between San Francisco and Indiana University, and freely pursues a way of life that would have landed her in a prison cell or gas chamber in the Third Reich or East Germany) has no clue how utterly out of touch she is with the solemn reality of this place—a place where fascism and communism are not abstract theoretical notions but have, in living memory, been brutal realities, and where the advent of demo-cratic capitalism was a blessed deliverance.

Next up is Roderick Ferguson, a young black man who teaches race and critical theory and chairs the Department of American Studies at the University of Minnesota, Twin Cities. Much like Stryker, Ferguson (who describes himself as a Marxist "who is trying to get Foucault and Marx to talk to one another") goes on at length about the 1960s and '70s without it even occurring to him to think about what it was like here—in what was then East Berlin—during those decades. Ferguson sneers at the separation of discourse about homosexuality from "critiques of race, imperialism, and patriarchy," about the fact that "queerness" has become "a subject of rights," and about committed gay relationships and their acceptance by establishment institutions—all of which defy the imperatives of "queer." An audience member gives Ferguson's paper a thumbs-up, arguing that "we have to see the richness of not belonging again."

At such moments, one's mirth at the inanity of Queer Studies gives way to distress and, yes, anger at its moral irresponsibility—its fashionable pretense that having equal rights and being treated with respect and dignity are somehow a matter of being "co-opted" by the establishment, of embracing the evils of "normativity," of sacrificing one's magnificent otherness. For these professors, who know that when their workday is over they will be able to walk the streets and go shopping at various stores and make their way home with a high degree of certainty that they will not be targeted for violence for their differentness, all of this rhetoric about "otherness" is nothing but a dishonest pose, which cruelly ignores the fact that for many gay people around the world today, the "normativity" these professors actually enjoy—even as they mock it—is something gay people in other societies can only dream of.

What is especially ironic about these professors' rhetoric of "otherness" and "queerness" is that they are, in fact, by any real-world measure, extremely conservative, lockstep, institutional, careerist creatures. Their sense of identification with their universities, their departments, and their fields of "study," not to mention the obvious way they size one another up by their titles, academic affiliations, and publications, is stifling. So are their endless pious references to Marx, Foucault, and Derrida, which bring to mind the obligatory nods to the Great Leader at some Communist Party congress.

Then there's their curious inarticulateness. One speaker after another, reading his or her own prose aloud, gets tangled up in its mottled, murky thickets. Indeed, some of them, despite their impressive résumés, seem borderline illiterate. José Esteban Muñoz, author of *Disidentifications: Queers of Color and the Performance of Politics*, is a leading figure in Queer Studies, got his Ph.D. at Duke, and is a professor at New York University, but he is one of the worst public speakers I have ever heard, taking excruciatingly long pauses, stumbling repeatedly over his text, concluding one sentence after another by asking "Right?" and mispronouncing simple words: he turns *library* into "liberry," says "denouncement" instead of "denunciation," stresses the third syllable of *nonsynchronous*, puts the stress in the adjective *adept* on the first syllable, and stresses the syllable "late" in *inarticulateness*, pronouncing it like the word *late*.

As the conference drags on, the endless rhetoric about "patriarchy" and the "intersection" of sexuality "with other formations such as race and gender" sounds more and more like Muzak. This academically approved rhetoric pretends to be unorthodox, deviant, threatening, and antinormative—but is, in point of fact, mind-numbingly conformist. There's plenty of talk about colonialism, most of it by American scholars whose domination of this English-language conference in a German-speaking country could itself well be viewed as a colonial enterprise. At one point between sessions, it occurs to me that here are all these gay men and women talking about matters supposedly touching on sex, and there's nothing remotely sexy about any of it—it's dry, boring, without a hint of a whiff of a *frisson*. How can anybody with the slightest libido say the words "sexuality as an artifact of institutionality" with a straight face?

As it happens, the setting of this conference is historically fitting—though I wonder how many of the participants realize it. For if Americans invented Queer Studies, it was Germans who invented its estimable predecessor, Gay Studies, of which Queer Studies—as we shall see—is an unfortunate betrayal.

Indeed, any proper account of the serious scholarly attempt to reckon with the reality of sexual orientation begins with the life stories of Germans like Karl-Heinrich Ulrichs, who, after losing his position as a government lawyer in 1857 when his homosexuality became known, went on to perform extensive research into human sexuality, to write several books (which were banned and burned across Germany), and to use his findings to argue for the decriminalization of homosexuality. To be sure, Ulrichs did not call himself a homosexual (a word that was not coined until 1869, by the Hungarian writer and human rights activist Karl-Maria Kertbeny), but an "Urning"—a word that Ulrichs adapted from Plato's

Symposium, and that many of his gay British contemporaries took up, translating it as "Uranian." Though many readers found the focus of his work scandalous, he was respected enough in certain academic circles to earn an honorary degree from the University of Naples. Perhaps the first gay person in history to "come out" publicly, Ulrichs died in exile in Italy in 1895.

His work strongly influenced Magnus Hirschfeld, a physician who two years after Ulrichs's death cofounded the Scientific Humanitarian Committee, which engaged in sexual research and continued Ulrichs's campaign for the abolition of the German law against homosexuality (an effort that won the open support of Einstein, Rilke, Thomas Mann, Hermann Hesse, and other luminaries). Hirschfeld also established the Institut für Sexualwissenschaft (Institute for Sexual Research) in Berlin, which in addition to studying human sexuality offered sex and marriage counseling, housed a sizable library, and promoted contraception, sex education, and the equal rights of women, gays, and transsexuals (a term that Hirschfeld coined). Hirschfeld was also the founder of the World League for Sexual Reform, which held conferences in several European capitals in the 1920s and early 1930s.

Though Hirschfeld's effort to liberalize public attitudes about human sexuality gained ground under the Weimar Republic, it ended abruptly when Hitler came to power. The Nazis closed the institute, seized its property, threw its director into a concentration camp (Hirschfeld was on a U.S. lecture tour at the time), and burned almost the entire contents of its library and archives. (It is believed that the Nazis saved the institute's mailing lists and later made use of them to round up gays.) Hirschfeld spent the rest of his life in self-exile in France, dying there in 1935; after the war West German courts upheld the Nazis' actions against the institute.

The research performed by Ulrichs and Hirschfeld was serious, scholarly, and responsible: they were traditional-minded, even conservative men of science who believed in objective research methods. They weren't propagandists but seekers of truth who felt that the truth would set them—and other gay men and women—free. Although both had theories that would later be discredited (Hirschfeld, for example, saw gay men as naturally effeminate), their work came to be recognized by serious scholars of sexuality as groundbreaking. Among those scholars is Wayne R. Dynes, a long-time professor of art history at Hunter College and a founder of Gay Studies in America, who points out that much of the work of his prewar German predecessors "was conditioned by evidence from ancient Greece and Rome, as one might expect from scholars with a thorough gymnasium training."

Gay Studies in America started out as a serious academic discipline in the tradition of Ulrichs and Hirschfeld. Its genesis is part of the early history of the American gay rights movement, which began in the 1950s with orderly, low-profile picket lines protesting antigay laws and policies (Frank Kameny, one of the movement's founders, was a World War II veteran who had been fired from his position as a U.S. Army astronomer for being gay) and entered a more aggressive and visible phase with the June 1969 Stonewall riots in New York, which are generally seen as inaugurating the "modern" gay rights movement. Dynes told me in July 2010 that it was in 1971 or thereabouts that his then best friend, a librarian named Jack Stafford, persuaded him to join a group of gay librarians working under the American Library Association's auspices, whereupon the two men "undertook, rather naively as it turned out, to produce a bibliography of gay and lesbian topics that would eschew, by and large, the old negative psychiatric junk." (At the time, it will be recalled, homosexuality was still officially considered a mental disorder.)

Some time later, Dynes "learned that a much bigger project... was under way at ONE, Inc. in Los Angeles." (ONE, Inc., had published *One*, America's first gay magazine, from 1953 to 1967.) "Its deficiencies soon became apparent, and I set out to work with W. Dorr Legg, head of ONE, to produce something better." In the end Dynes produced *Homosexuality: A Research Guide*, which remains the most substantial bibliography of information on the subject. "My mentor in these studies was the late polymath Warren Johansson, who impressed on me the need to read and ponder the enormous contribution of gay scholarship produced in Germany prior to 1933." In the fall of 1973, Dynes helped organize the first annual conference of the now-defunct Gay Academic Union (GAU) at John Jay College in Manhattan. "The quality of the presentations varied, with some scholarly, others just pep talks. But in talking to some of the better people I could see a convergence towards the idea of Gay Studies. We saw, of course, that there would be problems getting the proposals through the appropriate college committees. But we were on our way—or so we thought." So began "Gay Studies as an academic discipline" in America.

"In order to avoid reinventing the wheel," Dynes recalls, "Warren and I thought that one should begin the new chapter of gay studies...on the foundations of the German one"—which, he notes with admiration, had been "guided by the motto *Per scientiam adjustitiam* [Through science to justice]. That is to say, cumulatively the assemblage of objective knowledge would persuade society to eliminate laws and discriminatory policies regarding homosexuality. This was a continuation of the Enlightenment project of *Sapere aude* [an expression, meaning 'dare to know' or 'dare to discern,' that stems from Horace and that Immanuel Kant selected as the motto for the Enlightenment]. Warren and I resigned ourselves to the fact that most people were going to ignore the German contribution, but we drew heavily upon it in our own work. We assembled a small group of ten or so people meeting at regular intervals in my Morningside Drive apartment. Out of this collaboration came the *Encyclopedia of Homosexuality*"—a comprehensive and extremely well-received volume that included informative entries on everything and everyone from Alcibiades, Suetonius, and Theocritus to Jean Cocteau, Yukio Mishima, and Noel Coward. Dynes emphasizes that he and his colleagues weren't out to create an "epistemic rupture"—that is, they had no intention of overturning prevailing Enlightenment notions about reason, evidence, logic, and the nature of knowledge. "We thought that Gay Studies would become a department in most universities, not unlike the departments of, say, Spanish and chemistry." Alas, other gay academics, who were more politically oriented and aligned with the New Left, didn't share what they saw as the "assimilationist" views of Dynes and his colleagues, and, in Dynes's words, "sought to break with the existing edifice of knowledge." "Some of these dissidents," Dynes says, "left academia, while others stayed behind to snipe from within." And snipe they did. There were other problems, too: "During the seventies there was a great hullaballoo about the need to give full representation to lesbians and lesbianism. In vain we pointed out that historically there was much less data about gay women than gay men. We were tarred with the label of misogynist. In 1981 AIDS was first detected, and many diverted their research to that subject, perhaps understandably."

Then, in the late 1980s, Lesbian and Gay Studies began to be transformed by a "social-constructionist" view of sexual orientation—a transformation that Dynes describes as nothing less than a "tsunami" and that was furthered by three books published in 1990: John J. Winkler's *The Constraints of Desire: The Anthropology of Sex and Gender in Ancient Greece*; *Before Sexuality: The Construction of Erotic Experience in the Ancient Greek World,* edited by David Halperin, John Winkler, and Froma Zeitlin; and—most influential of all—Halperin's *One Hundred Years of Homosexuality: And Other Essays on Greek Love*. Social-constructionist positions on sexuality vary in their purity: some social constructionists simply argue that the nature and expression of human sexuality are highly dependent on social and cultural factors; others go so far as to insist that sexual orientation does not exist as such, and that what an individual perceives as his immutable sexual identity is in fact entirely the product of his society and culture.

This new way of thinking about sexual orientation derived strongly from the work of the French philosopher Michel Foucault (1926–84), who wrote in *The History of Sexuality*: "We have had sexuality since the eighteenth century, and sex since the nineteenth. What we had before that was no doubt flesh." In the same intellectual spirit, the fact that the word *homosexuality* was not coined until 1869 has led many social constructionists to claim that homosexuals as such didn't even *exist* before 1869. (This view explains, for example, the otherwise ridiculous-sounding subtitle of Jonathan Ned Katz's 2003 book, *Love Stories: Sex Between Men before Homosexuality*.) As Dynes notes, social constructionism has generally limited its adherents' field of study to "Western Europe and North America in the last 150 years or so." Typical of social-constructionist views are the assertions made in "Capitalism and Gay Identity," John D'Emilio's essay in *The Lesbian and Gay Studies Reader*, that "gay men and lesbians have *not* always existed" and that "[t]*here are more of us* than one hundred years ago" (his emphasis) because "ideological conditions" have made it "easier for people to make [the] choice" to be gay. In his insistence on the concept of "choice" and his acknowledgment that his claim "confirms the worst fears and most rabid rhetoric of our political opponents," D'Emilio contradicts the felt experience of the overwhelming majority of gay men.

The social constructionists invented a term to describe those who did not share their views: they were *essentialists* and were typically described as denying that people in different cultures and eras have had different understandings of the nature of sexual identity. But no one denies that understandings of sexual identity have changed over time; a fairer description of the "essentialist" view is that sexual orientation is a fact of nature and that homosexually oriented individuals have existed in roughly equal proportions in all societies across the generations—even though those individuals' way of thinking about their sexuality has surely varied in accordance with social and cultural factors. In the foreword to *Lesbian and Gay Studies: An Introductory, Interdisciplinary Approach* (2000), Mary McIntosh echoes the prevailing attitude of many social constructionists toward "essentialists" when she writes that "we in lesbian and gay studies are remote from the ordinary gay world and from the gay movement because we are aware of the lesbian and gay identities as the product of a particular period or culture, whereas the average lesbian or gay has a folk-essentialist view and, indeed, likes to think that 'we' have always been there, throughout historical and cultural oppression." Note how the social-constructionist view is here simply taken for granted as the truth—a truth recognized as such by the properly educated members of the gay academic left—while the essentialist view is dismissed with imperial condescension as the product of sheer ignorance.

Social constructionism took over Lesbian and Gay Studies so quickly that by 1992 the philosopher Richard D. Mohr, who writes about homosexuality from a traditional academic perspective, was bemoaning the fact that "the social construction of homosexuality... has achieved hagiographical status within lesbian and gay studies" and lamenting Gay Studies scholars' "generic worship of Saint Foucault." Mohr's lack of reverence for Foucault so outraged Halperin that he wrote a book, *Saint Foucault* (2004), in which he accused Mohr of seeking to tame him. But Halperin wasn't about to be tamed:

> Far from being intimidated into towing [sic] a more normative line by the prospect or threat of getting herded together with Foucault into the stigmatized company of "militant," "radical," or "extreme" gay male intellectuals and activists, I have been driven by an instinct of survival to want to expose the political operations that have brought about such a phobic construction of Foucault in the first place. [Note: Mohr, whose criticism of Foucault Halperin is apparently characterizing here as homophobic, is openly gay.] And in the course of pursuing that project, my admiration for Foucault and my identification with his discursive and political positioning have increased exponentially.
>
> So let me make it official. I may not have worshiped Foucault at the time I wrote *One Hundred Years of Homosexuality*, but I do worship him now. As far as I'm concerned, the guy was a fucking saint.

Halperin goes on to praise the Frenchman for having "grasped his total political situation as a gay intellectual and scholar better than anyone else has ever done.... *Michel Foucault, c'est moi*," he says, explaining that he shares with Foucault "the problem of how, as a gay man, an academic, and a public intellectual, I can acquire and maintain the authority to speak, to be heard, and to be taken seriously *without* denying or bracketing my gayness." Halperin engages in this kind of self-dramatization throughout *Saint Foucault*, depicting himself as a victim or potential victim of "silencing," when in fact he has never been silenced, and has, on the contrary, been abundantly celebrated and rewarded (for example, with a 2008—2009 Guggenheim fellowship). He depicts himself as a beleaguered truth-teller—"What Foucault and I have in common...is our vexed and inescapable relation to the sexual politics of truth"—when in fact he is a voice of Lesbian and Gay Studies orthodoxy and an enforcer thereof. He has actually written books called *How to Do the History of Homosexuality* and *How to Be Gay*—titles that make it clear that in Halperin's eyes there are most assuredly right and wrong ways to do the former and be the latter.

Halperin endorses what he calls Foucault's "dark vision of modernity, of the liberal state, and of progressive, Enlightenment-era values (such as freedom, truth, and rationality)." Deep down it's all about power, which according to Foucault is "everywhere." Halperin explains:

> When he says that "power is everywhere," Foucault is not talking about power in the sense of coercive and irresistible force (which in his lexicon goes by the name not of "power" but of "determination"); rather, he is referring to what might be called *liberal power*—that is, to the kind of power typically at work in the modern liberal state, which takes as its objects "free subjects" and defines itself wholly in relation to them and to their freedom.... The kind of power Foucault is interested in, ...far from enslaving its objects, constructs them as subjective agents and preserves them in their autonomy, so as to invest them all the more completely. Liberal power does not simply prohibit; it does not directly terrorize. It normalizes, "responsibilizes," and disciplines. The state no longer needs to frighten or coerce its subjects into proper behavior: it can safely leave them to make their own choices... because...they *freely and spontaneously* police both their own conduct and the conduct of others....

In other words, the most formidable and disturbing kind of power at work in the world today is not the brutal totalitarianism of a country like North Korea, but the kind of power wielded by the government of a country like the United States—because in the latter, people think that they are free, even though they behave according to rules and norms that they have unconsciously internalized. Because the "modes of domination" in the modern liberal state do not present themselves as such, they are, as Halperin puts it, "all the more difficult to challenge or oppose"; freedom in the West, then, is nothing but a lie because its exercise is "conditional upon personal submission to new and insidious forms of authority, to ever more deeply internalized mechanisms of constraint"—otherwise known (as we have seen) as *hegemony*. It should come as no surprise to anyone familiar with Foucault's Orwellian philosophy—in which freedom is totalitarianism and totalitarianism is freedom—that he was a Communist Party member in the 1950s and a Maoist in the 1960s and '70s. His "dark vision" of the free world enables Halperin—who is, of course, fortunate to be living in a time and place in which gay people enjoy more rights and respect than ever in history—to depict himself as a heroic victim of well-nigh unparalleled subjugation. He speaks of what "gay men in the United States…are up against in our struggles to survive this genocidal era"—an era marked not, to be sure, by "explicit oppression" but rather by "pervasive and multiform strategies of homophobia that shape public and private discourses." Lesbians and gay men, says Halperin, need not "bewail the passing of…liberal, humanist notions, [or] be threatened by their demolition" because gays have been the targets of "a new kind of terror" carried out in the name of liberalism, humanism, and individual identity, "a terror all the more terrible in that its nature *as* terror is effectively concealed beneath the disguise of the supposedly nonarbitrary authority of freedom, truth, and rationality." Describing Foucault's objective as being "not *liberation* but *resistance*," Halperin makes it clear that he shares this aim, insisting that "[t]he most radical reversal of homophobic discourses consists not in asserting…that 'gay is good' [a slogan coined by Franklin Kameny] but in assuming and empowering a marginal positionality."

To this end, Halperin prefers the term *queer* to *gay* because while "gay identity…is…rooted in the positive fact of homosexual object-choice, queer identity need not be grounded in any positive truth or in any stable reality" but rather—and here Halperin is articulating an orthodoxy that we will explore more fully in the succeeding pages—"acquires its meaning from its oppositional relation to the norm. Queer is by definition *whatever* is at odds with the normal, the legitimate, the dominant. *There is nothing in particular to which it necessarily refers.* It is an identity without an essence," and is therefore "available to anyone who is or feels marginalized because of his or her sexual practices." Halperin makes it clear that this includes child molesters. "[O]ne can't *become* homosexual, strictly speaking: either one is or one isn't. But one can marginalize oneself; one can transform oneself; one can become queer." And for Halperin, queerness is the goal: "Foucault insisted that homosexuality did not name an already existing form of desire but was rather '*something to be desired.*' Our task is therefore 'to *become* homosexual, not to persist in acknowledging that we *are.*' Or, to put it more precisely, what Foucault meant is that our task is to become queer.... Self-invention is not a luxury or a pastime for lesbians and gay men: it is a necessity." Apparently, lesbians and gay men who have no desire "to become queer" have failed at a task that is obligatory for them, whether or not they are aware of it. Halperin, like Foucault, in short, is yet another busybody who has an agenda for other people's lives.

As it happens, the facts of Foucault's own personal life have a direct relevance to his philosophy. Foucault called for "the intense pleasures procured by means of drugs, sadomasochistic eroticism, and anonymous sex"—and he practiced what he preached, which helps explain why he ended up dying of AIDS at age fifty-seven. Some of his disciples find the more excessive aspects of Foucault's private life a source of embarrassment; but not Halperin, who considers Foucault's private life to be triumphantly consistent with his philosophy. For in Foucault's view, sex was not just sex: it was a political act, and gay bathhouses were sites of "resistance." Forget the fact that gays who frequent bathhouses in, say, Amsterdam or Berlin aren't "resisting" anything; they're just having fun, and nobody tries to stop them. (Foucault the Maoist, by the way, was apparently unbothered by the fact that under Chairman Mao such places would have been destroyed and their patrons exterminated.)

Now, Foucault's fetishes were certainly his own business, but he plainly meant to suggest that they made him more *correctly* queer, gay, transgressive, and oppositional than others. We are expected to understand, then, that what may seem like self-indulgence on his part was, in fact, heroism. For Foucault, it was not sufficient to do what he enjoyed doing and leave it at that; no, he needed (for whatever psychological reason) to represent it as a philosophical and moral response to institutional power. Halperin describes Foucault as gaining "insights into the transformative potential of sex…from his experiences in the bathhouses and S/M clubs of New York and San Francisco…." Insights! Some might find it odd for a man so preoccupied with and unsympathetic to the exercise of power to be as powerfully drawn as Foucault was to violent acts of sadomasochism. But Foucault had an answer to this: the search for "new" sexual pleasure in a world in which power is all leads naturally to the power-obsessed phenomenon of sadomasochism. However much it may seem otherwise, "'domination' in S/M," writes Halperin, is for Foucault "not a form of a personal or political subjugation." To sum up, then, the sexual domination in S&M is *not* domination, while what seems to be the nondomination that characterizes free societies *is* domination.

As Halperin puts it, S&M involves "the strategic use of power differentials to produce effects of pleasure instead of effects of domination," and thus "some of Foucault s clearest indications of what might count as *queer praxis* occur in the context of his discussions of S/M." Indeed, the more you look at it, the more Foucault's entire philosophical project looks like a road map to S&M—a justification for Foucault's own sexual practices, and more than that: an implicit argument that his own sexual practices are the *proper* sexual practices for homosexuals. "More powerfully than any other thinker I know," writes Halperin, "Foucault *politicizes* both truth and the body" because he "reconceptualize[s] sexuality as a strategic device" and "thereby converts sex into the basis for a radical critique of, and political struggle against, innumerable aspects of modern disciplinary culture." In short, Foucault was—and Halperin is—out to sign up recruits for a revolution against human freedom, individual identity, Cartesian reason, and Enlightenment values.

Imagine believing that it's your obligation as a "queer" to view your every sexual encounter as an act of political resistance! Foucault goes on endlessly about oppression, but he doesn't come off as someone who has been oppressed (nor does Halperin)—he comes off as an overgrown brat who wants to have his cake and eat it, too, and who has worked up elaborate, sophisticated-sounding reasons for why he should not only be allowed to do anything he feels like but be idolized for it. Even as he celebrated himself for his exploits, he flatly refused to acknowledge the damage these activities can, and did, cause both medically and psychologically. Social constructionism, after all, became a force in Lesbian and Gay Studies at a time when some gays in certain cities were forming what Halperin describes as "a subculture that...has been pioneering new forms of life." To refuse, as Halperin does, to draw any conclusions about Foucault's philosophy from the consequences of the "new forms of life" that he advocated is, by any objective standard, morally irresponsible. (Then again, to a pure social constructionist even the AIDS that killed Foucault was nothing but a social construct.)

Yet in Halperin's view, any criticism of Foucault's totalitarianism is beyond the pale. More than once, Halperin refers to Foucault's critics as "gay-baiting detractors." How dare anyone not worship at Foucault's altar? Halperin devotes a good deal of *Saint Foucault* to a savaging of James Miller's book *The Passion of Michel Foucault*—which, although it is in fact a hagiography, is nonetheless insufficiently worshipful for Halperin, who complains that Miller "reverses [Foucault's] entire political program." Yes, he does—by uncovering the ugly personal impulses that informed Foucault's philosophy. Similarly, Halperin accuses "Foucault's gay detractors" of being "just as crude as any professional, right-wing homophobe: Bruce Bawer, for example, is not ashamed to write, 'The greatest single influence on Gay Studies today is the late French theorist Michel Foucault, an enthusiast of sadomasochism who analyzed sexual relations almost entirely in terms of power' (not a bad place to begin such an analysis, now that you mention it!)." In other words, I was entirely correct to describe Foucault in this way—my offense was not in misrepresenting him but in disagreeing with him. By the end of *Saint Foucault*, it is clear that Halperin shares Foucault's brutal preoccupation with power: Foucault saw himself as being at war with tyrants and terrorists, and felt justified in being as brutal as he thought they were; and the same is true of Halperin.

"[W]henever those of us who feel ourselves to be in Foucault's embattled position, or who share his political vision, hear those who aren't, or who don't, invoke the notion of 'truth,'" writes Halperin in the last sentence of his book, "we reach for our revolvers." This is, of course, a line from Goering.

For a representative picture of Gay Studies under social constructionism, we can turn to *The Lesbian and Gay Studies Reader* (1993). Edited by Henry Abelove, Michèle Aina Barale, and Halperin, it contains forty-two articles, two-thirds of which are by women (even though the actual proportion of gay men to lesbians in the general population is approximately the other way around). The editors describe their discipline as follows: "Lesbian/gay studies is not limited to the study of lesbians, bisexuals, and gay men. Nor does it refer simply to studies undertaken by, or in the name of, lesbians, bisexuals, and gay men. Not all research into the lives of lesbians, bisexuals, and gay men necessarily qualifies as lesbian/gay studies." To "help to clarify this point," the editors introduce an "analogy with women's studies":

> [W]omen's history seeks to establish the centrality of *gender* as a fundamental category of historical analysis and understanding.... Thus, women's studies is not limited to the study of women's life and contributions: it includes any research that treats gender (whether female or male) as a central category of analysis and that operates within the broad horizons of that diverse political and intellectual movement known as feminism.
>
> Lesbian/gay studies does for *sex* and *sexuality* approximately what women's studies does for gender.

In other words, just as Women's Studies is not about women but about gender (which explains why many Women's Studies departments or programs have added words like "Gender" and "Sexuality" to their names), Lesbian and Gay Studies is not about lesbians and gays but about sex. The editors note that there is a "degree of overlap" between the two fields. They also point out that like Women's Studies, Lesbian and Gay Studies has "an oppositional design" and "straddles scholarship and politics." At many institutions, in fact, Gay Studies is treated, in some way or another, as a subdivision of Women's Studies. Stanford's Feminist Studies Department, for example, offers an undergraduate minor in Lesbian, Gay, and Bisexual Studies. At many universities, such as the University of Illinois at Champaign-Urbana, departments of, or programs in, Gender and Women's Studies offer courses or minors in Queer or Lesbian, Gay, Bisexual, and Transgender Studies. Some institutions offer Lesbian Studies under the aegis of Women's Studies (at South Puget Sound Community College, for example, you can earn a graduate certificate in Lesbian Studies from the Women's Studies Program). But none of these departments or programs offers degrees in Gay Male Studies. (Barry D. Adam, after examining a representative sampling of books in the field, notes that while half of them "address lesbian studies, and half gay and lesbian or queer studies...none offers an exclusively gay male focus.")

Indeed, *The Lesbian and Gay Studies Reader* reads in large part like a Women's Studies primer. For example, the contribution by Marilyn Frye, then a professor at Michigan State, addresses such subjects as the "parasitism of males on females" and the supposed preoccupation of many literary works by men with "the theme of men getting high off beating, raping, or killing women." Among Frye's assertions are that "[m]any awakening women [that is, women whose consciousness has been raised by people like Frye] become celibate or lesbian," that "[m]ale parasitism means that males *must have access* to women; it is the Patriarchal Imperative," and that "[t]he woman-only meeting is a fundamental challenge to the structure of power," for "[t]he slave who decides to exclude the master from her hut is declaring herself not a slave." Rather than seek to understand sexual categories, the late University of Arizona professor Monique Wittig declares in her essay, "One Is Not Born a Woman," the need to "destroy...the categories of sex" and maintains that a woman can escape servitude only "by refusing to become or to stay heterosexual. We are escapees from our class in the same way as the American runaway slaves were when escaping slavery and becoming free."

A gay man reading *The Lesbian and Gay Studies Reader* discovers soon enough that he is expected to acknowledge (and admit his complicity in) the oppression of women by men through the centuries; to recognize that women's revolution against patriarchal domination is central to the contemporary study of sexuality and sexual orientation; and to accept the appropriateness of discussing *all* sexuality, including his own, within a radical feminist framework. He is expected, in short, to embrace the view that gay male sexuality can be properly studied only in light of the alleged plight of women, and to understand, therefore, why Gay Studies is often a subsidiary of Women's Studies. Even to suggest that it might be worthwhile to examine gay male identity, history, and experience as a topic unto itself, without constant reference to the alleged evils of patriarchy and the oppression of women, is to identify oneself as sexist.

Indeed, *The Lesbian and Gay Studies Reader* is testimony to the fact that the gay male, or at least the gay white male, is welcomed into the precincts of Lesbian and Gay Studies only, as it were, on a tentative, probational basis—for as a white man he is by nature simply too implicated in the patriarchy for the comfort of his more multiply-oppressed fellow homosexuals. A lesbian, after all, cannot disguise her gender, and a black man cannot hide his color, but a gay white man can keep his sexual orientation a secret and thereby function smoothly as a member of the oppressor class. In *The Lesbian and Gay Studies Reader*, the essays that do deal with gay men are disproportionately concerned with such subgroups as gay *African* males, gay *African American* males, gay *Mexican* males, and gay *Indian* males (not to mention pre-Columbian Native American *berdaches* and medieval Chinese transsexuals), suggesting that it's far more legitimate in the eyes of Lesbian and Gay Studies professionals to belong to any one of these categories than to be a gay white male. The anthology, to be sure, includes several essays on AIDS, which suggest that gay white men who are visibly infected with HIV are at least *somewhat* redeemed in the eyes of the Lesbian and Gay Studies community, plus not one but two articles about photographer Robert Mapplethorpe, the criticism of whose often quasi-pornographic work by conservatives made him a left-wing hero and thus, for the gatekeepers of Lesbian and Gay Studies, that rare thing—a gay white male worthy of admiration.

Indeed, the hostility that rises up from the pages of *The Lesbian and Gay Studies Reader*—and there's quite a lot of it—is directed far less toward heterosexuals than toward men of whatever orientation. Take the book's most famous contributor, the poet Adrienne Rich, who in her essay wonders why gay men and straight women exist, since women should obviously be the primary objects of affection for both men *and* women. Isn't female heterosexuality, she asks, an aberration? Employing a popular radical feminist trope, Rich all but equates heterosexual sex with rape, speaks of the "terrorism of women by men," and approvingly cites a description of "adult male sexual behavior" as "a condition of *arrested sexual development.*" And she insists: "To equate lesbian existence with male homosexuality because each is stigmatized is to erase female reality once again." Women who think they are heterosexual, she writes, are suffering from "false consciousness." She praises as "revolutionary" the "refusal of some women to produce children," hails "[w]oman identification" as "a source of energy" and "a potential springhead of female power, curtailed and contained under the institution of heterosexuality," and acclaims "lesbian experience" as "an electric and empowering charge between women."

This kind of rhetoric was ubiquitous in gay newspapers and magazines in the late 1980s and early 1990s, and I wasn't the only gay man who found such fanatical man-hatred less than congenial. In 1993, the year *The Lesbian and Gay Studies Reader* came out, I published a book, too. In part, it was a response to the disinformation spread by public figures like Pat Buchanan, who in his now-notorious "culture war" speech at the 1992 Republican convention essentially declared war on gay people; in part, it was a reply to the radical nonsense of people like Adrienne Rich and groups like Queer Nation (founded in 1990 and known for the slogan "I hate straights") and the Lesbian Avengers (established in 1992). What was striking was that the two sides presented the world with almost identical views of gay people: we were depicted as philosophically lockstep subversives who despised America, religion, and capitalism; whose lives revolved around sex far more than straight people's did; and whose proper place was not in mainstream society but at its margins. On one issue after another, both camps were in total agreement—for example, both fiercely opposed gay marriage and the right of gays to serve openly in the military. For gay-left activists, marriage and the military, along with corporations and organized religion, were the enemy; a gay person who wanted to have anything to do with any of these things was, in their view, a pathetic creature begging for admission into straight institutions, rather than a soldier in the heroic struggle to establish specifically gay and lesbian institutions. Instead of wishing to be welcomed into mainstream American society, lectured the gay left, gays should be seeking to transform it radically from top to bottom.

A Place at the Table: The Gay Individual in American Society (1993) was my attempt to effect a change. I wanted to illuminate for straight readers a subject that made them uneasy; to persuade gay readers who'd unthinkingly embraced the gay left's narrow line to open their minds; and, especially, to help young gay people to understand that they needn't accept anybody else's prescriptions for their lives. There was no single "right" way to be gay. The public debate about homosexuality had been controlled by people at the ideological poles; I wanted to move the discussion to the center, the mainstream—where most individuals, gay and straight, actually lived.

A Place at the Table was followed, in 1996, by Andrew Sullivan's *Virtually Normal*, which systematically decimated the arguments of both the antigay right and queer left, and by the anthology *Beyond Queer*, in which several writers, most of them gay, took on gay-left orthodoxies. These books were part of a sea change for gay Americans, and the response from ordinary gay readers was enthusiastic. But both the antigay right and the gay left attacked us mercilessly. The former, of course, viewed us as apologists for something they found abominable; the latter saw us as traitors to the Queer Nation. "We don't want a place at the table," lesbian activist Donna Minkowitz railed at me on the *Charlie Rose Show*. "We want to turn the table over!" In a

1994 article, "Who Stole the Gay Movement?," Stephen H. Miller provided a snapshot of that moment in gay history: "The lesbian and gay left," he wrote, "has declared war against the growing numbers of moderates, libertarians, and out-and-proud conservatives (along with other ideological deviants) within the gay movement." What the gay left was actually irked by, suggested Miller, was "the gay community's failure to embrace what [Tony] Kushner and others conceive of as a grand alliance of the radical left." Miller quoted Richard Goldstein of the *Village Voice*, who had complained that "gay conservatives" ignored "the vital bond between queers and feminists," and Urvashi Vaid, former executive director of the National Gay and Lesbian Task Force, who in *Virtual Equality: The Mainstreaming of Gay and Lesbian Liberation* (1995) condemned that "mainstreaming" as the work of "a racist, sexist gay and lesbian Right" and called for "a full-scale frontal assault" on its members. "This," observed Miller quite rightly, "is pure Stalinism—silencing anyone who opposes the hard left's dominance of the gay movement by labeling us racist and sexist."

The "gay conservative" movement made a difference. It helped innumerable gay Americans to realize that they weren't alone—that there were other gays who, like them, didn't identify with the ideas and images promulgated by the gay left. Thanks in part to that movement, millions of gays came out during the 1990s—and the more gays came out, the clearer it became that the "gay conservatives" were right: the great majority of gay people weren't the political extremists or sexual subversives that both the antigay right and gay left said we were; in most ways, we were ordinary people, who could be found not only in Greenwich Village, the Castro, and West Hollywood, but also in Queens, Oakland, and Burbank—not to mention in cities, towns, and rural areas across America. We worked at every imaginable kind of job and ranged across the social, political, and cultural spectrum. In short, aside from our sexual orientation, we were very much like our heterosexual siblings. The rise of the Internet during this period also played an immensely important role: suddenly, young gay people whose counterparts a decade or two earlier had felt utterly isolated could go online and discover kindred spirits.

The result of these changes has been a society that, for gay people, is light-years away from the one in which I wrote *A Place at the Table*. For more and more gay youth today, the closet is a historical curiosity; thanks to the presence in their lives of openly gay adults (and the increasing number of openly gay celebrities and TV characters), they're able to recognize their own homosexuality at amazingly young ages and, rather than being plunged into the intense confusion, anxiety, and sense of isolation that plagued earlier generations of young gay people, can matter-of-factly come out to their families and friends and be met with matter-of-fact acceptance. They don't see themselves as different in any significant way from their straight friends; they don't view themselves as members of a subculture or feel that their homosexuality obliges them to become political radicals or sexual libertines or to live in gay ghettos. To show young gay people today a gay newspaper or magazine from 1990 or earlier is to introduce them to a world that is completely alien to them. The issues over which gays argued back then seem, to them, quaint and baffling; they take for granted that gays should be allowed to marry and serve openly in the armed forces.

In the 1990s, the conflict between us so-called gay conservatives and the gay left was widely framed as a debate between "assimilationists" (I have always preferred "integrationists") and "liberationists." Today it's clear that the "assimilationists" won the battle among ordinary gay Americans. Our arguments, once mocked by the gay left, are now taken for granted as common sense by the overwhelming majority of gay people. Yet you'd never know this if you spent some time in a typical Gay Studies classroom today.

I've outlined the conquest of Lesbian and Gay Studies by social constructionism. But this was only the beginning of the discipline's slide into irresponsibility, irrelevance, and incoherence. It provided the foundation for something even worse—namely, Queer Theory, founded by two women who studied philosophy at Yale at a time when it was the American headquarters of French poststructuralist theory: Eve Kosofsky Sedgwick (1950–2009), who became a professor at Duke and, later, the Graduate Center at the City University of New York; and Judith Butler (born in 1956), who has taught at Johns Hopkins and Berkeley.

The term "Queer Theory" itself was coined in 1990 by Teresa de Lauretis, an Italian-born author of several books on feminist theory and lesbian sexuality, at a conference at the University of California, Santa Cruz, where she still teaches. Indeed, for Queer Theory today, it's almost as if time stopped somewhere around 1990. For as far as most of its proponents are concerned, the arguments presented by Sullivan, me, and others in the 1990s might never have been made; and if they *are* acknowledged, they're treated as wildly reactionary. Similarly, Queer Theory's practitioners recognize the advances made by gays in American society over the last couple of decades—how could they do otherwise?—but the fact that these changes represented a triumph of so-called assimilationist ideas over their own views is dropped down the memory hole.

What is Queer Theory? In *A Genealogy of Queer Theory* (2000), William B. Turner affirms its debt to Foucault as well as to feminism: "the concerns of queer theorists for sexuality, gender, and the relationships between the two, as well as their political and intellectual ramifications, grow distinctly out of feminist political and scholarly activity as much as, if not more than, out of gay political and scholarly activity." If earlier practitioners of Lesbian and Gay Studies had made it clear that their work didn't necessarily have anything to do with homosexuality, and if social constructionists had further weakened this connection, Queer Theory entailed, among other things, an even greater distancing of what had been called Gay Studies from its putative subject. Being "queer," in the eyes of Queer Theory, isn't about sexual orientation at all, really, but about the same kind of marginality, radicalism, and differentness preached by Kushner, Vaid, Queer Nation, and company in the late 1980s and early 1990s. "Could it be that everyone is queer?" asks Turner quite seriously.

"Queerness indicates merely the failure to fit precisely within a category.... Sedgwick has suggested that the only definitive indicator of queerness is the inclination of an individual so to designate her- or himself." In the tradition of Foucault, moreover,

Queer Theory is also about power. Queer theorists reject what they regard as the use of simplistic identity labels (aside from the label *queer*, of course) because such labels result in people having more or less power based on the label that is attached to them, with the power always going to those who are committed to an "unqueer reading of identity."

Indeed, Queer Theory is preoccupied with what its practitioners purport to regard as the endlessly problematic concept of identity and with what Turner calls the "working through of the specifics of variously overlapping, disjunctive, cooperative, clashing identity categories." As a result of this "working through," he says, "[t]he logic of identity looks increasingly peculiar—increasingly queer—under the lens of queer theory." Turner approvingly quotes David Halperin's explanation that "'queer' does not name some natural kind or refer to some determinate object" but rather "acquires its meaning from its oppositional relation to the norm. Queer is by definition *whatever* is at odds with the normal, the legitimate, the dominant." Sedgwick herself was a perfect example of the term's flexibility: although she identified herself as "queer," she was a heterosexual woman who spent forty years in a monogamous marriage to a man. Note, however, that while Turner accepts that a straight woman can legitimately be labeled "queer," he would refuse to use the word to describe, say, a man who is married to a woman but who secretly has sex with men. Nor would he call such as man gay. For in the eyes of Queer Theory, identity—sexual or otherwise—is not about an individual's intrinsic nature (such as a sexual orientation that the individual may act upon or not, may either acknowledge to himself or be in denial about, and may admit to others or dissemble about). No, what matters—*all* that matters—is that the individual in question embrace the label. It's all about the act of declaration, of self-labeling—an action that exists entirely apart from any essential quality, desire, or identity, let alone activity.

Like Halperin, Turner targets Richard D. Mohr, in this case for defending the view that an individual's sexual orientation is what it is, and that whether he owns up to it or not doesn't change the facts. By taking this position, complains Turner, Mohr is missing "the performative aspect of sexual identity." A person's sexual identity, you see, does not exist in and of itself, apart from what that person says about it to other people; you are what you call yourself. You may be a man who has no attraction to other men at all and has never had sexual conduct with another male, but if you choose to call yourself "queer," that's what you are; by the same token, you may be a man who is exclusively attracted to men and has had sex with thousands of them, but if you present yourself to others as heterosexual that's what you are. This emphasis on "performance" derives from Sedgwick, who argues, in Turner's paraphrase, that "[i]n order to prove oneself 'truly' queer, one need only have the impulse so to designate oneself."

For its practitioners, Queer Theory is nothing less than the Grand Unified Theory of human nature, and any other intellectual discipline, any other form of knowledge, is necessarily subordinated to it. Take, for example, Turner's statement that "[a]ttempts to find biological bases for either gender difference or sexual orientation reflect the desire to shift political discussions into the realm of science." In short, never mind sexual orientation; even *gender difference*, in the eyes of Queer Theory, is not properly a biological but a political question upon which it is the prerogative not of biologists but of Queer Theorists to pronounce. For a reader who, like Ulrichs and Hirschfeld, actually cares about the psychological well-being, social acceptance, and legal rights of gay men and women, Queer Theory can feel like a mischievous, exploitative activity—a vacuous, pretentious, and ultimately pointless rhetorical game that detached, self-absorbed academics—some of whom aren't even gay—play on the backs of gay people.

Queer Theory, manifestly, exists in a bizarre academic time-warp. Even as homosexuality has grown increasingly accepted in mainstream America, and as the institutions of the closet and the gay ghetto have steadily evaporated, Queer Theorists continue to cling to the old separatist agenda—continue to try to reinforce the idea that gays are strange, marginal, anti-establishment, contrarian, and rebellious—and continue to try to pretend that when they echo the tired twenty-year-old platitudes of Kushner, Goldstein, and Vaid they are saying something new.

*   *   *

It is one of the curiosities of Queer Studies that the person who is almost universally considered its founding mother made a point of the ordinariness of her private life. In her 1999 book. *A Dialogue on Love* the stout, grandmotherly Sedgwick described herself as engaging in "vanilla sex, on a weekly basis, in the missionary position, in daylight, immediately after a shower, with one person of the so-called opposite sex, to whom I've been legally married for almost a quarter of a century." Yet this is the woman who, as Maria Russo put it in an obituary for *Salon*, made "literary studies...sexy." Wrote Russo: "Through the lens of high theory, scholars began injecting libido into once dry and staid academic realms." This seems to me the very opposite of what Sedgwick really accomplished: there is nothing "sexy" whatsoever about the ugly, murky language of Queer Theory, and to speak of the glories of literary criticism—from Dryden, Johnson, Coleridge, De Quincey, and Hazlitt through Arnold, Macaulay, Pater, and Ruskin to Eliot, Jarrell, Trilling, and Orwell (to name only a few of the great critics who have written in English)—as "dry and staid" is to not know what you are talking about. When Russo calls Sedgwick's work "sexy" she is thinking about such notorious efforts as the 1989 MLA lecture "Jane Austen and the Masturbating Girl," the very title of which, at the time, caused a stir in academic circles and became a touchstone for this odd new species of critical activity. Sedgwick claims, in her lecture, that she has discovered an undercurrent of repressed sexuality in *Sense and Sensibility*—a claim that she supports by laboriously reading sexual meanings into innocuous statements and gestures throughout Austen's novel. This, in a nutshell, is the approach Sedgwick takes throughout her *oeuvre*; this is what it means to "queer" literary works. If one expects substance, meaning, and insight from literary criticism, the spectacle of Sedgwick's "queering" of the masterpieces of the ages cannot seem anything but a distortion of the literary works themselves—just as her rhetoric can seem a reckless game being played with gay people's lives by a heterosexual woman who finds in those lives a convenient screen onto which to project her fantasies.

Epistemology of the Closet (1990) is regarded by all and sundry not only as Sedgwick's most important book but as a (if not *the*) founding text of Queer Studies. In Sedgwick's own words, the book's central argument is "that an understanding of virtually any aspect of modern Western culture must be, not merely incomplete, but damaged in its central substance to the degree that it does not incorporate a critical analysis of modern homo/ heterosexual definition." But Sedgwick "proves" this point by focusing on a handful of literary works (among them Wilde's *Picture of Dorian Gray*, Melville's *Billy Buddy*, Proust's *À La Recherche du temps perdu*, and Henry James's "The Beast in the Jungle") whose homosexual content has never been a state secret, and—as in "Jane Austen and the Masturbating Girl"—by forcing sexual interpretations upon these works at every turn.

Sedgwick also engages in the now-popular academic pastime of comparing different kinds of oppression and insisting on the complexity and ambiguity of the plight of individuals who are the supposed victims of multiple kinds of oppression (such as gay black women): "it was the long, painful realization, *not* that all oppressions are congruent, but that they are *differently* structured and so must intersect in complex embodiments that was the first great heuristic breakthrough of socialist-feminist thought and of the thought of women of color." Sedgwick calls this a "realization," but it sounds like a commonplace—assuming that one buys the proposition that everybody in America other than straight white men is "oppressed." She goes on: "This realization has as its corollary that the comparison of different axes of oppression is a crucial task, not for any purpose of ranking oppressions, but to the contrary because each oppression is likely to be in a unique indicative relation to certain distinctive nodes of cultural organization." In other words, every kind of oppression works in a somewhat different way. And the oppression of gays? "The *special* centrality of homophobic oppression in the twentieth century…has resulted from its inextricability from the question of knowledge and the processes of knowing in modern Western culture at large." She speaks of "the now endemic crisis of homo / heterosexual definition, indicatively male"—apparently meaning, as Mark Masterson (now of the Victoria University of Wellington) has explained, that our culture is unable to answer the following questions: "Is sexuality an orientation or is it a choice?; are homosexuals born or are they made?; essentialism or social construction?; nature/nurture? These are all part of the effect of this crisis in modern sexual definition. Sedgwick believes, and I agree with her, that it is impossible to adjudicate between these."

Yet although Masterson goes on to speak of this "mass of contradictions that adhere to homosexuality," the pairings in his list are all really different ways of putting the same thing—and there is no reason whatsoever to claim that it is "impossible" to ultimately decide between them. On the contrary, most gay people will testify, and an increasing majority of heterosexuals have come to understand, that sexuality is a matter of orientation and not of choice, period. To pretend that there is some "crisis of definition" surrounding this question is to create an appearance of confusion and melodrama where there is none. Plainly, Sedgwick's purpose here is not to ascertain or clarify objective facts but to be "performative." As Masterson himself admits, she is not out to resolve questions but to make the purportedly unresolved questions themselves her subject.

Unlike most of her female colleagues in Queer Theory, Sedgwick is often described as having identified with gay men. But she was consistently sarcastic and dismissive of heterosexual men. She referred with imperial condescension, for instance, to any sign of "heterosexual male self-pity," sneering contemptuously about the "vast national wash of masculine self-pity" that she claimed to witness regularly in the *New York Times* "About Men" column, in "dying-father-and-his-son stories in *The New Yorker*" and in "any other form of genre writing aimed at men." She mocked the "sacred tears of the heterosexual man," that "rare and precious liquor whose properties, we are led to believe, are rivaled only by the *lacrimae Christi*...." Is there any other group that could get away with mocking like this in today's academy? Sedgwick, note well, was not just criticizing sentimentality; she was essentially suggesting that straight men's feelings are in some way illegitimate. "What charm, compared to this chrism of the gratuitous," she writes, "can reside in the all too predictable tears of women, of gay men, of people with something to cry about?" The point here is that straight men, by definition, have nothing to cry about, ever—since, after all, they hold all the cards in contemporary society. What's bizarre is that the author of these words spent forty years of her life married (happily, by all accounts, including her own) to a straight man. The only way to reconcile such rhetoric with her actual life and feelings is to recognize that Sedgwick truly is engaged in an act *of performance* here—playing a role, putting one over on us.

For the most part, however, the "performance" in *Epistemology of the Closet*, as throughout her work, consists of an often impenetrable display of jargon—an exhibition whose primary purpose is not to communicate ideas but to create an impression. Meandering and repetitious, *Epistemology of the Closet* fails again and again to build toward any clear point; Sedgwick wanders through the texts under consideration—summarizing plots, describing characters, pouncing on this or that word or expression and going on at length about its supposed hidden meanings—yet nothing remotely resembling a coherent argument ever comes into focus. One feels somewhat as if one is watching the rushes of a movie—scenes that have been shot over and over but have yet to be edited together in a way that make narrative sense. And then there is the prose:

> In dealing with the multiple valences of sexuality, critics' choices should not be limited to crudities of disruption or silence of orthodox enforcement.

> In "The Beast in the Jungle," written at the threshold of the new century, the possibility of an embodied male-homosexual thematics has, I would like to argue, a precisely liminal presence.

> [I]t is mostly in the reifying grammar of periphrasis and preterition [in "The Beast in the Jungle"]...that a homosexual meaning becomes, to the degree that it does become, legible.

> [T]he structuring metaphor...here seems to be peculiarly alimentative.

Sedgwick's most distinctive stylistic attribute is the tendency to insert words like *liminal* and *preterition* and *alimentative* into sentences, much in the manner of a malicious child shoving a stick into the spokes of a moving bicycle. The intent in both cases is the same: to show off—and to throw off.

Naturally her disciples take a different view. Masterson says that it is precisely because *Epistemology of the Closet* is "one of the key texts of queer theory" that it is "a challenging book to read. It is primarily for an academic audience. Others perhaps could follow its arguments, but without a connection to an academic setting, the persons who read it may find that they will have to keep the interesting insights they have acquired to themselves. This book is not for the layperson." Masterson's candor here is refreshing. For in these few sentences he points to a hard fact that is central to Queer Theory: *none* of it is meant for the educated common reader, whether gay or straight; unlike Ulrichs and Hirschfeld, its practitioners do not seek to bring understanding and insight to the multitudes (or to anybody) or to have any impact whatsoever upon public thinking about homosexuality and gay rights. On the contrary, Queer Theory is—and is intended to be—the exclusive property of ivory-tower initiates.

If anything, to be sure, Sedgwick's prose style is less opaque than that of her fellow Queer Theory founder Judith Butler. From 1995 to 1998 the scholarly journal *Philosophy and Literature* sponsored a Bad Writing Contest, and in 1998 Butler won first prize for the following sentence from her article "Further Reflections on the Conversations of Our Time," which had appeared the year before in the journal *Diacritics*:

> The move from a structuralist account in which capital is understood to structure social relations in relatively homologous ways to a view of hegemony in which power relations are subject to repetition, convergence, and rearticulation brought the question of temporality into the thinking of structure, and marked a shift from a form of Althusserian theory that takes structural totalities as theoretical objects to one in which the insights

into the contingent possibility of structure inaugu-
rate a renewed conception of hegemony as bound
up with the contingent sites and strategies of the
rearticulation of power.

As Denis Dutton, who established the Bad Writing Contest,
explained in a 1999 issue of the *Wall Street Journal*, "To ask what
this means is to miss the point. This sentence beats readers into
submission and instructs them that they are in the presence of a
great and deep mind. Actual communication has nothing to do
with it." Dutton emphasized that saying such a thing about Judith
Butler's prose did not make one a philistine: "As a lifelong student
of Kant," he pointed out, "I know that philosophy is not always
well-written. But when Kant or Aristotle or Wittgenstein are most
obscure, it's because they are honestly grappling with the most
complex and difficult problems the human mind can encounter."
By contrast, prose like Butler's amounts to "a kind of intellectual
kitsch" produced by self-styled "theorists" who "mimic the effects
of rigor and profundity without actually doing serious intellectual
work" and whose "jargon-laden prose always suggests but never
delivers genuine insight." (Or, to quote Nietzsche, "Those who
know that they are profound strive for clarity. Those who would
like to seem profound to the crowd strive for obscurity.") Sarah
Salih, writing in *Critical Quarterly*, defended Butler, in good Queer
Studies fashion, by invoking the concept of performativity: "Butler
is attempting to do something with her prose; in other words, the
language she deploys is performative rather than constative"—the
latter being a philosophical term that means "relating to a statement, question, or command that can be considered true or false."
(Salih was on firm ground, given that Butler is in the habit of
making statements—such as the claim in her 1990 book *Gender
Trouble* that even the idea that there are two biological sexes is a
social construction—that cannot be taken seriously as "constative.") But Butler herself, presumably having decided that using
the performativity defense would only expose her to further public
ridicule (performativity, after all, being a concept that one could
hardly expect noninitiates outside the academy to understand or

appreciate), fell back, in a *New York Times* op-ed and a letter to the *London Review of Books*, on the safer argument that difficult ideas require difficult language.

In the summer of 2010, Butler again drew a degree of attention outside the academy. While in Berlin for Gay Pride events, she praised Hamas and Hezbollah, which she described admiringly as organizations of the left, and turned down an award from a German gay organization, which she accused of "Islamophobia" because it had criticized the Muslim-on-gay violence that is widespread in Germany. In this instance, it seemed clear that Butler was not being "performative" but was, rather, making "constative" remarks that were meant to be seen as applying to the real world. Her readiness to side with the tormentors of gay people because those tormentors belonged to a group that is generally considered sacrosanct on the orthodox left underlines the fact that Queer Studies is *not* about advancing the rights and security of gay people, but is rather a movement of the left whose leaders are prepared to support allegedly leftist groups and causes even if they represent a clear and present danger to gays.

In any event, one question about performativity has never been satisfactorily answered by any Queer Theory practitioner I know of: what is the point of the "performance"? And here's a second question: why must the "performance" be so dull?

In 2001, Arthur Kramer, the rich heterosexual brother of Larry Kramer, cofounder of the AIDS activist group ACT UP and author of the play *The Normal Heart*, gave Yale a million dollars to establish the Larry Kramer Initiative for Lesbian and Gay Studies (LKI). "I wanted gay history to be taught," the playwright explained in a 2009 speech at that university. "I wanted gay history to be about who we are, and who we were." But it didn't work out that way. What LKI actually turned out to be was a potpourri of courses with titles like "Gender and Sexuality in Popular Music," "Gender Transgression," "Beauty, Fashion, and Self-Styling," "Gendering Musical Performance," "Gender Images: A Psychological Perspective," "Queer Ethnographies," and "Music and Queer Identities." Kramer was stunned and outraged. "When I set LKI up I didn't know that gay studies included all kinds of other things and these other things ruled the roost: gender studies, queer studies, queer theory." Had he known, he said, he'd have

> insist[ed] that my brother's money be funneled via the history department rather than leave it up to Yale, which plunked LKI just where it should not have been, in the women's and gender studies department. The various queer and gender theories I came to quickly realize as relatively useless for a people looking to learn about our real history drowned us out completely. Month after month, over these five years, as I was sent constant email announcements of lectures and courses and activities that reflected as much about real history as a comic book, I slowly began to go nuts.

He protested vehemently and won the support of the celebrated gay historians George Chauncey and Martin Duberman, both of whom, according to Kramer, said, in effect, "Yale is doing it wrong. You do not teach gay history via gender studies, via queer theory. You are making the same mistake every other gay program makes." But the complaints were to no avail. To the outrage of the man whom it was named for, LKI remained a "queer" institution. Kramer made his feelings about this word clear in his Yale speech: "I am not queer! And neither are you! When will we stop using this adolescent and demeaning word to identify ourselves? Like our history that is not taught, using this word will continue to guarantee that we are not taken seriously in the world." Surely Ulrichs and Hirschfeld would have agreed.

*　　*　　*

To be sure, not all practitioners of Lesbian and Gay Studies are hardcore adherents of Queer Theory. Some lesbians, for example, resist the disappearance of "lesbian" under the rubric of "queer" and feel more at home with Women's Studies than with Queer Studies. There are also lesbians as well as gay men who practice a less theory-intensive version of Gay Studies (usually at less prestigious institutions). This doesn't mean, however, that their approaches to the subject are necessarily more responsible than those of the Queer Theorists. Indeed, if the Queer Theorists' offense can be summed up by saying that their heads are stuck in thick clouds of rhetoric that float far above the quotidian preoccupations of the real world, some Gay Studies teachers err in the opposite direction, teaching classes that are devoted to banal, often subliterate personal confession in the form of coming-out stories, diary-writing, and the like. The course descriptions make them sound like self-help groups, and indeed they tend to encourage students to consider every aspect of their daily lives fascinating and meaningful simply because they are gay.

An example of this strain of Lesbian and Gay Studies can be found at the website of the oldest Gay Studies department in the United States, which was founded in 1989 at the City College of San Francisco (CCSF). The site looks and reads less like an academic department's website than like the home page of, say, a ladies' bowling team. When you click on "faculty," you're presented with a mishmash of casual snapshots of the professors; click further—for example, on the picture of Ardel Thomas—and you'll get her astrological data: "I am an Aries—a fire sign. I am born in the year of the Dragon—another fiery symbol. That means I have tons of energy and am very excited about life." She tells us that she received a Ph.D. from Stanford, after which she went on to direct the Community Service Writing Program at that institution. Then:

> In 2004, I decided to leave Stanford University because I wanted to teach in the community college setting. I got a tenure track job in Lexington, Kentucky. I had also lived in San Francisco (not Palo Alto) for 12 years! YIKES! CULTURE SHOCK!
>
> Then, in January 2005, I found an ad for LGBT Studies at CCSF. City College of San Francisco?????? LGBT Studies???????? My dream job if only I could land it! Soooo. . . . .

> Here I am now in my second year—my first year as chair. I am having such a FABULOUS time teaching LGBT Studies and English 1A at CCSF!!!!!

One wonders if Professor Thomas tells her students that it is a good idea to use all caps and multiple question marks and exclamation points in expository prose.

When I looked at CCSF's website in 2010, instructor Mo Brownsey, who was identified as a stand-up comic, solo performer, director and writer of films and videos, and columnist for Match.com (a dating website), was teaching a course in "Queer Creative Process" in which "[f]inal projects are a personal work of art, highlighting your unique process." Herb Green, who has master's degrees in American Studies from Brown and in Ethnic Studies from Berkeley, was teaching "Gay Culture and Society," which "examines significant styles from leather to lipstick and from drag to disco and assesses the evolution of sensibility and identity in various Queer cultures and communities." Now, "gay culture and society" is certainly a subject worthy of academic study, but when I read about Green's focus on "leather to lipstick" and "drag to disco" I couldn't help thinking about Ulrichs and Hirschfeld, who could discourse eruditely about the epiphenomena of homosexuality in Periclean Athens, and about Dynes's *Encyclopedia of Homosexuality*, which contains a wealth of knowledge whose surface is barely scratched by curricula like Green's.

Then again, Green's course sounded like heavy lifting compared with the rest of the department's course offerings, the emphasis of which was largely therapeutic. Ed Kaufman's faculty page explained that his "joy in teaching the course Gay Male Relationships comes from the opportunity to help gay and bisexual men develop and sustain meaningful intimate relationships." Trinity Ordona was teaching "Issues in Lesbian Relationships," for which the required books were *Lesbian Couples: A Guide to Creating Healthy Relationships* and *If the Buddha Dated: A Handbook for Finding Love on a Spiritual Path*. The 2010 schedule also included such courses as "Healing through Journal Writing," "Commitment to Self: Singlehood, Solitude & Being Myself in Relationship(s)," and "Healing a Broken Heart: Recovery & Reconciliation." This is a long way from social constructionism and Queer Theory—but it's also a long way from anything that might remotely be considered serious higher education.

There are, to be sure, Queer Studies professors who manage to combine the "performative" jargon of Queer Theory with a relatively engaged (if predictably radical) approach to actual human life. Meet Ian Barnard, a gay white South African who teaches at California State University, Northridge, and whose stock-in-trade is bringing race and sexuality together. In the first line of his book, *Queer Race: Cultural Interventions in the Racial Politics of Queer Theory* (2004), he writes that the term "queer race"

> juxtaposes two nonanalogous demarcations of iden-
> tity, sexuality and race (assuming for the moment
> that "queer" refers to sexuality and that the word
> "race" is self-explanatory) in order to inaugurate
> a third term that conjured up a cacophony of new
> epistemological questions, identificatory possibil-
> ities, and theoretical problematics I want to vari-
> ously pursue, articulate, and contest precisely as
> each problematic is suggested, enabled, abjured, and
> reinvented by the others.

Barnard says that he does "not see sexuality and race as dispa-rate constituents of subjectivity or axes of power" but rather as two "systems of meaning and understanding that formatively and inherently define each other." While other Queer Theorists might describe, say, a Chicana lesbian as "triply oppressed" because she is a woman, a Chicana, and gay, Barnard argues that breaking down such a person's identity into three individual categories "erases" her compound identity as a Chicana lesbian, the properties of which, in his view, are no closer to being the sum of its constituent elements' properties than, say, sulfuric acid combines the properties of hydrogen, sulfur, and oxygen. For this reason, Barnard celebrates Gloria Anzaldúa's "disrupt[ion]" of "canonical genre designations" as offering a "vision for the future of queer theory," saying that "a political queerness is an especially urgent imperative now, given the increasing visibility of right-wing gays in the United States in recent years." (As examples of these "right-wing gays," he names me, Stephen H. Miller, and Marshall Kirk and Hunter Madsen, authors of the 1989 book *After the Ball: How America Will Conquer Its Fear and Hatred of Gays in the 90's*.)

Barnard clearly considers the "visibility" of gays who reject Queer Theory and radical-left politics a menace. Part of what makes Miller, me, and others so threatening, as he sees it, is that we're gay white men who choose not to flail ourselves for being white and male; and one reason why he's so high on Anzaldúa is that her way of using the word *queer* "allows for...a conceptualization of identity that is different from definitions of lesbianness and gayness revolving around sexual orientation only, and thus normalizing middle-class white (often male) experience." He praises Anzaldúa for insisting that "[a]ll parties involved in coalitions need to recognize the necessity that women-of-color and lesbians define the terms of engagement." This "principle," Barnard argues, must be followed by queer activists and theorists: "feminism and anti-racism, queers of color and white female queers and their experiences, and colored female queer theory must set the agendas and delineate the parameters of these agendas if queer is not to become a synonym for gay white men." And this is a gay white man talking! If he really believes what he's saying, how can he justify writing *Queer Race*, in which he certainly seems to be setting agendas and delineating parameters?

Barnard discusses at length, and admits to being fascinated by, both O. J. Simpson and the serial killer Jeffrey Dahmer. This fascination is disturbing, and Barnard's way of writing about these two men has the effect of trivializing the murders they committed. For Barnard there appears to be no such thing as objective morality, just group categories and group justice; he refers repeatedly to the "erasure" of this or that kind of compound identity—black women, gay black men—and it can sound as if such perceived "erasures" are, for him, realer and more offensive than an actual "erasure" in the form of cold-blooded murder. Although he is careful not to explicitly label Dahmer a hero, Barnard's discussion of Dahmer's serial killings frames them in large part as strikes against conventionality, homophobia, and racial and sexual pigeonholing—as, in short, "queer" actions. Because Dahmer was an apparently racist white man who denied he was homosexual, but had sex with (and killed and ate) men of color, most of whom also identified as heterosexual, Barnard feels that "[t]he Dahmer case helps us to redefine queer in several ways." For "only to discern queer in terms of a conventional understanding of progressive politics is to impoverish the potential of queer theory to diagnose the function of codifications of desire precisely where such discourses are successively formative: the moments when the meanings of queer generated by the interstices of gay desire and racial identification are most elusive and disturbing. This is something like the invention or discovery of queer race. The queer in queer race is thus doubly queer both insofar as it queers queer and destabilizes the (disconnection between queer and race."

In short, Dahmer, in a grotesque way, becomes for Barnard a poster boy for queerness. To be sure, a few pages after telling us that "queer race" "queers queer," Barnard says that it "un-queers queerness...by eroding sexuality as a unique ground of knowledge." (Presumably we are expected to accept this bald contradiction on the understanding that Barnard is being performative, not constative.) Barnard devotes an entire chapter to Dahmer, and later returns to him, this time dropping the jargon and diving into confession:

> What is so special about Dahmer? Or is this about me being white and gay? Or is it about something else for me? My desire for Jeffrey Dahmer? My desire for Jeffrey Dahmer's desire? I feel sorry for him. I was born in the same year that he was. He played the clarinet; so do I. I am attracted to him, his voice, his glasses at his sentencing.

Dahmer isn't the only mass murderer whom Barnard turns into an erotic object; elsewhere in *Queer Race* he claims that "some gay men were infatuated by the white, boyish, crew-cut [Timothy] McVeigh's television images, an infatuation that had subversive potential in the context of the mainstream media's racist and imperialist first assumption that the bombing had been the work of Middle-Eastern terrorists." (So having a crush on a terrorist who took the lives of 168 people, including nineteen small children, somehow strikes a blow against racism and imperialism?) Barnard also spends several pages on the O. J. Simpson trial, maintaining that because Simpson was a black man who was accused of murdering a white woman, "black women disappear from the O. J. Simpson trial as completely as it renders any possibility of queer black men unthinkable"—a statement that can hardly be improved on as a representative example of Queer Studies hyperbole.

*　　*　　*

On a sunny day in September 2010, I stroll up Unter den Linden in Berlin to the main building of Humboldt University, where I will soon be hearing Susan Stryker's opinions about democratic capitalism. A plaque facing the street informs passersby that it was here that Max Planck came up with quantum theory. Alas, I'm here for a conference about another theory whose name begins with a *q*. Organized by the university's Queer Research Group and by the Department of English and American Studies, the conference is titled "Queer Again? Power, Politics, and Ethics."

As I'm signing in at the registration desk, the young woman on duty prepares me for "an embarrassing question." It turns out to be "Do you have a Ph.D.?" Not that I would be turned away if I didn't; they just want to know which attendees have Ph.D.s and which don't. Queer Studies pretends to be about fearlessly overturning all established categories, but here, as everywhere else in academe, establishment credentials actually matter a great deal.

The opening event is held in a lecture hall that is packed almost to capacity. The great majority of my fellow attendees are lesbians in their twenties or thirties, and a surprising number of them are cute and skinny, with short haircuts, T-shirts, and a body language that make them look like teenage boys. We're welcomed by "Dr. Prof. Eveline Kilian" (Germans love to double up on the academic titles), a middle-aged woman who explains the "embarrassing question":

221

it turns out that the conference receives funding from the German Research Fund, which requires that the organizers provide a list of participants with Ph.D.s and another list of those without (the Germans love drawing up lists of names). Kilian asks that we "forget about the ideological implications of this"—never mind that the whole premise of Queer Studies is that it *never* overlooks the ideological implications of *anything*.

The conference, we are informed, is intended as a sort of response to the 2004 book *No Future: Queer Theory and the Death Drive* by Lee Edelman, a professor at Tufts University. Edelman's book is arguably the most influential work in the field at present, and underlies what is described as "the antisocial turn in Queer Theory." Edelman depicts human society as being permeated by a mentality that he labels "reproductive futurism"—a preoccupation with the future and with the "Child" (a word he capitalizes consistently) that serves as "the emblem of futurity's unquestioned value."

Since gay couples cannot naturally reproduce, gays are widely viewed as the enemies of the future. The traditional "liberal" gay response to this "ascription of negativity to the queer," Edelman says, is to dismiss it outright; but since Queer Theory views queerness by definition as oppositional, it is more appropriate, maintains Edelman, for queers "to consider accepting and even embracing" the "ascription of negativity" to themselves, and to explicitly reject any stake in or concern for futurity." Gays should, he suggests, "listen to, and even perhaps be instructed by, the readings of queer sexualities produced by the forces of reaction." So when Donald Wildmon of the American Family Association rails that acceptance of gays "will result in society's destruction," gay people, instead of denouncing such rhetoric in good liberal fashion, should "pause for a moment to acknowledge that Mr. Wildmon might be right—or, more important, that he *ought* to be right..."

In other words, queers *should* be the threat, the menace, that Wildmon describes; we should turn our backs on "[t]he structuring optimism of politics," whether of left or right, because all politics is about hope for the future and is thus linked to a "life drive." Briefly put, we should embrace "queer negativity"—we should embrace "the death drive," which "names what the queer, in the order of the social, is called forth to figure: the negativity opposed to every form of social viability." Edelman acknowledges that this approach would not bring gay people goodness, happiness, or self-knowledge; on the contrary, it would promise "absolutely nothing," and would certainly yield nothing in the way of a "positive social value"; its sole value would lie in "its challenge to value as defined by the social, and thus in its radical challenge to the very value of the social itself." Edelman's argument is widely viewed in today's Queer Theory circles as brilliant, pathbreaking, and explosive. But in fact it is not even original; it is simply a more explicitly nihilistic version of the case against gay "assimilation" that was promulgated by far-left activists back in the 1980s and '90s. But of course even to call it an argument is to give it credit it does not deserve: it is nothing but another Queer Studies "performance," a cynical piece of claptrap that has no imaginable application to real gay persons' lives. *No Future* is stunning in its moral irresponsibility and sheer fraudulence: this is, after all, a career-making book by a patently ambitious member of the professoriate who pretends to have given up any concern for the future and who pretends to be counseling his fellow Queer Theorists to join him. And indeed many of them, recognizing which way the Queer Studies winds are blowing at present, have—in the interest of their own futures—climbed onto the *No Future* bandwagon. It's all a despicable charade, and what makes it despicable is the naked lack of concern on the part of some of the world's most fortunate gay people for the futures of the most vulnerable of gays—among them the innumerable young people who are living with, or who have been thrown out of the house by, homophobic parents, and who may well not see much of a future before them; and the gay people, young and old, living in places where homosexuality is still punished harshly, in some cases with death.

This is what Queer Studies has come to: a breathtaking combination of purported nihilism and sheer academic careerism. With *No Future*, Queer Studies would seem to have arrived at its natural destination—a perfect moral and intellectual void.

CHAPTER 5
The Dream of Aztlán: Chicano Studies

Over our lunch in Monterey, I ask Shelby Steele about Chicano Studies. "There's always a conflict between them and Black Studies," he says. "At the University of Utah I was designing this [Black Studies] program, so they came forward very quickly. Their hustlers were as good as our hustlers. They wanted a piece of the action. So they said to me when the white man left the room, 'Look here, this is the West, this is our territory.' And they beat us out. We had one program, with one director for Black and Chicano Studies, and they got the director. It's pathetic. It's sad and funny at the same time. They did it that way throughout the Cal State system. Monterey Bay State came into existence when Clinton took the White House and said he would use the 'peace dividend' to close down Fort Ord and create a new campus in Monterey. The unspoken implication was that this would be a Chicano campus. They'd put a white [college] president in charge, but he'd be on a leash. From its inception, the idea was that this would be the Hispanic campus.

"Identity politics really shapes the contours of the Cal State system in this way."

And from the very beginning of Chicano Studies, the Cal State system has been its ground zero.

*   *   *

It was indeed the black civil rights movement that—along with the farmworker activism of César Chávez (whose birthday is now an official holiday in several states)—helped spark the Chicano movement; and it was the birth of Black Studies that gave some Mexican American activists the idea that they, too, deserved their own academic discipline. To be sure, it cannot be said that they had a very clear idea of what the actual objective of these programs should be, and in fact all these years later the purpose of Chicano Studies remains a highly debated question. What is not debatable is the intensity of the passions that gave birth to Chicano Studies. The 1960s Chicano movement—known simply, and universally, as *el movimiento*—was for its participants a matter of ardent commitment to *La Causa* and *La Raza*, though there was much disagreement as to what exactly they were committing themselves to. Were they simply fighting for greater educational and job opportunities and the like? Were they out to transform the American system entirely? Or did they seek to secede from the United States? For many Chicano activists, especially in those early days, the goal (however Utopian or quixotic it might now seem) was indeed one of secession: they sought nothing less than to tear the parts of the United States that had once been Mexican territory—including, roughly speaking, the present states of California, Nevada, Utah, Colorado, Arizona, New Mexico, and Texas (which many activists, using the Spanish word, chose to refer to as *Tejas*)—asunder from the Union and form a new nation. This nation already had a name: it would be called *Aztlán*, borrowing a place-name from Aztec history.

In 1969, two large national gatherings took place at which Chicano activists came together to produce manifestos. In Denver, the First National Chicano Youth Liberation Conference was organized by activist Rodolfo "Corky" Gonzales. Born in Denver (his father was a Mexican immigrant), Gonzales was a successful featherweight boxer and founder of a group called the Crusade for Justice. He was also the author of the movement's equivalent of "The Battle Hymn of the Republic" (or, perhaps, *Howl*), a 1967 poem called "I

Am Joaquín," which is widely credited with helping to advance the Aztlán agenda. The poem, whose full text—several pages long—is to this day enshrined in several major Chicano Studies anthologies and textbooks, begins as follows:

> *Yo soy Joaquín,*
> *Perdido en un mundo de confusion…*
>
> I am Joaquín, lost in a world of confusion,
>
> caught up in the whirl of a gringo society,
>
> confused by the rules, scorned by attitudes,
>
> suppressed by manipulation, and destroyed by modern society…

As the poem continues, the protagonist identifies in turn with a Mayan prince, with Emiliano Zapata, and with other figures from Mexican history; he draws strength from both his Indian and his Spanish heritage. "I am Aztec prince and Christian Christ," he writes. But identify with the Anglos and their dream of capitalist progress? No way. For Joaquín, the only true path—the only proper course to take in response to Anglo domination, the only means of preserving and being true to his heritage—is that of revolt.

The influence of Gonzales's poem can hardly be overstated. As George Hartley of Ohio University writes, it

> was mimeographed and widely circulated in order to be read during public demonstrations and organizing campaigns.… Beyond its immediate public activist function, however, *I Am Joaquín* also functioned as the inaugural work of what is now seen as the Chicano Literary Renaissance, lasting from the late '60s to the mid '70s. *I Am Joaquín* provided the groundwork, then, for all Chicano poetry to come. Yet what is perhaps more interesting is its

role in serving as the founding literary work for all previous Chicano literature. What I am saying is that before 1967 Chicano literature did not exist, but after 1967 the whole history of Chicano literature from the 1600s to the 1960s suddenly, retroactively came into being. Moreover, I contend that prior to 1967 and the publication of *I Am Joaquín*, Chicanos did not exist, and yet after that moment we can see that they had been around for centuries.

It was not Gonzales, however, but another young activist (and poet) who wrote the manifesto that emerged from the Denver conference. "El Plan Espiritual de Aztlán" was the work of Alberto Urista Heredia, a student at the University of California, San Diego, who published poetry under the pseudonym Alurista. His manifesto began as follows:

In the spirit of a new people that is conscious not only of its proud historical heritage but also of the brutal "gringo" invasion of our territories, we, the Chicano inhabitants and civilizers of the northern land of Aztlan from whence came our forefathers, reclaiming the land of their birth and consecrating the determination of our people of the sun, declare that the call of our blood is our power, our responsibility, and our inevitable destiny. We are free and sovereign to determine those tasks which are justly called for by our house, our land, the sweat of our brows, and by our hearts. Aztlan belongs to those who plant the seeds, water the fields, and gather the crops and not to the foreign Europeans. We do not recognize capricious frontiers on the bronze continent.

Brotherhood unites us, and love for our brothers makes us a people whose time has come and who struggles [*sic*] against the foreigner "gabacho" [gringo] who exploits our riches and destroys our culture. With our heart in our hands and our hands in the soil, we declare the independence of our mestizo nation. We are a bronze people with a bronze culture. Before the world, before all of North America, before all our brothers in the bronze continent, we are a nation, we are a union of free pueblos, we are Aztlan.

The manifesto went on to call for "total liberation from oppression, exploitation, and racism." Chicanos would "driv[e] the exploiter out of our communities, our pueblos, and our lands" and "defeat the gringo dollar value system." U.S. government authorities were described as "the occupying forces of the oppressors." Finally, the manifesto called for the "[c]reation of an independent local, regional, and national political party" whose ultimate goal was "[a] nation autonomous and free."

The Denver conference took place in March 1969; the next month, at a symposium in Santa Barbara, the Chicano Coordinating Council on Higher Education drafted *El Plan de Santa Barbara: A Chicano Plan for Higher Education,* which brought together Chicano student groups under the name Movimiento Estudiantil Chicano de Aztlan (Chicano Student Movement of Aztlan), or MEChA. The manifesto read, in part:

> For the Chicano the present is a time of renaissance, of renacimiento. Our people and our community, el barrio and la colonia, are expressing a new consciousness and a new resolve....
>
> The ethic of profit and competition, of greed and intolerance, which the Anglo society offers must be replaced by our ancestral communalism and love for beauty and justice. M.E.Ch.A. must bring to the mind of every young Chicano that the liberations of this people from prejudice and oppression is in his hands and this responsibility is greater than personal achievement and more meaningful than

degrees, especially if they are earned at the expense
of his identity and cultural integrity.

...[A]ll attempts must be made to take the
college and university to the barrio, whether it be
in form of classes giving college credit or community centers financed by the school for the use of
community organizations and groups.... The idea
must be made clear to the people of the barrio that
they own the schools and the schools and all their
resources are at their disposal.... Many colleges and
universities have publishing operations which could
be forced to accept barrio works for publication.

But how exactly did Chicano Studies fit into the goals of the
Chicano movement? Even the leaders of *el movimiento* weren't sure.
After all, the demand by Chicano activists for an academic discipline of their own was rather illogical from the outset, given that
the academy was a part of the very establishment that they viewed
as their enemy and claimed to want to overthrow or secede from.
Alurista himself would later admit that "Chicano Studies was
created by students, by Chicano students, and as students we had no
concrete idea of what it was that a department of Chicano Studies
would accomplish in view of our recognition of the corruption and
decadence of the American educational system." In other words,
from the very birth of Chicano Studies, there was no *there* there.
Yet the student activists didn't let that stop them. They pressured,
bullied, and/or guilt-tripped one university after another (mostly in
California and other southwestern states) into establishing Chicano
courses, departments, and centers—though they played little or no
role in actually shaping the discipline that resulted.

And how *did* the discipline get shaped? To borrow a distinction made by Michael Soldatenko, who chairs the Chicano Studies
Department at California State University, Los Angeles, at the outset
there were two main ways of doing Chicano Studies. One, born out
of the Quinto Sol collective and articulated in *El Grito: A Journal of
Contemporary Mexican-American Thought* (both founded at Berkeley
in 1967), entirely rejected the premises of the traditional humanities

and social sciences, and is labeled "perspectivism" by Soldatenko because Octavio I. Romano, *El Grito*'s editor, "proposed to initiate Chicano(a) research from the perspective of the Chicano(a) subject." For Romano, traditional scholarly methods were so intrinsically prejudiced against Chicanos that "the very nature of objectivity...had to be rejected." This emphasis on subjective testimony brings to mind Edward Said's dismissal, in *Orientalism*, of the work of great scholars of Islam and Arab culture who didn't happen to be Muslims or Arabs themselves.[1] Soldatenko actually says, without a hint of criticism or mockery, that Romano "provided Chicanos and Chicanas with a radical weapon in their battle with the academy and knowledge."

Yet by the 1980s perspectivism had lost out to the approach promoted in *El Plan de Santa Barbara* and articulated in *Aztlán: Chicano Journal of the Social Sciences and the Arts*, which was established in 1970 (and which soon altered its subtitle to *International Journal of Chicano Studies Research*). This approach, which Soldatenko dubs "empiricism," was less personal and more political: while perspectivists sought to turn the academy into a place where they could express "the entire spectrum of feelings that are the soul of the barrio," empiricists saw the university "as a political tool" that they sought "to capture" in order "to continue the fight to transform the barrio"—a "place to battle for self-determination and Chicano liberation." The empiricists, says Soldatenko, saw "[a]cademic work" as "ancillary to political work" and hence accepted traditional academic models only because "they had no vision for intellectual work." Most of them, he adds, began as Chicano "nationalists" but later gave up the dream of an independent Aztlán and became ordinary "liberal, progressive, or Marxist" academics.

---

1 That writing about groups to which one doesn't belong is still a source of anxiety in Chicano Studies is reflected in *"This Land Was Mexican Once": Histories of Resistance from Northern California* (2007), in which author Linda Heidenreich frets that "[c]ritical works by Indigenous scholars such as Devon Abbot Mihesuah and Greg Sarris...problematize any works by non-native scholars" and assures us that in writing about the Napa tribe, she's "address[ed] these problems" by "engag[ing] in a dialogue with Earl Couey, the Wappo Tribal Consultant, in an attempt to ensure that the stories I see and hear when I look to the Napa region 'do no harm.'" In short, spokespeople for certain groups now vet the work of historians—not to ensure that what they write is *true*, but to ensure that it "does no harm."

For a time, the debate within empiricism focused mainly on whether Anglo oppression of Chicanos was more properly identified as racism or classism. Those who said classism were, of course, Marxists; those who went with racism saw Anglo oppression as "internal colonialism"—for them, Chicanos in the United States were, like Indians in the British Empire, the subjects of a colonial power. The "internal colonialism" crowd was no less revolutionary than the Marxists; nor were the two positions mutually exclusive. Indeed, if their goal was supposedly to "analyze" the oppression of Chicanos, Chicano Studies practitioners increasingly combined internal colonialism *and* Marxism in their efforts to describe Anglo domination.

In the 1970s, as fewer and fewer Chicano Studies professors pretended to have any intention of translating their radical rhetoric into radical action, many leading figures in the field lamented what they saw as its increasing "moderation"; political scholar Theresa Aragón de Shepro of the University of Washington called for a new birth of radicalism; and Chicano historian Mario García complained in 1973 that "Chicano Studies…now represents a bureaucratic organization laden with incompetent and opportunistic faculty members whose sense of commitment to the students and the Chicano Movement leaves much to be desired." Apropos of García's charge, it is hard not to notice that even some of the most celebrated figures in Chicano Studies write astonishingly poor prose. (A brief example: Rodolfo Acuña, author of the leading Chicano Studies textbook, refers to "[t]he hue of one's skin color.")

In Soldatenko's retelling, the original dream of using the academy as a fortress from which to launch a Utopian revolution eventually got turned inside out: instead of overthrowing the oppressive Anglo establishment of which the university was a part, and founding a People's Republic of Aztlán, Chicano Studies would make it its goal to "revitalize moribund [academic] fields," thereby "sav[ing] traditional academic disciplines" such as social science. Soldatenko lists several supposed developments in Chicano Studies that he plainly views as evidence that the discipline, during the 1970s, was a beehive of high-level intellectual activity: he tells us enthusiastically, for example, about the rise of "objectivism of social science" in Chicano Studies; the call by Tomás Atencio of La Academia de la Nueva Raza (Academy for the New Race) for the creation of "a learning experience through dialogue—his famous *resolana*" (*glare*); Samuel C. Martinez and Roberto Vargas's concept of *razalogía* (*raceology*), which "evolved out of the attempt to conceptually describe our approach for developing knowledge that heals, liberates and transforms"; and *chicanismo*, described in the magazine *Con Safos* as an attempt at expressing the entire spectrum of feelings that are the soul of the barrio."

Then there's the work of Juan Gómez-Quiñones, whom Soldatenko considers "the senior Chicano Studies historian in the University of California system." Soldatenko describes Gómez-Quiñones's 1982 book, *Development of the Mexican Working Class North of the Rio Bravo*, as a key "social-Marxist" work and his 1977 essay "On Culture" as a "pivotal essay in the consolidation of Chicano Studies scholarship and canon formation" because it "provided an understanding of the structures of oppression that would result in action research," "ratified the empiricist agenda and dismissed all other versions of Chicano studies and returned to a Leninist-Stalinist form of Marxism," "left little doubt that a Leninist-Stalinist form of materialist analysis was the only acceptable research epistemology and the only effective expression of action research," and ensured that henceforth Chicano Studies scholars would seek "to understand the condition of the Mexican American as the result of either the structural weakness of the American system or the oppression of a racist and/ or capitalist structure" and would "then devise solutions for this condition—whether a set of reformist policies to ameliorate the American system or revolutionary action to overthrow an unjust and unequal system." (Action, then, was still, at least theoretically, a part of the picture.) For Soldatenko, the 1981 publication of the second edition of Acuña's *Occupied America* was a momentous event, signaling a definitive shift from "the internal colonial model" to a Soviet-style "class analysis." Acuña's "turn...to historical materialism," writes Soldatenko, was widely seen as marking "the demise of internal colonialism" and "the victory of dialectical materialism." The problem with "internal colonialism," Chicano scholar Estevan Flores commented, was that it offered no "class perspective" and was thus "ultimately reformist" rather than revolutionary.

But even as empiricism, with a focus on "Leninist-Stalinist… analysis," was solidifying its hold on Chicano Studies, the anthology *This Bridge Called My Back: Writings by Radical Women of Color*, edited by Cherríe Moraga and Gloria Anzaldúa and also published in 1981, introduced a radical feminist perspective into this and other disciplines. Many male Chicano activists felt threatened by feminism; no less a figure than Rodolfo "Corky" Gonzales, author of the universally revered "I Am Joaquín," expressed concern that Chicanas would fall prey to "white European thinking" and "lose their *Chicanisma* or their womanhood and become a frigid *gringa*." There was—and still is—plenty of debate among Chicana feminists as to whether they should therefore ally with Chicano men or with Anglo women. Those who choose the latter risk being smeared as traitors to their people and sellouts to bourgeois Anglo materialism. At a Chicana workshop at the first National Chicano Student Conference in 1969, Enriqueta Longeaux y Vásquez spoke of the "dual oppression" Chicanas experienced— both sexism and racism; two years later, at the first National Chicana Conference in Houston, Mirta Vidal went Longeaux y Vásquez one better, speaking of not dual but triple oppression—as Vidal put it, Chicana women were oppressed "as members of an oppressed nationality, as workers, *and* as women."

But who was oppressing whom? And which was the bigger problem, racism or sexism? Predictably, many Chicana activists blamed everything on Anglo capitalism: "It is the economic structure that forces the Chicano to oppress the women because the whole world oppressed him," wrote Anna Nieto Gomez, proffering a common view. "We aren't oppressed by Chicanos, we're oppressed by a system that serves white power," wrote Velia Garcia in 1971, so "our men, not white women" are "our natural allies." So it went. Some Chicana women remained loyal members of *el movimiento*; others focused on feminism; others were Marxists who avoided both movements. In 1986, Chicano Studies practitioner Alma M. Garcia decreed that "a combination of all three approaches" was "the only way to redefine the study of women within Chicano studies." But a generation later, the squabbling continues; one Chicana scholar after another has written about "multiple oppression" and called for "research" into gender, race, and class as if such things had not already been said a thousand times before.

And after feminism came all the rest of it—the invasion of Chicano Studies (along with every other sector of the humanities and social sciences) by structuralism and poststructuralism, Queer Theory, and what Soldatenko calls "a 'cultural turn'"—that is, a shift from straightforward take-to-the-barriers revolutionary rhetoric to the kind of "research" that might focus on anything from, say, Chicano music to Chicano dressmaking while still incorporating the obligatory anticapitalist, anti-Anglo clichés. Soldatenko, for one, isn't pleased with this "cultural turn": "While Chicano(a) scholars have won the academic battle, we have lost the war for justice. The ability to transform our neighborhoods and our places of work remains Utopian." He calls for an "ethical turn" in Chicano Studies and an end to "unmediated theorizing"—which presumably means more rallying cries and calls to action. In his letter welcoming participants to the thirty-seventh annual convention of the National Association for Chicana and Chicano Studies (NACCS), the organization's chair for 2010–11, Devon G. Peña, strikes a similar note. "Chicana & Chicano Studies has followed new directions and this has included a major shift toward preoccupation with post-modern deconstruction of texts and narratives and a narrowing of our political work into acts of interpellation in discursive politics." As a result,

> academic-based Chicana & Chicano Studies has continued to lose much of its focus on participatory community-based social action research. However, the focus on discursive politics appeared to be running its course. It seems to be in stasis, as an epistemological project, largely because our students and community activists are increasingly losing interest in Chicana/o Studies if it remains committed to a stale form of discourse fetishism that characterizes too much of [the] so-called "cultural studies" Left in academia.

...[A]s bonafide academic intellectuals, we probably became less relevant to the more "gritty" efforts to directly intervene and participate in the myriad social, economic, and political challenges facing our communities. One is right to ask: How many times can we deconstruct a text before we realize that this is more an exercise in intellectual navel-gazing than a socially and politically useful form of knowledge that advances the struggles of our predominantly working-class and indigenous Diaspora communities?...

Making our voices heard is no longer enough! We must move beyond discourse to actual mobilization for campaigns against all forms of oppression and exploitation and the structural violence that allows neoliberal capitalism to colonize every single gay, lesbian, transgendered, and straight body on this planet: Race, class, gender, sexuality, and place are all real complex structures of difference that are used to keep our communities under control and suppress our potential as indomitable forces for social change and emancipation.

Whatever one thinks about the directions it has taken, Chicano Studies has undoubtedly thrived. The website of the Department of Chicano Studies at Cal State Northridge recounts its proud history: "[i]n 1968 African American and Chicana/o students demanded that the university [then San Fernando Valley State College] recruit more minority faculty, establish programs that would meet the needs of these students, and provide the necessary support services so that they would succeed and graduate. They took over the Administration Building, were arrested, and presented a series of demands to the President of the university." The administration gave in, establishing "the Educational Opportunity Program (EOP) and a variety of support programs" as well as departments of Chicano and Pan African Studies; in the autumn of 1969, the first semester of forty-five Chicano Studies courses began under the direction of Rodolfo

Acuña. Today the department at Cal State Northridge, now called the Department of Chicana and Chicano Studies (with Acuña, under the title of professor emeritus, still at the helm), is the largest department of its kind in the United States and offers "a major, a double-major, a minor, and a Masters in Chicana/o Studies"; as of mid-2010, it boasted, according to its website, "25 fulltime and 35 part time professors" and "160-170 class sections" per semester.

Then there's the University of California, Los Angeles, where the Chicano Studies Research Center was founded in 1969 and an interdisciplinary Chicano Studies program was established in 1973. In 1990, a MEChA-organized protest demanded the elevation of the program to departmental status. After three years of "discussions," UCLA's chancellor rejected the proposal. There ensued a sit-in at the Faculty Center and acts of vandalism that caused thirty thousand dollars' worth of damage and resulted in more than eighty arrests; but the action that proved decisive was a hunger strike by nine Mexican Americans, including several students and anatomy professor Jorge R. Mancillas, who told the *New York Times*: "This is not a symbolic act. We either get a department of Chicano studies or we will die here." After fourteen days the chancellor agreed to turn the Chicano Studies program into a "center" named for the recently deceased Cesar Chávez; in 2005, the program and center became a full department. Today the Cesar E. Chávez Department of Chicana and Chicano Studies has twelve full-time faculty members, five joint faculty members, ten affiliated faculty members, and seven visiting faculty members and lecturers, and offers an undergraduate major and minor as well as M.A. and Ph.D. degrees in Chicana and Chicano Studies.

Chicano Studies isn't confined to the Southwest. The program at the University of Minnesota dates back to 1972 and was also the result of activist tumult. "Under pressure from the Latin Liberation Front," reads the history department at the program's website,

> a student-led group of Chicana and Chicano students from colleges in the Twin Cities, the University of Minnesota began to address financial aid, campus employment for students, and recruiting. In particular, the Latin Liberation

Front strongly encouraged the creation of a Department of Chicano Studies at the University of Minnesota. Dissatisfied with the pace of the University response, on October 26, 1971, twenty Chicano students occupied the Twin Cities administration building, Morrill Hall.... Following a two hour meeting with administration officials, Manuel Guzman presented the group's demands: "If we do not have concrete evidence of the establishment or implementation of a Chicano Studies Department within 72 hours a vote will be taken to strike against the university administration and its policies."

Although an initial response from the college raised the possibility of the new department being combined with another existing department, Latin Liberation leaders rejected the idea, arguing that it would be crucial for the department to have a distinct identity. Within three days of the occupation and ultimatum, College of Liberal Arts committees approved the proposal for a free-standing Chicano Studies Department.... Chicano Studies accepted its first students in the fall of 1972 and was the first Chicano Studies program in the Upper-Midwest.

One of the activists there at the beginning was David Diaz. He got a B.A. at Cal State Northridge, was awarded a doctorate in urban planning at UCLA, and then became a lecturer at Northridge, where he held a joint position in Urban Studies and Chicano Studies and stayed for twelve years. Now he's a colleague of Soldatenko's at Cal State Los Angeles. One sunny afternoon in the spring of 2010 I make my way to Diaz's office on campus in East Los Angeles. The door is open, and he waves me in affably as he rises from his chair.

Diaz looks every inch the aging sixties radical. He's stocky, with long, messy hair, and is dressed in a loose, rumpled, casual shirt and jeans—a Chicano version of David Crosby. Every aspect of his appearance seems designed to communicate the message that although some might consider him a member of the establishment, he's still a radical and isn't about to smooth out his rough edges for anybody. At his invitation, I sit down on his couch. I do a quick survey of his office; it's crowded with pictures, posters, mementos, and assorted knickknacks that are charged with political meaning and that I wish I had a chance to check out more closely. (When, during our conversation, I mention that I'm gay, he pulls back a curtain and proudly shows me the "No on Prop 8" poster in his window.)

"We were teenagers in the street," he recalls, and proceeds to wax nostalgic about his involvement with such movement figures as Vicki L. Ruiz (author of *Cannery Women, Cannery Lives: Mexican Women, Unionization, and the California Food Processing Industry, 1930–1950*), Gloria Anzaldúa, and Rodolfo "Corky" Gonzales. Diaz reminisces about Gonzales's Crusade for Justice and about the conference that issued *El Plan Espiritualde Aztlán*. He also talks about the Raza Unida Party, which for a time after its establishment in 1970 enjoyed considerable support among Chicanos in Los Angeles, and about the "Chicano Moratorium," which organized anti—Vietnam War demonstrations, including a 1970 march in East Los Angeles in which thirty thousand protesters took part.

Diaz is an expert in state and federal environmental law, but was "always an activist," focusing on public works and housing. He puts it succinctly: before he became an academic, "people hired me to stop things." He has what he describes as "a legacy of opposition against the state." I ask him how he reconciles being both a scholar and an activist. "For me it's easy," he says. "I came to the academy in mid-career," and becoming a Chicano Studies professor was "a natural evolution," because "interwoven in my field is a legacy of activism." He writes op-eds frequently for *La Opinión*, which is the largest Spanish-language newspaper in the United States and the second-largest daily in Los Angeles, and in them he has, among other things, "gone after mayors." And none of this has caused him any problems in his academic career? "So far," he says, "no."

Diaz has been at Cal State Los Angeles for three years now, and here, as at Northridge, he teaches both Urban Studies and Chicano Studies—two subjects that, for him, are intimately connected. He's preoccupied with "issues of gentrifying, eminent domain, displacement"—"attacks on cities" such as the construction of the "freeways that dissect East L.A.," forcing the destruction of homes. Diaz, who grew up right here in East L.A., as well as in the small neighboring cities of Whittier and Montebello, and whose 2005 book, *Barrio Urbanism: Chicanos, Planning and American Cities*, is described by its publisher as "the first book on Latinos in America from an urban planning/policy perspective," says that as a young man he observed a "parallel between the bombed-out cities in Europe and what I saw around me."

When I ask him what his objective is as a teacher of Chicano Studies, he says it's to "recapture Chicano history for young students who have little clue about history," especially the history of labor and politics; to get them to "appreciate their own historical and cultural legacy," and to instill in them the "inquisitiveness to further explore" that legacy. "My ultimate goal is that students appreciate the value of knowledge and become engaged in society, in community service. Expecting them to become political activists in an apolitical society is expecting too much." At present he's teaching a class on diversity, in which the reading list consists of "eight works on why diversity didn't happen in America." He says the questions that animate the course are "What is a diverse society? What will diversity look like in the middle-class future?" I ask about his students. He describes them as "working-class and self-supporting"; one-third, he says, are "struggling," and one-third are "competing." Many lack basic academic skills—writing, outlining, doing research. Most, though Chicano, speak English as their mother tongue. "Language has not been super-problematic over the last fifteen years. What is problematic is writing skills." (Of course, a major reason why writing skills have declined is that students, instead of learning to develop and articulate their own ideas, are taught to parrot ideology.)

I ask him about Acuña. "I criticized him when I was in college—my peers were shocked—because he said that we needed to form alliances with other minority communities. Acuña thought our numbers would increase and we'd all be leftist activists together. I was always someone who believed in broader activism, though as a youth Aztlán was a powerful image to motivate me and my generation. We hoped that [an independent Aztlán] would occur in the future, but it was obviously Utopian, idealistic." So the dream of Aztlán is dead? "Today it's ..." He pauses. "I don't even hear the term anymore myself, but I situate it in the historical moment of the 1960s and '70s, as a motivating factor for that generation."

Edén Torres also waxes nostalgic. She's an older woman, amply built—a Mother Earth type with the long white hair of an aging sixties rebel and a constant, if rather inscrutable, smile. She's very light skinned—you'd never guess in a million years that she identifies herself as a Chicana—and her personality (or at least her present mood) is one of steely good humor: on this day and at this place, anyway, she combines a wry, lively demeanor with (as one discovers soon enough) a tough-as-nails ideological rigidity and, yes, a skillfully suppressed anger. Author of one book, *Chicana Without Apology/Chicana sin vergüenza: The New Chicana Cultural Studies* (Routledge, 2003) and an associate editor of *Aztlán*, she's an example of the ever-widening phenomenon of studies crossover: at the University of Minnesota, she's both an associate professor in the Department of Gender, Women and Sexuality Studies and the chair of the Department of Chicano Studies, and has also taught American Studies. It doesn't take long to realize that she knows exactly what she thinks and has known it for a long time. It's also clear that she has a sense of absolute security and authority in academic settings and is used to being taken seriously in them.

Today, the setting in question is a session at the 2010 annual NACCS convention in Seattle, and Torres is here to air a complaint. Her youth, she recalls, was dominated by a "rage-filled aesthetic." When she was young, politically active Chicanos like herself dreamed of Aztlán. But her Chicano students today? Nope. For many young Chicanos nowadays, Chicano identity just doesn't mean what it did to her. They're apolitical. They don't see themselves as "different." They don't aspire to secede from the United States. They're "complicit in dominant formations"—which means that they consider themselves members of mainstream American society and buy into its values.

Nor are they interested, she tells us, in hearing about institutional oppression. They embrace "mainstream narratives" of their people and are taught—not by her, but by others—to identify with the goals set for them by Anglo society. They want economic success! More and more of them are "middle-class students who are no longer the first in their family to attend college"—and are thus disturbingly aloof from the issues raised by the revolutionary texts they read in her classes. Worst of all, they don't feel oppressed—they don't feel despair. This plainly infuriates—and baffles—her. How is it that diversity and multiculturalism have produced a generation of young Latinos who affirm their cultural identity, yet who "remain so politically naïve" that they embrace oppression, imperialism, and colonialism? Many of them have parents who have told them race no longer matters; many have grown up in diverse, affluent communities. In short, the American dream has come true for them—and *she can't stand it*.

Not that she puts it quite this way herself. As far as she's concerned, the American dream was, and is, an illusion. Latinos—even young, successful, fully integrated Latinos—remain oppressed, whether they realize it or not. The problem, she explains, is that they simply don't recognize "Western cultural imperialism" when they see it. She tells us about one of her Latino students who lamented—yes, lamented—that he'd never experienced racism. She makes it clear that she finds this preposterous: of *course* he'd experienced racism; he just hadn't recognized it as such. What that student didn't realize is that you don't need to be called a "spic" or "wetback" to be a victim of racism; no, racism takes a variety of forms, and what's so tricky about the forms it takes nowadays—and in identity studies today this is a truism, a mantra, a creed—is that those forms have grown ever more subtle and subcutaneous, ever more unconscious and unarticulated.

It's all about *hegemony*. And if hegemony is the problem, Chicano Studies—which Francisco H. Vásquez describes in *Latino/a Thought* as "an anti-hegemonic, liberation movement"—is the antidote. In Torres's eyes, the pathetic fact about the life of that Latino student of hers is that thanks to American hegemony he'd experienced racism—institutional racism, systematic racism—every day since he was born, and hadn't even been aware of it! Like the Jim Carrey character in *The Truman Show*, he'd spent his entire existence in a world of illusions, trapped in the oppressor's web, and had been lured by that oppressor into embracing a false image of himself and of the hegemonic empire, which he had foolishly believed to be a free country and of which he had so misguidedly considered himself a full and equal citizen.

For Torres, it's a disgrace. Young people today are permitted by mainstream American society to be Latino—but only if they accept middle-class values. "Perhaps," she admits, "I'm a political dinosaur who wants to retain a difference...a brownness." (This last bit sounds unintentionally funny, considering how pale she is.) For unless we cling to our non-Anglo self-image, she insists, we're doing the capitalists' work.

*   *   *

Among those who share Torres's ire at young Chicanos today who fail to recognize themselves as oppressed is Rodolfo Acuña, the aforementioned paterfamilias of Chicano Studies at Cal State Northridge and author of the definitive Chicano Studies textbook, *Occupied America: A History of Chicanos*. First published in 1972, the book—now in its seventh edition—has shaped the thinking of Chicano Studies students ever since the birth of the discipline, and the changes it's undergone over the years have both reflected and influenced the changes in Chicano Studies itself.

In his preface to the seventh edition, Acuña explains that when he first wrote the book he simply "wanted to get the historical narrative down for the purpose of supporting a political argument." Since then, however, various developments have required adjustments in the text. The most important change, as we've seen, is that the late 1960s generation of Chicano students who raged at oppression and agitated for Chicano Studies programs—thus making *Occupied America* possible—has been succeeded by a generation or two of Chicano students who, quite simply, aren't particularly upset. "About the mid-1990s," writes Acuña, "I realized that the story [of Chicano history], which was so personal to me, was not as clear to the students and working-class people of that generation. Their life experience differed from my own."

How? Acuña's answer is essentially identical to Torres's: "Racism is today not as easily defined, and the illusion of the American Dream has gripped many younger Mexican Americans; in some cases it blurs the civil rights struggles of the Mexican American and Chicano generations." In other words, too many young Chicanos nowadays aren't focusing on grievances but on getting an education and making a living. Which, for Acuña as for Torres, is an alarming development, because it represents the erosion of the very victim mentality on which Chicano Studies is built. Acuña complains that today's young Chicanos don't appreciate their forebears' sacrifices, that they're embracing alternative labels such as "Latino" and "Hispanic," and that they've "chosen to be part of the illusion that they are equal partners in the great society."

How dare they not see themselves as perpetual victims! They may *think* they're full members of American society, but Acuña—like Torres—knows better, and he's determined to open their eyes and replace their complacency and ambition with bitterness, resentment, and a full-blown entitlement mentality. Above all, he's out to quash their individuality and draw them back into the herd, reminding them that they're members of a *group*—and heirs to a magnificent cultural legacy that the Europeans destroyed. In order to put across this last point, Acuña romanticizes the "great civilizations" that the Spanish explorers found in the New World. This is standard Chicano Studies practice: the Aztecs and other pre-Columbian civilizations are routinely depicted as having been highly developed and essentially peaceful—and are routinely contrasted with their European conquerors, who are almost consistently portrayed as ignorant and bloodthirsty.

Moreover, while praising the vanquished New World civilizations' "sophisticated culture" (Acuña boasts that "their mathematical discoveries were a thousand years ahead of European[s']" and that their "cosmological understandings were in advance of those of other civilizations"), Chicano Studies practitioners routinely gloss over the more ticklish historical details. When Acuña complains that "some choose to dwell on the bizarre practices such as human sacrifice" that were an essential feature of these "great civilizations," he is surely not referring to any major players in Chicano Studies, for virtually all of them have followed Acuña's lead by *not* dwelling on such matters—even as they focus unremittingly on every horrible detail that they can find of Anglo abuse of the descendants of Aztecs and Mayans.

Never mind that the Mayans routinely sacrificed children when dedicating temples. (A Mayan mass grave of sacrificed children was excavated as recently as 2005.) Never mind that the Aztecs appeased the fire god, Huehueteotl, by burning live captives and tearing out their hearts, and paid tribute to the god Tláloc by burning children to death. (Archaeologists have discovered mass graves of both Aztec and Toltec children—the latter of whom had been decapitated.) And never mind that nearly every important event on the Inca calendar appears to have called for the murder of children—and not just any children, but those who were the healthiest, most well formed, and most beautiful, the better to please the gods. You'd never know any of this by reading Acuña or by perusing most Chicano Studies texts, which seek almost universally to cultivate in students a sentimental view of these ancient civilizations—and a concomitant notion of Europeans as inherently more brutal than the Aztecs, Mayans, or Incas. Still, the Spanish aren't the number-one enemy in Chicano Studies. While students are expected to learn to resent Spain for having conquered the Aztec, Mayan, and Inca paradises, it's far more important for them to despise Anglos for having taken over so much of Mexico after its independence from Spain. This explains why Acuña's preface is followed by a two-page map depicting Mexico in 1821. The map's size can't be accounted for by abundance of detail—on the contrary, only one city, Mexico City, is marked. No, it's an unusually spare map, and its purpose is clear: to dramatically impress upon students just how much of the present-day United States was once part of Mexico. (It's followed by another two-page map showing "Cradles of Civilization" around the world, and here again the point is obvious: three to four thousand years ago, there was no "civilization" in Europe or the present-day United States, but there *were* "civilizations" in the places that are now southern Mexico, Central America, and western South America.)

Another aspect of Acuña's book that's typical of Chicano Studies is his thoroughly one-sided characterization of U.S.-Mexico relations. America is portrayed consistently as racist, aggressive, corrupt, and violent, and Mexico (with very rare exceptions, such as when Acuña criticizes the dictatorship of Porfirio Díaz) as a helpless, virtuous victim. In his retelling, "Euro-Americans"—to use his term of choice for descendants of English settlers—are cast almost exclusively as squatters, cattle rustlers, vigilantes, members of lynch mobs, and so forth. For Acuña, America's acquisition of territory won in the Mexican War, gained through the admission of Texas to the Union, and bought in the Gadsden Purchase was "theft," pure and simple—and if not for this colossal transgression, he argues, Mexico would have been a far richer country, owing to the oil deposits and arable land it lost to Uncle Sam. (His assumption, of course, is that Mexicans would have developed California and Texas as energetically and imaginatively as "Euro-Americans" have done.) At one point Acuña acknowledges that "[l]ike [sic] all history, there are two sides to the story"; but almost without exception, his sympathy is entirely with Mexicans and Chicanos, and his book reads like an anthology of the worst things ever done to and said about Mexicans by "Euro-Americans"—a term that, in his hands, comes off as little more than a slur.

While Acuña is quick, moreover, to leap on any statement that might remotely be construed as reflecting anti-Chicano prejudice, he doesn't hesitate to defend even the most violent anti-white language. For example, he writes about a 1969 press conference at which José Angel Gutiérrez of the Mexican American Youth Organization (MAYO) "called upon Chicanos to 'Kill the gringo.'" Acuña assures the reader that what Gutiérrez meant by this was "that the white rule of Mexicans should end." Indeed, instead of criticizing Gutiérrez, Acuña attacks Representative Henry B. González of Texas, who replied to Gutiérrez's explicit incitement to violence by calling for a grand jury investigation of MAYO. Acuña characterizes this action as an "attack" on Gutiérrez; his clear message is that González, not Gutiérrez, was the troublemaker. It's typical of Chicano Studies that it holds up people like Gutiérrez, rather than people like González (a Mexican American who served in the House of Representatives for nearly four decades), as role models.

*　　*　　*

One thing the reader of *Occupied America* will notice very quickly is the preoccupation with labels. "Throughout the book," Acuña writes in his preface, "I use the terms *U.S. Mexican, Mexican American, Chicano*, and occasionally—toward the end of the book—*Latino*. The use of the term *Chicana/o* recognizes the Chicana struggle for gender equality within the group." He goes on to explain that the intermarriage of people with different national backgrounds has made labeling problematic, but argues that "caution must be exercised in concluding that we are Latinos or Hispanics to the exclusion of Chicana/o or Mexican American" and that "it is also important for other groups such as the Salvadoran and Guatemalan to evolve their own identities."

Such tireless attention to labels is so common in Chicano Studies that it can sometimes seem as if the whole discipline consists of nothing *but* discussions about labels. In *Latino/a Thought*, Francisco H. Vásquez notes the proliferation within Latino culture of "names that refer to how dark the skin may be (*güero/a, trigueño/a, moreno/a, prietola, negro/a*) or to hair texture (*pelo liso* or *pelo quebrado*)—straight or wavy hair)" and goes on for a couple of pages about these distinctions and the intragroup prejudices that have resulted from them. (One often gets the impression that there's a never-ending contest under way as to which sub-sub-sub-group is *most* discriminated against.) Similarly, at the beginning of "*This Land Was Mexican Once*": *Histories of Resistance from Northern California* (2007), Linda Heidenreich discusses at length the labels she's chosen to use for different groups and subgroups: "Those immigrants who arrived under Spanish rule, I call simply 'Spanish'/ or 'Spanish colonizers.'...I call those arriving or living in California after 1821 'settler-colonizers.'... For those colonizers and settlers who were raised in California, I also use the term by which they identified themselves, *Californianas/os*.... I refer to Californios and Mexican immigrants collectively as 'Chicanas/os.'" She devotes more than a page to all this, explaining in detail why she's chosen to refer to "the dominant population" as "Euro-American."

Groups, subgroups, and the names for them: the centrality of these matters to Chicano Studies becomes crystal clear at an

NACCS conference session titled "NACCS for Beginners," which is intended to introduce newbies to the basic facts about the organization. It's an April day in 2010, and people are still standing around chatting when a bright-eyed, energetic young woman steps up to the podium and identifies herself as Cynthia Durate, secretary of "knocks." (It takes me a few seconds to realize that that is the way you're supposed to pronounce NACCS.) Durate serves up a Power-Point presentation about the highlights of NACCS history. Most of the highlights are name changes. Founded in 1972 as the National Caucus of Chicano Social Scientists (NCCSS), the organization became the National Association of Chicano Studies (NACS) in 1988. Later years saw the introduction of the Chicana Caucus and the Lesbian and Gay Caucuses; the latter two subsequently changed their names to the Lesbian, Bimujeres, and Trans Caucus and the Joto Caucus (*joto* is a traditionally derogatory Mexican term for an effeminate, "passive" partner in gay male sex). In 1995, to show more sensitivity to its female members, the NACS changed its name to the National Association of Chicana and Chicano Studies (though sometimes one sees it written with "Chicano" first and "Chicana" second).

All this attention to name changes might seem a bit puzzling: surely the NACCS must have racked up a few, you know, actual *achievements* during its nearly forty-year history? True, all of these identity studies can seem to be about nothing more or less than the proper naming of identity groups; still, perhaps none is more fixated on this subject than Chicano Studies. For one thing, as the name of the NACCS indicates, it's no longer appropriate to call it just Chicano Studies. No, you're supposed to call it (a) Chicana and Chicano Studies, (b) Chicana/o Studies, or (c) Chican@ Studies, where the "@" is understood to be a combination of "a" and "o."

Chicano Studies may profess to reject Anglo-European culture and thought, but its ideology, like that of every other brand of identity studies, owes a great deal to at least one Anglo-European intellectual tradition—namely, Marxism. Early in *Occupied America*,

Acuña informs us that his account of Chicanos "is inspired by the British historian E. P. Thompson"—a leading member of the British Communist Party. Among the few other non-Chicano historians whom he quotes with admiration is E. J. Hobsbawm, also a communist. Consistently, Acuña portrays capitalism as a destructive force. Indeed, his use of political labels makes it clear that for him, pretty much any group that isn't outright communist is "far-right" or "ultra-conservative." Acuña compares the Texas Rangers (the state police, not the baseball team) to the Gestapo; he compares the treatment of Mexican Americans during World War II to the treatment of Jews under the Nazis; he puts the words "free world" in scare quotes; and he cites a speech by Fidel Castro with emphatic sympathy, depicting Castro as the savior of the Cuban people from U.S. capitalist hegemony (or, as he puts it, as "the symbol of Latin America's anticolonial struggle with the United States") and an inspiration to all Latin Americans who seek to resist that hegemony. "That [Castro] had overthrown a dictator put in power by the United States during the 1930s," maintains Acuña, "was not lost on Latin America." There's no hint whatsoever that Castro himself is a dictator; his manifold violations of human rights and individual liberties go unmentioned. A student would never know from Acuña that not all Latin Americans—and not all Cubans—revere Castro (whose image actually appears on both the front and back covers of the fifth edition of *Occupied America*), and would certainly never get the foggiest idea from Acuña's book of what it really means to live under a communist regime. Of course, if Acuña provided his young readers with even a thumbnail portrait of life under totalitarian communism, it would put all of his horror stories about the United States into their proper perspective—and that's hardly what Acuña is out to achieve here.

Quite the contrary: when Acuña gets around to recounting the history of Chicanos during the early Cold War years, he sneers in familiar left-wing fashion about the "red scare" and "Red hunters," writing about communism as if it were no real threat, accusing anticommunists of "paranoia" and referring to "the so-called Communist expansion." He mocks "the Euro-American belief of [*sic*] a monolithic, worldwide conspiracy directed from Moscow" (as if there *hadn't* actually been a monolithic, worldwide conspiracy directed from Moscow). He praises a group called the American Committee for Protection of Foreign-Born (1933–82), but instead of acknowledging that it was a communist front organization founded—and funded—by the American Communist Party, he puts it this way: "Superpatriots labeled the ACPFB a Communist-led organization...." And once his narrative brings us into the 1960s, the text becomes a blizzard of acronyms, most of them the names of Mexican American activist organizations: AWOC, CSO, NFWA, UFWOC, PASO, MAYO, UFW, LULAC, MASO, MASA, MAYA, MAPA, AMEA, UMAS, LRUP, WGP, CCHE, MEChA, CPLR, PADRES, MALDEF, CRLA, CMAU, CLF. It's a useful reminder that this isn't an objective history of a people but a propagandistic account of a political movement. Acuña fills page after page with capsule biographies of political activists—the obvious implication being that these are the principal figures worth knowing about in Chicano history. There's no mention of such accomplished Mexican-Americans as *Peanuts* animator Bill Melendez, novelist John Rechy, dancer and choreographer Jose Limón, Nobel Prize chemist Mario J. Molina, singers Vikki Carr and Ritchie Valens, and actors Anthony Quinn, Dolores del Rio, Gilbert Roland, Ricardo Montalbán, Eva Longoria, Salma Hayek, Edward Furlong, and Jessica Alba—not to mention innumerable famous athletes and several astronauts. But of course the success of such people in American society challenges the very premise of Chicano Studies.

Eventually (in chapter 14), and rather indirectly, Acuña does acknowledge that not all Chicanos share his own politics, noting that according to a 1983 *Los Angeles Times* poll most of them actually prefer to be called Mexican, Mexican American, Latino, or Hispanic. But to Acuña this choice, freely made, is not just an innocent matter of individual preference, but the consequence of sinister "conservative" efforts to destroy the entire Chicano rights project. And as he moves into the 1970s, Acuña takes the opportunity to praise such groups as the Socialist Workers Party, the Mexican Communist Party, and a Maoist faction called the ATM (short for August 29th Movement) for "raising the consciousness of students" and "enhancing the political consciousness of Chicano students."

Acuña's book is largely about poverty, and taken for granted throughout is the proposition that Great Society-style programs, by definition, benefit the poor. There's nothing remotely resembling an objective examination of this issue, and those with sincere alternative views are consistently treated as duplicitous apologists for heartless capitalism. But when it comes to economics, there's an amusing twist: after having complained for hundreds of pages about Chicano poverty—which, naturally, he blames entirely on "Euro-American" exploitation—Acuña suddenly does a turnaround, griping about the increasing prosperity of Chicanos since the 1960s, a development that, in his view, has made them more complacent and less radical. As he puts it, while the "growth of the Chicano middle class…gave Chicanos more of a voice in government and society," it also led "middle-class Chicanos" to acquire "social and economic interests differing from those of the working class" and caused them to be "coopted by the mainstream, making them agents of social control, intermediary gatekeepers, power brokers, or influence peddlers between the Chicano community and the ruling class."

What's intriguing here is that Acuña is all but admitting that the problem isn't—as many practitioners of Chicano Studies claim—that the American dream is a "lie," but rather that it's a dream that *does* come true and that, once fulfilled, poses a threat to radical Chicano politics (and to the empire that Acuña and others have built on those politics). The ugly truth, from Acuña's point of view, is that Chicanos who have attained material comfort thanks to the capitalist system don't *want* to overthrow it. For Acuña, one particularly unpleasant fact is that, in recent years, the Latino vote has grown increasingly Republican, owing to Latinos' deep-seated religious and cultural conservatism. Acuña plainly doesn't feel comfortable addressing this reality, because it challenges his compulsion to identify Chicanos and their culture with "progressive" ideals—and to depict them as victims of conservatives, not as conservatives themselves. A similar situation arises in connection with the case of Puerto Rico, which he describes as a victim of continued (and, it goes without saying, oppressive) U.S. "colonialism," saying that some Puerto Ricans want their island "to become a state" while others support independence; what he avoids mentioning is that Puerto Ricans have voted consistently in referenda for the retention of their oppressive "colonialism"—otherwise known as commonwealth status—which affords them ample benefits without subjecting them to federal taxes.

Needless to say, Acuña deplores integration—the idea, as he puts it, that Mexican Americans "will go the way of Italian Americans"—because it means accepting "white male" and "capitalist" norms. He describes those who try to prevent illegal immigration as "racist nativists" whose motive is "to keep America White" (even though immigration controls are supported by millions of nonwhite Americans, including millions of Latino Americans). And in his epilogue he celebrates "[t]he beauty of the term *Chicano*," which "defined and continues to define purposes" by "acknowledging] a history of oppression...." Or, as Eden Torres puts it at the NACCS convention, a Chicano "is a Mexican American with a non-American image of himself!" One of the purposes of American higher education, one should think, is to help young citizens to understand, respect, and build upon the values on which their nation is founded; Chicano Studies was born in—and, to this day, continues to inculcate—opposition to such thinking.

If Acuña's book is the standard Chicano Studies textbook, Soldatenko's *Chicano Studies: The Genesis of a Discipline* (2009) seems well on its way to being regarded as the standard history of the discipline's development up to 1982. The book, I discover at the Seattle conference, is even the subject of its own session. Soldatenko, the star of the panel, proves to be a gregarious, down-to-earth type with a ready laugh who reminds me a bit of a middle-aged Ernest Borgnine. The presentations and subsequent comments by audience members make it clear that nobody present has any serious quarrel with Soldatenko's account of what Chicano Studies has been; but there's lively discussion of the question of what Chicano Studies *should* be. The room is packed (mostly with men), the conversation lively, the air charged with testosterone. (It occurs to me later that at this conference, with its abundance of gay, lesbian, and feminist panels, this was, in effect, a straight-guy session.) Many of the attendees are plainly eager to speak their minds. One suggests that Chicano Studies needs to "stop navel-gazing and come back to something more real"; another insists that "good research doesn't necessarily lead to greater justice"; somebody complains that "the whole function of American education is to protect American exceptionalism" and that "Chicano Studies reified American exceptionalism in its doctrines." Participants raise questions: Can we use science to get at "the answers"? Is the "cultural turn" problematic? What about the connections between Chicano Studies—and Chicano activism—and revolutions in Africa, Latin America, and (of course) Cuba? After a man in the audience tells us that "at Berkeley they wanted Third World Studies, not Ethnic Studies," there's a lively exchange about whether there's a need for new disciplines with names like Power Studies and Sociogenic Studies. Soldatenko beams broadly through it all, plainly enjoying the give-and-take, and even tosses out the occasional joke, as when he playfully insults one of his fellow panelists by suggesting that he's a mere "liberal" rather than a Marxist. (In these precincts—as at a GOP convention—*liberal* is a dirty word, though for rather different reasons.) Everyone seems sincerely engaged; if you watched this session with the sound turned off, you'd think you were witnessing an urgent, substantial debate about matters of the first importance.

One subject that doesn't come up—although there's an ample amount of it on display in Soldatenko's book—is anti-Anglo racism. For example, Soldatenko quotes a remark by a Chicano journalist deploring Chicano Studies' dependence on the Ford Foundation's "private gringo bureaucracy." He sums up an article by a member of the Brown Berets, "a Chicano(a) nationalist youth group," who argued that "Anglo values are the product of the capitalist system—a system that removes humanity" so that "for the Anglo, everything is reduced to a contest, while for Chicanos, it is family, memory, and ultimately humanity." At no point in the book does Soldatenko even hint that he finds any of this hate rhetoric offensive—and at no point in the session devoted to his book does any of the eager participants bring up the topic.

Nor is there any mention of another aspect of Chicano culture that's clearly alive and well—namely, the fierce hostility to gay people (and especially to gay men) that still reigns (especially among heterosexual men) in Mexican-American communities. In order to get a sense of how this ticklish topic is dealt with in these precincts, I find my way to a session bearing the bemusing title "Toxicity within the Body of Chicano Studies? Exploring Our Queer Bodies and the Toxic within Our Sacred Sites." Pablo Alvarez of Cal State Northridge reads a paper consisting mostly of detailed plot summaries and very long quotations from the oeuvre of Gil Cuadros (the gay Chicano author, I learn, of a 1994 short-story collection titled *City of God*), plus occasional comments by Alvarez in which he essentially keeps repeating the same observation, namely that in Cuadros's work "the sacred emerges from a toxic body and a toxic society." His continual restatement of this point does not serve to make it any more comprehensible. Alvarez characterizes the auto-biographical protagonist of Cuadros's stories as "living with AIDS on the battlefield of Aztlán" (Cuadros died of AIDS in 1996 at age thirty-four), thus turning Aztlán into "AZT-land." (This kind of wordplay, of course, is omnipresent in the humanities and social sciences today.) The word *toxicity* recurs frequently in Alvarez's paper, only he pronounces it "toxidity."

Alvarez is followed by a bald, stocky Northridge colleague, Omar González, who begins by dedicating his paper to "two queer men of color" who were murdered the previous November for being gay. González contrasts the media silence about their deaths to the attention accorded the Matthew Shepard case. "There will be no made-for-TV movies about them," González says bitterly. Alvarez tells us he's a "gay Chicano living with AIDS" and quotes a colleague's observation that "the lack of attention to AIDS in Area Studies is striking." Mentioning two Chicano authors who died of AIDS, he gripes that their deaths will lead to "no movement within Chicano Studies": "Why change the curriculum for two dead faggots?" All of which leads him to ask: how do we eliminate "the toxic stigma" surrounding gay Chicanos? He tells us about groups (such as NARTH and PFOX) that claim to "cure" gays; about bogus treatments (once "aversion therapy," now "reparative therapy") for homosexuality; about a Chicano father who took his gay son to a therapist for a "cure," only to be told that the boy was just fine as he was. All this sort of thing is old news, of course, especially to gay people (and the audience, it seems to me, is 100 percent gay, or close to it), but Alvarez serves up his material as if he's boldly pulling back a curtain on earthshaking revelations. He worries aloud about the possibility of "preemptive genocide" of gay people in case a gay gene is isolated; I'm reminded of a disabled man at the Cultural Studies conference in Berkeley who was similarly concerned that selective abortion would result in the "genocide" of disabled people. (It's striking that these academics, who are forbidden by their professions' ideology to oppose abortion because it kills *individuals*, are permitted to worry about abortion as a threat to certain *groups*.)

For the most part, however, Alvarez's paper is not an argument but a narrative—an intense, stunningly personal *précis* of his own life, from being told by his confirmation class teacher that he would go to hell for being gay, to being thrown out of the house by his mother, to countless acts of unprotected sex that were his way of acting out and/or smothering his own rage. He makes generous use of religious language, characterizing his sex partners, for example, as "supplicants," and wondering aloud how many of the gay men he sees in Los Angeles bars "may be sacrificed at the altar of the AIDS epidemic." And he recounts at uncomfortable length a bizarre imaginary scenario in which his mother throws herself on his, Alvarez's, coffin in feigned agony. "I no longer fear *la muerte*," he says. "*La muerte* lives within me."

Heavy stuff. But Alvarez closes on an "up" note, telling us that he finally discovered an antidote to his rage. Where? In Chicano Studies! Though he felt isolated from both the Chicano and the gay communities because of their attitudes toward HIV-positive people, he's found a home—a refuge—in the Chicano Studies Department at Northridge. Chicano Studies, he has learned, can educate and empower; it can be a site for mentorship; it provides a "safe space" for "intergenerational queer support," where he can play "fairy godfather," helping younger gay people to develop healthy pride in their "*joteria*" (queerness). Summing up his paper, Alvarez claims that his purpose has been to "challeng[e] a heteronormative paradigm." This sudden injection of postmodern jargon into a piece of personal confession is disconcerting, for Alvarez's text isn't an academic paper but a salvation narrative: he once was lost, but now is found; was blind, but now can see.

Third and last up is Gibran Guido, a slim, handsome young man from San Diego State University. Guido also has experiences to recount. He works, he tells us, as an HIV test counselor. He talks about AIDS as a stigma and about AIDS stereotypes; he notes that HIV doesn't just attack gays; and he complains that AIDS continues to be overlooked by "our" community (that is, Chicanos). This is all, of course, terribly serious but, again, exceedingly familiar material: nothing that Guido has to say had not already been said a million times before he was born. After telling us a genuinely distressing anecdote about the first time he had to tell a client that he was HIV-positive, Guido serves up a series of sentences in which the key words of the session title, *toxic* and *sacred*, recur frequently. We must, he insists, "find the sacred in ourselves, each other, and *our cultura.*" He speaks of "trying to find the *sacred* within these sites of toxicity" and of "nurturing ourselves and realizing that we are connected to each other." He notes that personal stories, whether written or oral, have "proven to create community and acknowledge our connection to one another." He laments the current "toxicity of silence" and observes that "toxicity comes not only in the form of *violence* but in the form of *prejudice.*" Again, this is all quite touching personally—even if the overwrought rhetoric about toxicity and the sacred is more than a little baffling.

To his credit, and to my surprise, Guido actually challenges the political views that dominate Chicano Studies—specifically, the virtually universal affection for Castro and his revolution. Citing with approval Reinaldo Arenas, the gay Cuban author who died of AIDS and whose autobiography *Before Night Falls* is a powerful indictment of Castro's regime, Guido notes the widespread affection in Chicano Studies for the Cuban Revolution, then asks: "But revolution for whom?" He reminds the audience of Castro's concentration camps for gays. I must admit I'm impressed by this blatant violation of an unwritten Chicano Studies rule: thou shalt not speak ill of Fidel. But soon enough, alas, Guido reverts to type, complaining that "the [Anglo] enemy insists on dividing people into distinct groups"—an odd accusation, given that we're at the annual meeting of an association that prides itself on its division into groups, with straight men caucusing over here, straight women over there, gays here, lesbians there, and so forth. Approaching the end of his talk, Guido strikes a bemusing note: after all that has been said at this session about the traditional hostility of Chicano culture toward homosexuality and about what Guido himself has described as gay Chicanos' "ostracization from our own community," he calls for "us"—gay Chicanos—to "return to our cultural tradition" because "that [Chicano] culture can heal us." How? He doesn't say. By way of conclusion, he reminds us that "we all [on the panel] have a narrative" and that "our silence will not protect us."

Breaking the silence; telling your story: for many academics who have ridden to career success on the wave of identity studies, this is where it all begins and ends—with autobiography, whether one's own (as in the cases of Guido and Gonzalez) or someone else's (as in the case of Alvarez's paper on Gil Cuadros). For all the Marxist revolutionary slogans, Catholic spiritual imagery, and self-help and social work rhetoric, the real subject throughout was personal pain, personal confession, personal grievance; and the common theme was the indifference of mainstream American and/or Chicano society to the pain experienced by gay Chicanos, especially those with HIV. I feel immense sympathy for all these men, but I must add that, as a gay writer who lived in New York during the first two decades of the AIDS crisis, I've been reading and hearing stories like these for more than half my life now. That such material is apparently considered groundbreaking here at the NACCS seems to me only to underscore just how backward the Chicano "community" still is in regard to homosexuality and AIDS.

Indeed, what is ultimately most lamentable about the session is that although the participants acknowledge the prejudice against gays and AIDS sufferers that reigns in Chicano communities, their awareness of this prejudice doesn't translate into a greater regard for "Anglo" civilization and values (not to mention "Anglo" medicine), or into a rethinking of the question of who really *is* the "oppressor," at least when you're a gay Chicano with AIDS. On the contrary, these young men seem desperate to reconcile their

HIV status and sexual orientation with their Chicano heritage, desperate to locate a "place"—psychologically, spiritually, ideologically, geographically—where they can be their authentic individual selves while remaining true to their "people," their "culture," their group. Yet they appear to have gone to heroic efforts to resist recognizing that their only hope for the kind of wholeness they seek lies in the culture of the dreaded "Anglo," the alleged "oppressor"—a culture that has provided them with the very terms by which they define themselves sexually and with institutions and communities in which they've found safe harbor.

Look, for example, at Omar Gonzalez: he's been through so much, and yet his years of pondering his experience have resulted in nothing more than a barrage of highly emotional personal testimony (plus a touch of magic-realist fantasy in the form of the image of his mother throwing herself on his coffin). Indeed, it would seem that the whole point of telling one's story, in this setting, is not to follow it to its logical conclusion—not to *learn something from it*—but rather to strive to bring it into some appearance of harmony with at least certain aspects of Chicano Studies ideology. Especially for *jotos*, I reflect as I leave the conference room, the challenge at the heart of Chicano Studies is this: how can you honestly attack capitalist Anglo society as "heteronormative" when you yourself hail from—and are professionally compelled to celebrate—a culture notorious for primitive macho posturing, strict gender roles, and patriarchal family structures? And how can you claim that a return to that culture will be "healing" for gays?

After hearing and reading so much about Chicana feminism, I'm curious to see in person what it looks like these days. It's Saturday morning in Seattle, and the session is titled "Dancers, Mothers, and Grandmothers: Expression and Performance as Knowledge Production"—and it proves to be an ideal introduction not only to Chicana Studies today but to the sort of activities that Soldatenko is talking about when he describes Chicano Studies as having taken a "cultural turn."

All three speakers are female graduate students—Chicana Studies' future. First Jennie Luna of the University of California, Davis, reads part of her dissertation. It's about Señora Cobb, aka Mama Cobb, whom Luna describes as an "elder," "healer," "dancer," "teacher," "actress," "mother," "midwife," and "community resource," among many other things. She is apparently quite celebrated in certain circles, and is particularly famous, it seems, for having "transformed *danza*," a centuries-old genre of native dance in Hispanic America that both she and Luna appear to regard as a potential alternative (because it's both pre-European and nonpatriarchal) to the European male traditions associated with the Catholic Church. Born in 1932, Cobb became known as the "rainbow woman of the earth," says Luna, because she is supposed to have emerged from her mother's womb, the last-born of a set of triplets, and dropped to the ground just as a rainbow appeared in the wake of a storm. She went on to have nineteen children. Luna first encountered Cobb when the former was a high school student and the latter was a keynote speaker at an event encouraging "Raza youth" to get an education. Cobb spoke in her native tongue—the Aztec language, Nahuatl—and her presentation had a powerful impact on Luna. Later, when Luna became, as she puts it, "a college student and activist," Cobb spoke at events she organized. Luna also accompanied Cobb on "pilgrimages" to "sacred sites."

Luna mentions the concept of *palabra*. *Palabra* means "word," but more profoundly it designates a "sacred concept" that's "synonymous with responsibility and commitment," with "put[ting] one's integrity on the line." It's associated with the very "breath of life"—for "one's word is one's life." What does all this have to do with Señora Cobb? Well, according to Luna, some people say that if you don't come from the tradition of *danza* with which Cobb is associated, "you don't have *palabra*." For Luna, Cobb is a vital figure because she's helped to preserve the "indigenous tradition of sacred dance," which "has survived genocide [and] colonization"; Cobb's work constitutes a "reclamation" of the Chicano (and especially Chicana) past, supplies "an inclusive space for all who identify with Nahuatl," and provides an accessible starting point for young Chicanas who wish to make a connection with their own cultural history—for, as

Luna puts it, "knowledge of our past is the strongest tool we have against colonialism." She says she spent two years interviewing Cobb for this project, and informs us that Cobb, because of her devotion to the oral tradition, wouldn't let her use a tape recorder, telling her instead to "use your mind."

Luna serves up a grab bag of other details about Cobb, from whom she claims to have "gained a wealth of knowledge": Cobb once kicked customers out of a store so she could perform a blessing ceremony for the merchant's sick father; she makes *trajes* (dresses or suits); some people call her *loca* (crazy); at ceremonies she's been known to "call people out for wearing the inappropriate *traje*"; she worked for several years as a bounty hunter. Luna loads us up with information about Cobb—but doesn't explain successfully why any of it should matter to us and be seen as having a larger meaning. But within the context of Chicana Studies, the point is clear: Cobb personifies female, pre-European traditions (good) and symbolizes liberation from European colonialism and Catholic patriarchy (bad). Luna wants to redefine "tradition": in Mexico, she says, the word implies a connection to Catholicism, whereas when Cobb and Luna speak of tradition, they mean *la danza*. "It's important to document our stories and listen to our elders," concludes Luna, her words almost identical to those with which Gibran Guido ended his presentation at the *joto* session.

Next up is Eve Delfin of the University of California, Merced, who examines "the spirituality of *folklórico*"—that is, *baile folklórico*, or folkloric dance—in a "hegemonic society." *Baile folklórico* is an umbrella term for traditional Latin American folk dances that contain elements of ballet. Delfin maintains that "*folklórico* uses spirituality that affirms the importance of dance in our society," and she underscores the difference between *danzas* (which are purely native) and *bailes* (which betray European influences). The members of the "*folklórico* community," she explains, have various ideas and philosophies about exactly what it is that they do, and have regionally distinctive outfits, movements, and even politics. In the 1960s, she informs us, Chicanos made use of *folklórico* to come together, pitting "spirit, community, identity, belonging, imagination…against hegemony"; they became interested in *folklórico* in an effort "to find a spiritual link to their ancestors" in the face of a "hegemony that seeks to erase this link."

Delfin extols the "essentially spiritual nature" of dance; acknowledges the syncretism that brought Spanish influences to bear on native dance; recalls the way in which *folklórico* was used as "a nationalizing tool" after the Mexican Revolution, but also as "a form of resistance by indigenous people" and as a means of "repairing] breaks that result from hegemonic social structures in the United States." Aside from *baile* and *folklórico*, clearly, the key word here is *hegemony*. But Delfin seems far less interested in politics than in spirituality—for her, *baile folklórico* "gives people a sense of unity, of community, in which performers transcend time and space" and forges for the dancers a "connection to one another, to their *familia*, and to their ancestors." "We are inherently spiritual beings," she proclaims, asserting that dance provides "affirmation, a spirit of unity."

Last up is Larissa Mercado-Lopez of the University of Texas at San Antonio. A graduate student in English who also teaches Women's Studies, she's written a paper titled "Phenomenologies of Mestiza Maternity: Reading Transcorporeal Bodies as Sites of Knowledge Production." If Luna's and Delfin's papers were perhaps insufficiently jargon-ridden, Mercado-Lopez makes up for that deficiency and then some. In her work, she tells us, she is "theorizing [about] maternal bodies" and seeking "to identity the discursive intersections where I can locate and theorize about the maternal subject"; she's concerned about the "rhetorical warfare on brown bodies" and about "*mestiza* maternity" (a *mestiza* is a woman of mixed European and Native American ancestry) as "epistemic privilege"; she believes that "*mestiza* bodies can be read as sites of knowledge production," that our "analyses of embodiment must expand to recognize the material relationship between the psyche and the body, as well as the transformative potential of this interaction in the social world," and that "bodies such as maternal and transgendered bodies shift to produce multiple forms of consciousness." She has plenty to say as well about "the epistemological implications of maternal corporeality," "the body's relationship to power and consciousness," "the pregnant woman's phenomenological experience," and "the epistemological significance of *mestiza* maternity."

This session has neatly captured one of the conflicts at the heart of Chicana Studies: Chicana academics feel compelled to identify as feminist radicals and postmodern ideologues who are out to annihilate gender roles and traditional religion, but in their hearts they're often far more interested in spirituality and conventional female activities (dancing, clothes making). This conclusion is reaffirmed at the "Chicana plenary" later the same morning, the putative subject of which is the environment (the official theme of this year's conference). Welcoming us to this gathering, entitled "Mujeres Activistas," Mary S. Pardo explains that the "Chicana caucus was implemented in response to sexism" and notes proudly that it's "the largest caucus in the organization." She then introduces Gloria A. Ramirez, who works at the Esperanza Peace and Justice Center in San Antonio and edits a journal called *La Voz de Esperanza* (The Voice of Hope), which Pardo describes as offering "brilliant insights," such as the observation that "all of our first environments are the bodies of women." There follows a PowerPoint presentation about the evils of technology. (Looking around the sizable auditorium and examining the faces, I see no sign that *anyone* finds it amusing that PowerPoint is being used as an aid in a jeremiad against technology.) We're told that "environmental racism is the disrespect of our Mother Earth" (water is Mother Earth's blood, soil is her skin, etc.) and that "when you [non-Chicanos] started your Industrial Revolution, you started poisoning our Mother Earth, our air and our water. We took care of them for centuries. Within our DNA we know we belong to our Mother Earth. Humankind and nature are intertwined, cannot be disconnected."

One of today's most prominent Chicana activists and academics is Cherríe Moraga, co-editor of the pathbreaking feminist manifesto (femifesto?) *This Bridge Called My Back*. She exudes even more hostility for the Anglo establishment than most other Chicano academics—which is probably the main key to her success. "Chicano Nation," she has written, "is a mestizo nation conceived in a double-rape: first, by the Spanish and then by the Gringo." She's the author of several collections of bad poetry, all interchangeable with the work of any number of other narcissistic identity studies academics. But perhaps the most succinct summation of Moraga's views can be found in her essay "Queer Aztlán: The Reformation of Chicano Tribe." It opens (which isn't unusual in identity studies) on a self-congratulatory note: "My real politicization began, not through the Chicano Movement, but through the bold recognition of my lesbianism." Depending on the circumstances, it can indeed take courage to accept one's own homosexuality, but still, to describe oneself as "bold" is rather—well, bold. Perhaps it's because Moraga's essay goes back a few years (it's based on talks given in 1992) that the Chicano Studies students she describes aren't at all like the maddeningly integrationist kids Edén Torres moans about. "Radicalization among people of Mexican ancestry in this country," Moraga writes, "most often occurs when the Mexican ceases to be a Mexican and becomes a Chicano. I have observed this in my Chicano Studies students (first, second, and third generation...)…. They are the ones most often in protest, draping their bodies in front of freeway on-ramps and trans-bay bridges, blocking entrances to University administration buildings."

In other words, they've gotten into college—but instead of taking hold of this precious opportunity to be educated and become successful and productive members of society, they're making use of it to play at rebellion. "They are the ones who, like their Black, Asian, and Native American counterparts, doubt the 'American dream' because even if they got to UC Berkeley, their brother is still on crack in Boyle Heights [a section of Los Angeles], their sister had three kids before she's twenty, and *sorry but they can't finish the last week of the semester cuz Tío Ignacio just got shot in front of a liquor store.*" And what, according to Moraga, is the cause of all these family problems? Three words: "North American racism." Unlike her Chicano students, she notes, her Mexican immigrant students "have not yet had their self-esteem nor that of their parents and grandparents worn away by North American racism. For them, the 'American dream' still looms as a possibility on the horizon." This, in any event, is Moraga's analysis of the situation. It apparently hasn't occurred to her that because they've actually *lived* in Mexico, her Mexican immigrant students may in fact recognize and appreciate the opportunity for a better life that's been handed to them and want to make the most of it—whereas her Chicano students, who've grown up with welfare and affirmative action and the mantra of racism, may have been so crippled by the victim mentality that's been drilled into their heads ever since elementary school that they're incapable of taking responsibility for their own futures.

As a Chicana lesbian, Moraga is in the position of being able to complain in every direction, and complain she does—not only about the racism of North American whites, but also about the antigay and sexist attitudes of Chicano men (and of the male-run Chicano community and Chicano movement), the "privileges" of gay men, and "the misogyny of gay Chicanos." She's a victim so many times over that her less multiply-oppressed colleagues must wilt with envy. She slams gay Chicano men for their reluctance "to recognize and acknowledge that their freedom is intricately connected to the freedom of women." (This is yet another version of the claim—which, though utterly historyless, is an orthodoxy today in Queer Studies and Women's Studies—that the gay rights movement grew out of feminism.) "The earth is female," Moraga informs us more than once (she never says anything just once), and she also tells us that "the female body, like the Chicano people, has been occupied." She dismisses fellow Mexican American writer Richard Rodriguez—who has more talent in his little finger than she has in her whole body, occupied or not—as an "assimilationist" and attacks him for staying in the closet for many years (Rodriguez is now openly gay), which allowed him to "cling to privileges that make other people's lives more vulnerable to violence." The denunciation and smearing of truly gifted people like Rodriguez—people the Chicano community should be *proud* of—by the self-appointed gatekeepers of Chicano Studies is, alas, an everyday spectacle. (Did anyone in the Chicano Studies community even take note when Dana Gioia, who is one of the best poets of his generation and happens to be half Mexican American, was named chairman of the National Endowment for the Arts in 2002? No, because he made it on his merits and not by being a victimization hustler.)

For Moraga, the dream of Aztlán still lives: "Few Chicanos really believe we can wrest Aztlán away from Anglo-America," she admits, but adds: "If the Soviet Union could dissolve, why not the United States?" What an inspiring teacher she must be! Yet if her own Chicano students are good old-fashioned radicals, the Chicano movement itself is, in her view, only a shadow of its former self: "I mourn the dissolution of an active Chicano Movement possibly more strongly than my generation[al] counterparts because during its 'classic period,' I was unable to act publicly. But more deeply, I mourn it because its ghost haunts me daily in the blonde hair of my sister's children [presumably products of that evil phenomenon, miscegenation], the gradual hispanicization of Chicano students [i.e., the lack of resentment over the "loss" of Aztlán that is symbolized by their decision to call themselves Latino or Hispanic rather than Chicano], the senselessness of barrio violence [which is of course entirely the fault of *norteamericanos*], and the poisoning of *la frontera* from Tijuana to Tejas." She awaits a resurrection of the Chicano movement—only this time "in a 'queerer,' more feminist" form. She admires "Chicano nationalism, Black nationalism, Puerto Rican Independence,…the 'Lesbian Nation' and its lesbian separatist movement, and, of course, the most recent 'Queer Nation'"—and what she likes about each of these movements is "its righteous radicalism, its unabashed anti-assimilationism, and its *rebeldía* [rebelliousness, defiance]."

Moraga's essay is a howl of rage: *I rebel, therefore I am*. And what does this lesbian Che Guevara do for a living? Is she up in the mountains somewhere forming a guerrilla army to take Aztlán back from the gringos? No, she's a professor at Stanford University. She was a Rockefeller Foundation fellow in 2007 and won an NEA fellowship in 1993. And she was keynote speaker at the 2009 graduation ceremony for the Ethnic Studies program at Berkeley, where she urged the graduates to "finish this revolution."

If Moraga is a good example of the kind of Chicana who still embraces the dream of Aztlán, veteran Chicana activist Yolanda Alaniz and longtime feminist radical Megan Cornish, coauthors of *Viva la Raza: A History of Chicano Identity and Resistance* (2008), are good examples of the kind of hard-core Marxist-Leninists who consider "cultural nationalism" like Moraga's "regressive" and "disastrous" (their words) because it emphasizes ethnic identity over working-class solidarity. Rodolfo Acuña sets the tone of *Viva la Raza* with a foreword in which he laments the demise of the Soviet Union, which brought about "the death of many U.S. left mass organizations…such as the Communist Workers Party and the League of Revolutionary Struggle," and thus "had a devastating impact on communities of color in the United States." Alaniz and Cornish's dream is not of an exclusively Chicano Aztlán but of a multiethnic Marxist Utopia. In their version of Chicano Studies, Chicano history and culture become unimportant in and of themselves, and are valuable only to the extent that they can be used to further the workers' revolution. Alaniz and Cornish's explicit goal: "to topple capitalism and the racism, sexism and homophobia that sustain it" and replace it with "a system where resources and productive forces are publicly owned and run by workers for the benefit of all." Among their models: the Russian Revolution (quotations from Lenin crowd the first seventy-odd pages); Hugo Chávez's Venezuela; and Fidel Castro's Cuba, which Alaniz and Cornish celebrate, in a typical stretch of Orwellian prose, as

> the first victorious socialist revolution in the Western hemisphere, which audaciously burst forth at the very doorstep of the United States. Fidel Castro's charismatic leadership and Che Guevara's internationalist vision and martyrdom made them powerful models. The Chicana/o movement strove to emulate Cuba's monumental gains in eliminating poverty and racism and its courageous solidarity with global liberation struggles.

And as deeply as they admire the Cuban Revolution, Alaniz and Cornish mourn the post-Soviet "[e]conomic insecurity" that "led [Cuba] to adopt a foreign policy that was dominated by the desire for stable relations with the U.S. at the cost of providing radical leadership to Latin American, African and U.S. workers." A Cuba that provides "leadership" to "U.S. workers": such thinking is par for the course in Chicano Studies.

*　　*　　*

Enthusiasm for Marxism, and especially for the Cuban Revolution, is also on display—literally—at the NACCS convention, where one large room is set aside for the sponsoring publishers and other vendors (among them the University of Texas Press, the Bilingual Review Press, and the *Socialist Worker*) to show off their wares. I make a quick tour. At the table devoted to the latest titles from Pathfinder Books, the publisher's representative, a middle-aged woman, presses on me a copy of a newspaper Pathfinder publishes. "It's an excellent newspaper," she gushes. "I've been reading it since I was seventeen!" She also draws my attention to a slim book by Mary-Alice Waters, *Is Socialist Revolution in the U.S. Possible?* "Of course," the woman says with a big grin, "we think the answer is yes!" I pay a dollar for the newspaper, four bucks for the book. Later, looking at Pathfinder's website, I discover that in addition to publishing books by Marx, Lenin, and Trotsky, Pathfinder acts as an agent for the Cuban government; on the site you can subscribe to *Granma* and *Cuba Socialista*, the daily newspaper and quarterly theoretical journal, respectively, of the Central Committee of the Cuban Communist Party, as well as *La Gaceta de Cuba*, "Cuba's leading magazine on culture, politics, and the Cuban Revolution today."

If it isn't already clear that Chicano Studies today is, to a great extent, a locus for Marxist propaganda, consider *Latino/a Thought: Culture, Politics, and Society*, a major anthology in the field. In his introduction, the editor, Francisco H. Vásquez, asks why we should have an academic discipline called Chicano Studies and not, say, German-American or Italian-American Studies. His answer: "the U.S. Italian, Irish and German populations…have in due time been accepted as 'real' Americans. They do not need their own ethnic studies at the university." It doesn't seem to occur to Vásquez that one reason why these groups have been so successfully integrated is that they *didn't* have "their own ethnic studies at the university." Italian, Irish, and German Americans who went to college studied what everybody else studied. They didn't go to college to be "taught" about the one thing you could be sure they knew something about already—namely, their own ethnic subcultures—and to be encouraged to nurse grievances about them; they went to college to learn about things beyond their own experience and to do something useful with that knowledge.

Several times in his book Vásquez returns to a single historical incident that, in his view, is clearly central to the history of U.S.-Latino relations. The hero of the story is Ricardo Chávez Ortiz, a Mexican citizen who on April 13, 1972, hijacked a commercial flight that he had boarded in Albuquerque and demanded radio time "to talk about the unjust treatment of Mexicans." "He got the airtime," writes Vásquez, "but, as you might imagine, no major change occurred in the life of Mexicans in the United States. He paid with federal prison time for the right to speak to power." There's no hint that hijacking a plane may not have been the most appropriate means of gaining a podium.[2]

Vásquez says that his intention in his book is to promote "critical thinking." A subhead at the end of his introduction is more honest: "Becoming Politically Involved." Indeed, he is blatantly out to indoctrinate his students. He claims that the readings included in the book "differ in political tone and orientation" and warns students to "read with a suspicious mind, suspend judgment, and do not take statements as given truths.... [T]hink for yourself." Yet the range of opinions in his book is as broad as those at a Communist Party convention. And his version of the facts, time and time again, is breathtakingly dishonest. The Mexican, Russian, and Cuban revolutions, in his description, were "struggle [s] for civil and human rights for African-descent, indigenous, and Latino peoples and women, gays and other marginalized peoples." He refers to the "fight...between capitalist democracy and communist and social democracies," his obvious intention being to fool naïve readers into thinking that the Soviet Union and Castro's Cuba can be considered in any way to be (or have been) democracies. He equates Castro's revolution with the American Revolution—because both, he says, represented a rejection of colonialism. Not that he approves of the American Revolution: on the contrary, he takes an entirely cynical

---

2   Vásquez first tells the Ortiz story in his preface, repeats it on page 86 as if he hasn't already told it, and returns to it yet again on page 99.

view of America's founding, presenting the colonies' rebellion as a power grab by capitalist oppressors. By contrast, he describes Marxism, benignly, as "a political-economic analysis of society that is familiar in most of the world" (and thus, by implication, legitimate and respectable) but that "in the United States…is associated with 'godless communism'" and thus "reject[ed]…offhand" by "most people." Like Acuña, he doesn't bother to fill students in on the history of Marxism and what it has wrought (*The Black Book of Communism* is not in his bibliography); he says only that for students "it is important to become familiar with the concepts and terms of Marxist analysis" because many of the contributors to his book take a Marxist view, even though some of them regard it as "*a necessary but not sufficient analysis* for the understanding of Latino/a political realities." To read his anthology (which is riddled with quotations, many of them lengthy, from Marx, Engels, Lenin, Foucault, and Said) is to see a very wily Marxist teaching his undergraduates, step by step, to view the world through Marxist eyes.

Vásquez is unashamed in his propaganda. "Arguably," he writes, "Cuba got its freedom from the United States with the revolution of Fidel Castro; Puerto Rico remains, in the year 2008, the only colony in the world." Even to suggest that Cuba is free and Puerto Rico unfree is to feed students an outright lie. "[T]he next step of democratic evolution," Vásquez preaches, "is economic democracy.… [W]e the people need to set a bottom income and a ceiling to the wealth that can be acquired. That is an economic democracy." Such rhetoric, which is of course common among socialists, represents outright manipulation of students who have yet to learn the first thing about the history of human tyranny and individual liberty (not to mention economics), and who don't realize that the kind of government control Vásquez is recommending here is not "democratic" but rather takes us deep into socialist territory. Vásquez goes on to describe the Puritans as sharing "the nearly fanatical belief… that they were soldiers of Christ" and to suggest that "[e]choes of this notion can be heard in the justification for the war in Iraq." Invoking the Greek deities called the Furies as symbols of rebellion against injustice and citing the Declaration of Independence as one such rebellion, Vásquez says that "Al Quaida [*sic*] is the latest manifestation of the Furies," since it's a movement motivated by "memories of past injustices." ("No justice, no peace," he adds.) He even justifies suicide bombing, writing that when there's no "equality and justice" in a society, "the human body itself becomes the ultimate authority," explaining that "the difference between the ballot box and a suicide bomber is the difference between these two kinds of human rights."

Through all of Chicano Studies' twists and turns, *Aztlán*, founded in 1970, has remained its flagship journal. The magazine, which comes out twice a year, is beautifully (which is to say expensively) produced, with high-quality paper and illustrations. The topics of its articles run the gamut from literature, art, and culture to politics and society. The language is never crudely rebellious or violently anti-establishment—the clear objective is to produce a "respectable" academic publication—though the contents are consistently informed by an oppositional posture toward an America that is unwaveringly depicted as capitalist, imperialist, and oppressive. The spring 2010 issue is typical. In "Toward a Borderlands Ethics: The Undocumented Migrant and Haunted Communities in Contemporary Chicana/o Fiction," Pablo A. Ramirez of the University of Michigan argues that works of fiction by Chicano writers Helena Maria Viramontes and Daniel Chacon "help us understand that maintaining a Latina/o ethnic identity is…an ethico-political project that challenges the United States to form new visions of democracy and new relations with Latin America in order to maintain transborder communities and families." In "Líderes Campesinas: Nepantla Strategies and Grassroots Organizing at the Intersection of Gender and Globalization," Maylei Blackwell of UCLA builds "on Gloria Anzaldúa's theory of nepantla" to show "how campesina [female peasant] organizers create sources of empowerment from their binational life experiences and new forms of gendered grassroots leadership that navigate the overlapping hybrid hegemonies produced by U.S., Mexican, and migrant relations of power," thereby "challeng[ing] the racialized and gendered forms of structural violence exacerbated by neoliberal globalization." And in "The Curandera of Conquest: Gloria Anzaldúa's Decolonial Remedy," George Hartley of the Department of English and the Latin American Studies Program at Ohio University argues that Anzaldúa's "primary role...is that of the curandera [folk healer or witch doctor] of conquest, the healer of *la herida abierta* (the open wound) created by the borders imposed by capitalism, nationalism, imperialism, sexism, homophobia, and racism." Also worth mentioning is an essay from the fall 2009 issue titled "The Core Ideals of the Mexican American Gang: Living the Presentation of Defiance," in which Robert J. Durán of New Mexico State University denies "that criminality is the defining characteristic of gangs" and argues that "[g]angs maintain their cohesiveness and longevity through four core ideals: displaying loyalty, responding courageously to external threats, promoting and defending gang status, and maintaining a stoic attitude toward the negative conse-quences of gang life" and that "[s]tate-sponsored opposition to gangs only further solidifies these ideals"—meaning that gang members must be encouraged to "rechannel" their "collective energy" into "community empowerment."

Aztlán is published by the Chicano Studies Research Center at UCLA, one of four ethnic studies centers established at that univer-sity in 1969. (The others are the American Indian Studies Center, the Asian American Studies Center, and the Ralph Bunche Center for African-American Studies.) The director of the Chicano Studies Research Center and editor of *Aztlán* is Chon Noriega, whose back-ground is not in political activism but in art, film, and media; he's curated exhibitions, produced documentaries, and been involved in activities ranging from film restoration to archival work. As I find my way to the Research Center on a hot afternoon at the end of March—the first day of UCLA's spring quarter—I notice banners hanging from lampposts all over campus. They read: "Art, activism, access[:] 40 years of ethnic studies at UCLA."

I arrive on time for my appointment with Noriega, but he's still in a meeting. The secretary in his outer office invites me to take a seat and wait. I decide to walk around instead. I stroll up and down the hall, examining the bulletin boards outside the Chicano and Bunche centers. The ones outside the Chicano Center, I notice, are dominated by pictures of and clippings about Noriega. Twice I return to Noriega's secretary's office only to be told that he's still busy. Finally, after more than half an hour, Noriega and his guest come out of his office and Noriega, after giving him a chummy slap on the back, turns to me and apologizes graciously for making me wait. Everything about Noriega is gracious—elegant, sophisticated, smooth. He's an attractive middle-aged man in a fine suit that fits him like a glove; he's Latino in the way Ricardo Montalbán was Latino, except that he doesn't have the slightest trace of a Latino accent. Certainly the word *Chicano* doesn't seem to suit him at all, unless you can imagine a Chicano Cary Grant. Nor is there the remotest hint about him of the intense stew of radicalism in which the Chicano Studies movement was born, to say nothing of the Leninist-Stalinist ideology that dominates the field today; he talks in the soothing, civilized purr of the eminently reasonable academic administrator. He's the very model, indeed, of a highly successful member of that breed.

Briefly put, he could hardly be more different, at first blush anyway, from David Diaz.

He ushers me into his large, tidy office and we sit down—him in a chair, me on the couch. He offers me a piece of chocolate from a dish on the coffee table. It's delicious. I ask about the slogan on those banners: why, of all things, "art, activism, access"? Why, that is, those three particular words, of all the nouns they might have chosen? Noriega looks genuinely stumped. "Hmm, how *did* we come up with that?" he says with a hint of charming, Cary Grant-like bemusement. He really doesn't remember. In any case, he seems less eager to focus on activism than on art. "We have some pretty significant art holdings," he tells me. "We have the first Chicano mural painted at a university." He gets up, crosses the room, and comes back with a poster of the mural. Dating back to 1970, it's highly derivative of Diego Rivera—a busy, colorful celebration of working-class heroism. "Each center has a mural like this," Noriega tells me. "The African-American one was painted by a fourteen- or fifteen-year-old kid who is now a mid-career artist." He goes on for a while about the center's collection and promotion of Chicano art. "There are some amazing [Chicano] artists who aren't part of the history of world and American art," he says.

Noriega seems eager to distinguish his own Chicano Center from the Chicano Studies Department. "The center is different from the department, and precedes it. It was started forty years ago with no students, no faculty, and few resources. It was created along with a library, a press, and a community-relations program. It laid the foundations for the field intellectually—through publications and resources—and supported students and faculty in their development and training. By the late 1970s, it had helped bring about the creation of the department and the degree program." But he's less interested in talking about the Chicano Studies Department than about UCLA's other ethnic centers. "We work closely together through the Institute of American Cultures," he says. "We jointly administer grants and fellowship programs and collaborate on projects that are post-racial. We do Chicano and Latino projects, and more broadly framed projects as well. For example, projects involving voting rights and incarceration." It must be said that Noriega is extremely good at this; I might well be watching a promotional video.

"I've been the director for eight years now," Noriega continues. "I was and am in the Film Department. The center was a unique resource because it was campus-wide. Most people are in their departments and can't get outside them. The center had an impact across the campus—it could reach out across department lines. My role was to *formalize* much that was inherent. It was about *research*, not advocacy, not partisanship—research that would have an impact." So the center is about "activism," but not "advocacy"? "Research," he goes on, "that would reach out into community and have an overlap of interests. We needed infrastructure and increased resources. We needed some way of conveying our history and mission." It's impressive how smoothly Noriega steamrollers on; you get the impression that he could keep this up for hours. "We've provided a platform that pulls people in from across campus to collaborate on projects. For example, we have a grant proposal out right now relating to a San Fernando Valley hospital. My assistant has a Ph.D. in health sciences. We're trying to connect the Latino community with better health-care services. The question is, how do we set up an infrastructure whereby the right information can reach the Latino community?" If this is activism, Noriega makes it sound tame, moderate, unobjectionable.

"Health, education, arts, history—we need to identify different areas to prioritize. We have limited resources, so we can't take on everything. This center goes back forty years. It's evolved a lot over time. The consistent through-line is research that makes a difference. We try to define what that means. The gathering and production of knowledge should help where there are inequities, disparities, and ignorance. We work with the advocacy group the Mexican American Bar Association, for example, and try to find areas where our research matches up with what they're doing." So there *is* an advocacy element, after all? "We try to have a tangible impact—in the arts, in archival preservation, in media policy, in health-care services, in education. There's a history more tied to activism and access, and to the pressure to open up educational access. The situation is even more dire now forty years later. Forty years ago, Latinos were a minority population in Southern California. Now we're the majority population, but the level of access hasn't got much better." In Los Angeles, he tells me, Latinos make up 72 percent of the students in public high schools, but only 15 percent of the students at UCLA. (His use of the word *Latino* rather than *Chicano* is striking—an act that many of his Chicano Studies colleagues would consider treasonous.) What's striking about Noriega is not anything in particular that he has to say, but how different he is from David Diaz—that old radical at Cal State Los Angeles. Diaz looked and sounded as if he'd just come from a protest march in 1969. By contrast, the charming, dapper Noriega—the impeccably sophisticated face of UCLA's Chicano Studies Research Center—looks and sounds like a consummately skillful academic administrator. He makes the center sound as if it's accomplished exceedingly important—and *respectable*—things. Marxism? Leninist-Stalinist analysis? The dream of Aztlán? He makes these things sound as remote as the moon. Surely UCLA's Chicano Studies Research Center could not have a finer salesman.

CHAPTER 6
Studies, Studies Everywhere

1. "Every Damn Thing": Cultural Studies

Abortion, terrorism, sex toys, Hawaiian music, *The Wizard of Oz*, the French war in Algeria, the Rolling Stones, Brazilian male prostitution, Chinese opera during the Cultural Revolution, wartime British newsreels, the 2001 World Series, 1980s teen cinema, South African soap operas, the movie *The Day after Tomorrow*: all these subjects, and many others, were addressed in papers at the 2010 Cultural Studies Association conference. It's hard to imagine a social or cultural phenomenon that wouldn't be regarded as an appropriate subject for reflection under the purview of Cultural Studies, and it's equally hard to imagine a critical approach that wouldn't be considered valid. At one session alone, I heard papers on a French film about "organ transplantation in a transnational not-so-post-colonial context," obesity among black girls, and the ambivalence of the medical establishment toward women.

And, last but not least, the Hooters restaurant chain. Sarah L. Rasmusson, a middle-aged woman from the Institute of Communications Research at the University of Illinois, begins her paper by saying that she was once filled with "classic feminist rage that this cheesy, tacky-ass place even existed." But when she discovered that some of her students at Princeton were Hooters girls, she "had a kind of epiphany and realized the problem was me." Why, she wanted to figure out, "do I have such a compunction [*sic*] against this place?" Was it sheer condescension? So she got drunk, wrote a research proposal, was awarded a grant, and spent a year interviewing sixty girls at a Hooters in Champaign, Illinois, and traveling to several Hooters locations around the world.

After a brief detour into postmodern jargon ("neo-imperialist, neocolonialist…situating yourself at the nexus of global/body/sexualization"), Rasmusson veers back into autobiography, discussing the "schizoid split within myself" between the snobby academic and her own working-class past as a barmaid and cocktail waitress. She realized that in order to "own and honor" her past, she had to "exhume" it and "claim" it. Among the things she discovered in the course of her research, Rasmusson says, is that in the Midwest, Hooters has become a "safe space for gay men" as well as a "new postfeminist space" where, for example, sorority girls can campaign for breast-cancer awareness. Abroad, meanwhile, Hooters girls serve as "agents of globalization." In reply to questions from an audience of nervous women (I'm one of only two men present) who don't know how to react to this thumbs-up for an institution they've been taught to despise, Rasmusson says that Hooters helps young women work their way up, and that Hooters restaurants, far from being reactionary all-white enclaves, help forge cross-racial communities. Also, she admits she's turned on by Hooters girls.

In a way, I'm impressed by Rasmusson. Despite the occasional patch of academic gobbledygook, she at least has something fresh to say and is really out to understand something, instead of using it as an excuse to echo some orthodoxy. She's not concerned that her attitude toward Hooters is politically incorrect; unlike the middle- and upper-middle-class young women sharing the stage with her, this sometime barmaid has one foot in reality and is willing and able to look, think, form ideas, and actually speak her mind, at once challenging herself and others—which, in the humanities today, is far more than you can usually hope to expect, even if it's considerably less than you should ask for from something calling itself higher education.

My one question is: what makes Rasmusson's presentation Cultural Studies? Exactly how does it differ from old-fashioned sociology?

What *is* Cultural Studies? It's the soul of today's humanities—or is, rather, the empty space where that soul should be. In a time when the line between the humanities and social sciences is blurring, Cultural Studies is the prime location where that blurring is taking place. And in a time of intersectionality, it's the place where all the identity studies flow together on (as it were) neutral ground. In fact, a great deal of the "work" done in identity studies is, essentially, Cultural Studies.

Simply put, the idea of Cultural Studies is to explore the ideological and political ramifications of social and cultural phenomena, high and low, with the intention of better understanding the workings of hegemonic cultural power in everyday life. The term was first coined in 1964 by Richard Hoggart, founder of the Centre for Contemporary Cultural Studies in Birmingham, England, and at least in the beginning Cultural Studies was restricted largely to departments of literature. Now, however, though Cultural Studies continues to be headquartered, for the most part, in English departments, it has spread its tendrils throughout the humanities and social sciences. Though its original theoretical impulse, moreover, drew heavily on Gramsci, the nature of the "work" done by Cultural Studies practitioners has always been difficult to define. In a 2000 essay, Stephen Adam Schwartz admits that "the question of exactly what [Cultural Studies] specialists do is as yet poorly defined.... Its practitioners have long been loath to offer much in the way of a definition for reasons that, they tell us, have everything to do with the intellectual originality of the burgeoning field."

Since Cultural Studies is the postmodern phenomenon *par excellence*, it's probably fair to say that its indefinability is part of the point. Schwartz quotes the editors of the collection *Cultural Studies* as saying that the discipline "is not merely interdisciplinary" but "anti-disciplinary" and opposed to method. "To ask what cultural studies is, they imply, is to misunderstand this fundamental anti- or postdisciplinarity." It's opposed, moreover, not only to method but also to the idea of reaching a conclusion: it "sees itself not as an attempt to discover or uncover anything in particular about its objects of study, but as an intervention or performative discourse, an attempt to impose a view and a set of interests." In his encounters with the field, Schwartz claims to have detected "a certain anxiety that cultural studies might turn out to be 'every damn thing'" (the words "every damn thing" are borrowed from Stuart Hall, Hoggart's successor as director of the Birmingham center). And he observes that the "most tangible effect" of its rise "is the opening of the curricula and research agendas of literature departments to vast areas beyond the study of literature itself: not only popular art but everything from gas stations to drag racing to drag queens."

For Harold Bloom, the distinguished literary critic who is an English professor at Yale, Cultural Studies is nothing more or less than a grim interloper that has turned literary study into "one more dismal social science." When, over lunch in Philadelphia, I ask the distinguished University of Pennsylvania historian Alan Charles Kors about Cultural Studies, he shakes his head in dismay. "Cultural Studies," he laments, "is now dominant in all departments of literature and is increasingly big in history, sociology, and cultural anthropology, though less so in political science." His own capsule definition of Cultural Studies? "It sees culture as a means of assigning roles, power, obedience, and resources—and examines the way in which culture accomplishes that."

Kors first became aware of Cultural Studies in the 1980s. "I immediately saw that it was a wonderful Trojan Horse," he says, with its "notion of culture derived from Gramsci." By way of explaining the philosophy that was, at least originally, at the root of Cultural Studies, Kors notes that Marx saw "culture as a superstructure"—that is, as a phenomenon that existed outside of, or apart from, the socioeconomic structures that, in his view, made the world go around, and that was thus essentially irrelevant to those structures. Gramsci, by contrast, regarded culture "as a hegemonic force"—that is, a fundamental element of the power equation—and believed that "control of culture" was therefore "at least as important as the working class." For Kors, Cultural Studies is intellectually a considerable step below Marx: while "the Hegelians, the Freudians and even the Marxists," he points out, "felt obliged to try to demonstrate the truth of their ideologies," Cultural Studies rejects the very notion of objective reality and of an independent human will and mind—and when you eliminate those things, the only criterion left by which to judge any idea is its political or therapeutic effect. "Marx at least had an empirical claim he could make, namely class consciousness. If you wrote from the perspective of the proletariat, you were writing objectively"; but Cultural Studies practitioners "reject objectivity and take the perspective that their works have authority, meaning, and significance, whereas language does not." Apropos of this observation, Kors recalls belonging in the late 1960s and early 1970s to the American Society for Eighteenth-Century Studies (ASECS), a group in which historians and students of literature, music, and art history could get together in multidisciplinary fashion. With the Cultural Studies turn in literature, all that changed. "I went to a session on 'Patriarchy in Montesquieu,'" he recalls. "Three feminist literary scholars gave papers" that were perfect examples of the Cultural Studies approach. "In the Q&A, I said to one of the women, 'I found it very difficult to distinguish among your claims about what Montesquieu asserted about the relationship of men and women in the eighteenth century, and what was the relationship between men and women in the eighteenth century, and what ought to have been the relationship between men and women in the eighteenth century.' To which the woman replied, 'Of course you can't make those distinctions. You've obviously fallen prey to the fallacy of authorial intent.' To which I said, 'Would it be an example of that fallacy to say that Marx wrote *Kapital* as an analysis and critique of capitalism?' 'Yes,' she explained, and said you could also read *Kapital* in other ways." At which point he elegantly used her own ridiculous theory against her: "'Wouldn't it be an instance of the fallacy of authorial intent to say that you believe in the existence of something called the fallacy of authorial intent and that I have committed it?' To which she replied: 'You need to get serious about discourse.'" Many ASECS conferences, he notes, later became Cultural Studies conferences.

For a quick example of the standard language and politics of Cultural Studies, I would offer up "L'Ouragan de Flammes (The Hurricane of Flames): New Orleans and Transamerican Catastrophe, 1866/2005" by Anna Brickhouse, an associate professor of English at the University of Virginia, which appeared in the December 2007 issue of *American Quarterly*, a leading Cultural Studies journal. Brickhouse describes Hurricane Katrina as an example of a

> transamerican "ecoscape," a conceptual space regis-
> tering the interconnectedness of ecological with
> economic and political forces across the American
> hemisphere. We might begin to discern this partic-
> ular ecoscape in a series of humanitarian gestures
> and official statements of condolence that directly
> addressed the disaster as a shared tragedy of the
> hemisphere—one that would supersede, at least
> rhetorically, some of its most entrenched political
> antagonisms through a cooperative response to the
> disaster. Fidel Castro, for example, offered to send
> 1,100 Cuban doctors and several tons of medical
> and relief materials directly to the disaster areas.
> Hugo Chávez...offered to send Venezuelan fuel,
> humanitarian aid, and relief workers to the city....
> [But] the U.S. government declined all of these...
> offers of aid.

Briefly put: Castro and Chávez good; America evil. Brickhouse goes on to quote Castro at length, taking his propaganda at face value. She speaks of "Castro's humanitarian gesture," though she feels that his underlying goal was "his larger political project of unmasking the cruelty and indifference of the U.S. government and its version of democracy." She favorably contrasts Cuba's handling of a hurricane the previous year with the U.S. government's handling of Katrina. "Cuba—despite its longstanding poverty in the wake of U.S. embargoes—was ready to send its own 'young, well-trained professionals' where the U.S. president himself [Bush, not Obama, of course] had not bothered to show up."

At the Cultural Studies conference, I hear Mitra Rastegar of the City University of New York give a talk about how Muslims have been "demonized" in America since 9/11. Her case in point is the story of the Khalil Gibran Academy in Brooklyn, founded in 2007 by one Debbie Almontaser, a "respected" Muslim woman who became the target of what Rastegar describes as a "right-wing smear campaign" depicting her as an Islamist. Rastegar argues that while the *New York Times* defended Almontaser from these criticisms, Almontaser ended up having to resign because the image of her promulgated by "right-wingers" was "embedded in the paradigms" that had already been established by media portrayals of Muslims. Rastegar compares Daniel Pipes, who criticized Almontaser in a *New York Sun* article, to the Ku Klux Klan, Joseph McCarthy, and the government officials who sent Japanese Americans to internment camps during World War II.

The case against Almontaser pivoted largely on T-shirts reading "Intifada NYC" that were distributed to girls in New York by an Arab group that shared an office with a Yemeni organization for which Almontaser worked. The shirts caused a controversy, and Almontaser refused to condemn them, telling the *New York Post* that "intifada" simply means "shaking off" and that the shirts provided Muslim girls with "an opportunity…to express that they are part of New York City society…and shaking off oppression." Rastegar quotes this comment sympathetically, dismissing the *Post* as a "right-wing tabloid" and arguing that since "intifada was equated with terrorism" in the public mind, it was impossible for "a nuanced discussion of the word's fuller meaning" to take place. Rastegar concludes that "it was Almontaser s inability to dissociate herself from members of her community" that led to her downfall, and that "this is an outrage because of the tolerable/intolerable dichotomy that forces Muslims to fit a certain image fails the test of true openness to a variety of points of view within a community." In short, it was apparently wrong for anyone to expect Almontaser to renounce Muslim terrorists and their supporters; even to draw a line between the "tolerable" and "intolerable" members of the Muslim community was to force Muslims unfairly to choose between membership in "New York City society" and loyalty to even their most violent coreligionists, who would like to see New York City in cinders.

Why, I wonder, is Rastegar's apologia for radical Islam considered Cultural Studies? Is it simply proof that Cultural Studies does indeed include "every damn thing"? In any event, Rastegar is far from the first person to make such a case under the auspices of Cultural

Studies. Look, for instance, at the September 2007 issue of *American Quarterly*. In "Selling American Diversity and Muslim American Identity through Nonprofit Advertising Post-9/11," Evelyn Alsultany, an assistant professor of American culture at the University of Michigan, cites as evidence of America's anti-Muslim bias a 2004 Cornell poll finding that "74 percent characterized Islamic countries as oppressive to women," and that "47 percent indicated that the Islamic region is more likely than others to encourage violence among its believers." To Alsultany, these numbers do not reflect awareness of objective facts but "racism." She analyzes advertising campaigns, such as one by the Ad Council that was designed "in direct response to the hundreds of hate crimes against Arabs, Muslims, and Sikhs" and that she criticizes for "excluding unambiguous markers of Muslim or Sikh identity." She also complains about conservative criticism of the Council on American-Islamic Relations, which she finds incomprehensible given its "work in condemning terrorism and educating the public about Islam." (Never mind that it's a Hamas front group.) Still—sounding very much like Rastegar—she does fault CAIR for buying into "the good Muslim/bad Muslim paradigm."

I attend a session about "Marxist Cultural Studies" at which the lead speaker is Neil Larsen, a professor at the University of California, Davis, who tells us that in the 1970s literary theory became, quite simply, "Theory," and Cultural Studies wasn't even a part of the vocabulary. Back then, Larsen was opposed to Cultural Studies; but now he feels differently, because today's Cultural Studies "is so capacious that it contains everything." To be sure, he still questions its "underlying political…assumptions" (it's apparently not Marxist enough for him); but at this point, he says, it's pointless to tilt at that windmill. Larsen's talk is about Raymond Williams, a British Marxist critic who is seen as one of the progenitors of Cultural Studies, and about another British Marxist critic, Terry Eagleton, who "popularized" Williams. Larsen slings a lot of jargon about "Hegelian language" and "the experienced power of capitalism" and "the embarrassment of old literary theory." The "embarrassment" Larsen is referring to is apparently the fact that the entire corpus of literary criticism from Aristotle to T. S. Eliot is, in his eyes, pathetically inadequate because it isn't postmodern. Larsen is plainly acquainted with that corpus, but he's also plainly teaching his students to have contempt for a rich tradition with which they haven't even taken the trouble to become acquainted.

One thing I've noticed at this conference is the odd, unacademic way in which many of the participants have cheered one another on, like contestants on *American Idol*. It's striking, too, how fervently the speakers insist on the importance of "collective" thinking even as their own "work" reveals an inability to separate their "research" from their eagerness to talk about their own personal experiences, hobbies, enthusiasms, and grievances. Rampant individuality is okay, apparently, as long as it's framed as somehow having to do with group justice, collective oppression, commodification, capitalism, and so on. The fact is that while Cultural Studies professes hostility to American individuality, it is in practice, more often than not, an exercise in self-absorption and self-indulgence that has less in common with traditional studies in the humanities than with today's TV talk and reality shows and online social networks.

I hear a talk by Robert Irwin, a professor in the Spanish and Portuguese Department at UC Davis, who notes that the "legitimacy" of Cultural Studies "is still seen as a question mark" in Latin America, where many academics regard it as a fashionable new "colonialist import from North America" and as a threat to "traditional disciplines." In Irwin's view, the reason why scholars in other disciplines fear Cultural Studies is that its practitioners are "more sophisticated thinkers" than are their colleagues in fields like literature, history, and sociology. Irwin points out that many Cultural Studies scholars identify as political activists or artists rather than academics, for the goal of Cultural Studies is not mainly to produce scholars but to "foster the development of intellectuals," many of whom make "political incursions into the public sphere" instead of becoming conventional academics. Specialists in Cultural Studies, he says, "channel political desire into scholarly paradigms"; "we" begin not with "disciplinary tools" but with "questions."

"Sophisticated thinkers"! "Intellectuals"! It's Larsen all over, looking down with professed embarrassment at "old literary theory." Should one laugh or cry? Most of the people presenting papers at this conference are junior professors or graduate students who, by all indications, have only the most rudimentary familiarity with history, literature, philosophy, or any other legitimate field of learning. They haven't been educated in anything—they've only been trained to mimic their teachers' jargon and given license to pronounce on things about which they know next to nothing. To call them intellectuals distorts the meaning of that word in the most grotesque manner imaginable. Indeed, the discipline's jargon-ridden rhetoric is, in large part, a way to disguise one's ignorance of pre-Theory thought, art, literature, and, not least, history. Most of these people's knowledge of history would appear to consist of a few bullet points about Western imperialism and colonialism; routinely, they talk about slavery and the genocide of Indians as if these extremely well-known chapters of history are unknown to almost everyone except themselves. They never reveal the slightest familiarity with the ancient or medieval world, and know only one thing about the age of empire: whites bad, others victims. To examine objectively a complex topic like British rule in India (which brought pluses along with minuses) is beyond these people's competence, outside their interest, and entirely off their ideological radar.

When Irwin turns over the lectern to Tamara Spira of the University of California, Santa Cruz, she begins by telling us that she started out as a history student, but switched to Cultural Studies because she found history too "objective."

2. "Minorized Bodies": Disability Studies

If there is anything that is a slap in the face to social constructionism, it is physical disability. It is real. It *exists*. To suggest otherwise—to look into the eyes of people who are constantly in pain, people who require the daily use of wheelchairs or respirators, and to tell them that their afflictions are social constructions—mere linguistic epiphenomena—rather than the very real consequences of accidents or biological processes, is not only palpably untrue but cruel.

How, then, to shape a postmodern identity studies discipline around the fact of disability? Very carefully. While Disability Studies acknowledges the objective reality of disability, it goes as far as it can to diminish the place of biology and medicine in the discourse about disability and to focus on those aspects of the lives of disabled people that don't entirely resist social constructionist interpretations. The way in which practitioners in this field approach their subject is neatly summed up by the Society for Disability Studies.

The discipline, we are told, "should challenge the view of disability as an individual deficit or defect that can be remedied solely through medical intervention or rehabilitation by 'experts' and other service providers. Rather, a program in disability studies should explore models and theories that examine social, political, cultural, and economic factors that define disability and help determine personal and collective responses to difference." Of course, few would suggest that disability can be remedied "solely" by doctors or therapists. To pretend otherwise is to set up a straw man, thereby making Disability Studies look as if it is saying something new when it is not really saying much of anything at all.

Disability Studies, we are further informed, "should work to de-stigmatize disease, illness, and impairment, including those that cannot be measured or explained by biological science." This last flourish is typical, implying that, at least in certain cases, Disability Studies is able to go places that biology cannot, provide insights that it cannot, and supply some undefined, beneficial something-or-other that is beyond the purview of medical science.

Also, "while acknowledging that medical research and intervention can be useful, Disability Studies should interrogate the connections between medical practice and stigmatizing disability." Note the audaciously grudging nature of this "acknowledgment": *can be useful.* And note how this "acknowledgment" is immediately undercut by a vague slur against medicine—an implication that stigmatization of disability is intrinsic to the practice of medicine. Disability Studies is not interested in doctors who cure disabilities, or who spend their lives trying to; its focus is rather on describing the actions of doctors in such a way as to minimize the good they do and to maximize the bad, and thereby magnify the role of the Disability Studies scholar.

The *Disabled World* website admits that there are those in the field who distinguish "physical impairment from social disability," an approach that "in its most rigid form does not accept that impairment can cause disability at all." Yet "[s]cholars are increasingly recognizing that the effects of impairment form a central part of many disabled people's experience, and that these effects must be included for the social model to still be a valid reflection of that experience." In other words, some Disability Studies practitioners, in keeping with postmodern orthodoxy, have rejected the idea that physical disability is indeed, by its very nature, disabling, but have been compelled by a reality too overwhelming for even them to deny that certain handicaps can't be theorized away. Not surprisingly, as *Disabled World* acknowledges, "[t]he feminist slogan 'the personal is political' has been particularly influential" in the development of the basic premises of Disability Studies.

There are Ph.D. programs in Disability Studies, the first of which in the United States was founded at the University of Chicago in 1998. The Society for Disability Studies, founded in 1982 as the Section for the Study of Chronic Illness, Impairment, and Disability (SSCIID) and renamed in 1986, holds an annual conference and publishes a journal, *Disability Studies Quarterly*. Presentations in Disability Studies, moreover, are increasingly common at a range of identity studies gatherings.

At the Queer Studies conference in Berlin, for example, I attend a panel on "Queer Body Politics" at which a young Austrian woman, Heike Raab, discusses the similarities and differences between Queer Studies and Disability (or, as we saw earlier, Crip—short for "cripple") Studies. Both disciplines, she says, share a focus on "minorized [*sic*] bodies" (in both, she elaborates, "the body is entwined with cultural systems of knowledge"); but while gays have traditionally been closeted, disabled people used to be publicly displayed at freak shows. Raab speaks of "queering crip and cripping queer" and asks, "Are crip bodies queer bodies, and can we say that queer bodies are crip bodies?" What's most striking about Raab's paper (portions of which she displays in PowerPoint) is that she knows her Queer Studies jargon cold but keeps making simple mistakes in English (such as pronouncing *realm* "reelm")—the result being that her paper is even harder to follow than the typical Queer Studies text:

> Gender Performance, in the sense of Disability Studies, should aim a strategic confiscation from Gender rather than a deconstruction of Gender.

> In the contrary, as Sedgwick's dictum from *The Epistemology of the Closet* suggests, queer bodily practices and queer culture are for the most time in history marked from being in the closet.

> Queers on Wheels [an organization for gays in wheelchairs] tries an intervention in the hegemonic way of seeing from bodily difference.

Needless to say, the most sacrosanct issue of all in Women's Studies is abortion rights. In today's academy, the only remotely acceptable way to criticize a woman's unlimited right to terminate a pregnancy is to employ intersectionality—to trump the oppression of women, that is, with some other oppression. At the "Our Bodies, Our Shelves" session at the Cultural Studies conference in Berkeley, Daniel Caeton of the University of California, Davis, gives a presentation on "somanormativity," meaning bodily normality. Caeton, who describes himself as disabled (though the nature of his disability is not visible), fears that amniocentesis and other tests used to detect embryonic or fetal disorders will also be used to "identify and expunge deviants," and that as a result all potential disabled people will end up "in the medical waste incinerators." He describes this as "genocide." Yet how to prevent it? The only way, he tells a large and palpably uneasy audience, is to forbid mothers to abort children simply because they're disabled. In this regard, he says, "the reproductive rights movement"—indeed, feminism itself—"is at odds with the disability rights movement." Recalling that early-twentieth-century eugenics prescribed forced sterilization of the "feebleminded," he notes that "the rhetoric of eugenics has come together with the rhetoric of reproductive rights" to create a nightmare for the disabled.

Since Caeton doesn't want to be tagged as a right-winger for criticizing unfettered abortion rights, he strives to ground his position in left-wing principles. "In the leftist view," he says, "it is the mind that has rights, not the body." Also, while abortion rights are *individual* rights, disability rights are *group* rights—and every good leftist knows that the group's rights trump the individual's. Yet it's impossible for Caeton to avoid looking at the individual: he points out that "from the point of view of feminism, a fetus is a clump of cells in a woman's body," but "when we recognize the disabled fetus, we *do* recognize its separate identity.... We *personify* the fetus," he emphasizes, acknowledging that this divides him from the pro-choice movement, which accords fetuses "no independent human status." His challenge is clear: "Are adults who require machines to survive also to be considered expendable?" he asks, condemning "technology used to eliminate another person before that person can be recognized to be human." In conclusion, he insists on the need to "rethink" the relationship between feminism and disability rights. What he doesn't admit is that there's no way to "rethink" this matter in a way that will satisfy everyone—either women will continue to enjoy full abortion rights or they won't.

When it's time for Q&A, a woman in the almost entirely female audience notes that pro-choice activists and activists for the disabled are "allies" but laments that, indeed, "perhaps there is no solution" to the impasse Caeton has outlined. She questions whether it's legitimate for Caeton, a man, to address these matters at all; as for the fetus's rights, she suggests that "rights" is "an old concept" and that it is more *au courant* to think in terms of "reproductive justice." Caeton's reply: "I appreciate your historicizing that accurately." Someone ventures: "Is this a problem with the verbiage?" Caeton, underscoring that his intention was to "open dialogue" and "stage an intervention," insists that this isn't "just an issue of verbiage." Another audience member adds: "If we use the word *anthropomorphize*, don't we run the risk of aiding our enemies in the pro-life movement with their 'fetal personhood'?" Caeton replies that for him, as a disabled person, this is a life-and-death issue, and "the political expediency of avoiding the tactics of the enemy isn't worth it for me." His fellow panelist Lori Greenstone, mentioning that she has a disabled child, dares to ask: "Is there a place for a conversation in the middle—that is, it's not just pro-life and pro-choice?" Amy Barber (author of that paper on the Michigan Womyn's Music Festival) notes that while there are always disabled women at that event, she's never heard any mention of this conflict—on the contrary, she has friends who are at once feminist activists *and* activists for the disabled. A woman in the audience brings in the difference between second- and third-wave feminism, though she underscores that she is not trying "to incarnate that binary." Another panelist recalls what she describes as "the arc of discourse around the cochlear implant," reminding everyone that a couple of decades ago there was a debate within the "deaf community" about the use of such implants, which some activists decried because "hearing parents" were "eradicating deaf children" and thereby committing a "genocide of deafness"; today, however, the issue isn't so politically charged. (She also refers, absurdly, to "deaf individuals' aptitude to not hear.") Caeton, though acknowledging the danger of "the right co-opting this" issue, emphasizes that it's also dangerous "not to recognize the friction" between the pro-choice and disabled rights causes. Indeed, I can't help concluding that despite Caeton's strenuous effort to frame his argument from a left-wing, group justice perspective, what he's presented is, at bottom, a straightforward pro-life argument: the fetus *is* a human being; abortion *is* murder. But how mightily he has struggled to distance himself from that cogent formulation! Instead of just speaking the plain truth as he sees it, he has felt obliged, in this feminist setting, to serve up a boatload of double-talk under the guise of nuance and "problematizing."

Unsurprisingly, given the eagerness of professors and students of identity studies to claim as many labels for themselves as possible, some individuals have sought to expand the definition of disability to include...well, themselves. At the "Wrong/ed Bodies" session at the Cultural Studies conference, Angela Lea Nemecek complained that when she breastfed in her office at the University of Virginia, she was made to feel as if she had a disability. In short, her breastfeeding was "constructed in the workplace" as a disability. Therefore, she reasoned, breastfeeding *is* a disability and should be protected under the Americans with Disability Act. In addition to offering an example of social constructionist thinking in action, Nemecek embodies an academic phenomenon that might be called Disability Envy—the desire to have something about oneself recognized as a disability, thus increasing by one the number of victim groups one belongs to.

Meanwhile Emily Laurel Smith illustrated just how hostile Disability Studies can be toward medicine, therapy, and medical technology. Smith, a student of American Studies, Disability Studies, and Science/Technology Studies at the University of Minnesota, came to the Cultural Studies conference to talk about the forcing of technology—and thus of "cyborg" status, as she called it—upon disabled people. Smith explained that her mother has multiple sclerosis but refuses to use technology meant to make her life easier—an act that Smith celebrates as "resistance in the face of hegemony, as many of the vendors [of the technology] are able-bodied white men." Smith described those who invent new technology to aid disabled people as uncaring capitalists, and further asserted that "disabled-rights activists expose normalcy as a construction"—showing that there are, indeed, practitioners of Disability Studies who choose to reject reality and pretend that what disables disabled people isn't their disabilities but white men, capitalism, and all the other usual suspects.

3. "Health at Every Size": Fat Studies

In a 2010 article for the *Daily Beast*, Eve Binder reported on the rise of Fat Studies, a discipline that is, to a large extent, a subdivision of Women's Studies. Some Fat Studies students, wrote Binder, "are recovering from eating disorders." Esther Rothblum, a founder of the field and coeditor (with Sondra Solovay) of the 2009 *Fat Studies Reader*, says, "There would be no Fat Studies if there were no obesity epidemic." Yet other leading figures in Fat Studies vehemently reject the idea of an obesity epidemic. Linda Bacon, who teaches at City College of San Francisco and speaks frequently at colleges about the importance of "size acceptance," argues in her influential book *Health at Every Size: The Surprising*

Truth about Your Weight that what matters isn't slimming down but staying healthy at whatever weight is "right for you." The most remarkable thing in Binder's article may be her reference to a Women's Studies professor at the University of Michigan who, in Binder's words, worries that Fat Studies "may lead to social proselytizing rather than serious study." In short, identity studies are becoming so far removed from any hint of academic or intellectual legitimacy that even teachers of more established and only moderately asinine disciplines are reacting to the far more extreme asininity of newer ones.

At the National Women's Studies Association convention in Denver, it's clear that the overweight have won their places at the NWSA table. On Saturday morning, I attend a session entitled "Advancing Fat Feminism," featuring four white females. The author of the first paper, Amy Farrell of Dickinson College, was unable to come, so the moderator, Purdue's Michaela A. Null, reads it for her. It's a chapter from Farrell 's book *Fat Shame* about how images of fat women have been used for generations to denigrate women. For example, while the suffragists' own literature depicted them as thin, antisuffrage caricatures depicted them as fat. A century ago "fatness" was "seen as a marker of low status": in cartoons, blacks, Irishmen, and prostitutes were generally fat. And that's about all Farrell has to say. Next up is MaryAnn Kozlowski of Eastern Michigan University, who starts off by saying that she was worried she would have to buy an extra seat on the flight to Denver—the kind of injustice, she implies, that fat people are routinely compelled to endure. (I wonder how the person sitting next to her on the plane felt about the fact that Kozlowski, who is quite ample, was required to purchase only one ticket.) Kozlowski explains that she has "researched" representations of fat and weight in issues of *Seventeen* magazine published between 1967 and 1969. Her conclusion: that the magazine's anti-fat message, while not explicit, was nonetheless "insidious." For example, there were articles on eating right and on fitness. Over time, she adds, there was an increase in such "fat-phobic articles." And that's it.

Then there's Patricia Bowling, also of Purdue. She's an older woman—and apparently the token slim person on the panel. "As a beginner and a relatively thin woman," she says, she's hesitant to address "fat feminism" and "thin privilege." But she's chosen to do so anyhow. She discusses her own "lifelong addiction to exercise and discipline," which, she says, is the basis for her positive self-image—an image that, in her mind, is connected to "hard work." She worries whether she "know[s] enough about fat oppression" to teach the subject, and recalls that a colleague found it amusing when she saw that Bowling had *The Fat Studies Reader* on reserve at the library. While the hefty young woman sitting beside me chows down on tasty-looking baked goods, Bowling acknowledges that "there *are* health risks that are associated with being fat," yet adds that "fears are exaggerated" and that "fat people are getting treated as scapegoats." This said, she returns to her own "tight body," repeating that she's achieved her "bodily ideal" (in fact, she looks anorexic) as a result of "the sacrifices I've made all my life"—including swimming, exercising, and skipping meals. She says that "obviously" the "messages" about weight control that she's been heeding all her life are wrong, but she doesn't sound for a second as if she really means it (and to judge by her fellow panelists' facial expressions, they're not buying it). Bowling says that we need to "recognize thin privilege" and "fat prejudice," that fat people need "positive role models," and that we should reflect upon the links between "sizeism" and other isms and upon the problematic role of thin teachers such as herself who presume to speak for fat people. Her conclusion: like racism, fat prejudice "takes a visible obvious characteristic" as a basis for prejudice—and we must put an end to this. My conclusion: this is a passive-aggressive woman whose only motive for going into Fat Studies is to celebrate her own thinness.

Back to Null, who confesses to a "feeling of awkwardness when I talk about my work." Exhibiting a sweet, down-to-earth quality that one doesn't often encounter in Women's Studies (she actually refers to a female colleague as a "girl"), Null says that she "started at a place where I was fat-hating": she was a "fat activist but was still on the Atkins diet!" She urges us to "talk about what that word [*fat*] does." We need to "get past that word." Her closing thought: "What would it be like in a world where you didn't hate your body?" Last up is Sheana Director of Bowling Green State. "The most powerful word in the English language," she says, "is the F-word—fat." She provides a capsule history of fat activism: the National Association to Aid Fat Americans was founded in the late 1960s; a group called the Fat Underground came along a few years later. Since most fat activists were white women, they failed to address the "intersections" between classism, racism, imperialism, and "fatism." Director underscores the need to discuss these intersections, lamenting that all too often, in discussions about fat, "there are fat people, poor people, people of color, but never fat, poor people of color."

The next morning, there's another session about fat—kind of—titled "Outsider Feminist Inclusionist Perspectives on the Body." Patti Lou Watkins of Oregon State University kicks things off by introducing various "Fat Studies concepts." She hands out a flyer on which is printed the equation "Fatism" = "Sizeism" = "Looksism" and gives a PowerPoint presentation containing several "fat-positive images." And she mentions both intersectionality (pleading for the "need to bring in those other systems of oppression") and the "'health at every size' paradigm." While Watkins criticizes negative attitudes toward the word *fat* and preaches that "there are fat people who are very healthy," my eyes are on the young woman sitting directly in front of me. Rolls of fat pour around the back of her chair, and her rump protrudes beyond and hangs over, and under, the edges of the chair. She is very young. And here she is being told that her weight is a fundamental aspect of her identity and that any expression of concern about it is bigotry.

Watkins is followed by Lillian C. Taylor, a very big, lively, and charming young woman from the American Public University System (an "online university"), who describes herself as "a self-identified queer, fat, vegan, feminist" professor and whose topic is "inclusionism"—meaning the rejection of *all* isms, from looksism to ableism. After coming out as a lesbian at age thirty, she says, she took some Women's Studies courses. "Knowledge gave me courage," she testifies, and for a while she focused on her "queer identity." But she gradually recognized the "connections between oppressions" and began to see that "speciesism is at the root" of all other isms. "I started to see," she tells us, "that I had no right to the flesh" of other "sentient creatures." So she came out as a vegan—and got more hostility than when she'd come out as a lesbian. And much of the hostility, moreover, was from lesbians. (She says that some lesbians, not seeing the irony, actually tell her she's one of the "okay vegans" because she "doesn't flaunt it.") But what complicates the picture further, she says, is that while there are vegan-phobic lesbians, there are also "fat-phobic" vegans. She speaks of vegans who say that "fat people are gross" and who are suspicious of her presence at vegan get-togethers because they assume that since she's carrying around so much weight she can't possibly be a vegan and must be an "interloper" or "spy." She stresses that she's "not a vegan for health reasons" and that she refuses to drink milk, on feminist grounds: "Dairy is a feminist issue. Milk comes from a grieving mother." Comparing the physical abuse of cows and calves to abuse of women, she intones: "No human can be free while other species are oppressed."

Even more than at other sessions I've attended, the Q&A period this time around proves to be heavy on group therapy. Audience members exchange anecdotes about things doctors have told them ("Your BMI is too high"). Apropos of the "health at every size" paradigm, one woman warns: "You don't want to reinscribe another binary"—in other words, let's not privilege people who are fat and fit at the expense of people who are fat and unfit! Watkins worries: by preaching "health at every size," is she "pushing healthism" in the classroom? (Believe it or not, *healthism* is a real concept, introduced in the 1980s and '90s by academics who, drawing on Foucault, argued that encouraging people to watch their health is a coercive and potentially fascist act linked to capitalism, racism, and Nazi-style eugenics.) Several women complain about media coverage of the "obesity epidemic" (though none of them will admit that such an epidemic exists)—coverage that they view as "blaming and shaming." Asked about the role of capitalism in all this, Watkins cites the diet industry's lust for profits, in response to which a slim, beautiful young vegan with Pippi Longstocking braids pipes up: "I did a Marxist analysis.... It blows my mind how capitalism has worked to erase these things."

I hear about fat not only at the Women's Studies conference in Denver but also at the Queer Studies conference in Berlin, where Rachel White, a heavyset young lecturer in Women's Studies and sociology at the University of Westminster, gives a paper titled "No

Fat Future?" Just as Lee Edelman, she notes, depicts "queers" as people who embody no future because many of them do not have children, so, she says, fat people are often depicted as having "no future" by a society that is constantly linking fatness to mortality. In a PowerPoint presentation, White shows us British tabloid head-lines and advertisements linking inactivity and fatty diets to weight gain and, in turn, to death, and the audience joins her in laughing at these visuals, even though there is nothing particularly unreasonable about the concern expressed therein about the health risks related to obesity. Echoing Heike Raab's observation about disabled people, White concludes that fat people "disturb the heterosexual picture," thus making them "potentially queer."

4. "Why Are Men So Awful?": Men's Studies/Male Studies

On an early spring day when the campus of Monterey Peninsula College—a motley collection of utilitarian, barracks-like buildings which looks like a military base (and for good reason: this used to be Fort Ord)—is almost totally deserted, I find my way across it to David Clemens's tiny, book- and paper-cluttered office. Clemens, a professor of English, welcomes me and we start to chat. There's much to talk about, including the college's Great Books program, which Clemens introduced. But what makes my head turn is the news that one of the six courses he's teaching this term is about "literature by and about men."

Men?

"Most literature," Clemens explains, "is universal and intellec-tual. But some of it can be looked at through sex, through gender." He put together the course because courses on literature by and about women abounded in American universities, but nobody, he says, was teaching about literature and men.

The course covers books, poetry, and films that explore such topics as men at war and fatherhood and that illuminate male codes, such as chivalry and the samurai code of *bushido*; the syllabus includes the Faulkner story "The Bear," stories by Sam Shepard, Robert Hayden's poem "Those Winter Sundays," James Dickey's *Deliverance*, and the films *Seven Samurai* and *Fight Club*. One issue that comes up in the classroom is misandry, or hostility toward men, which is, of course, alive and well in today's academy and which also shapes a good deal of contemporary film and literature (although Clemens suggests that this tendency "disappeared after 9/11"). One interesting detail: several of the students in his men's lit course are females who signed up at least in part because they feel their fathers have been denigrated by society.

The men's literature course caused problems: at first, students who took it and later transferred from MPC to universities in the California state system were denied transfer credits on the ground that it was too "narrow" a course and had no counterpart elsewhere in the system. But when the National Association of Scholars (NAS) took up the issue, "someone very high up in the university system said, 'Let s just make it transferable and get out of this.'"

For all the radicalism of David Clemens's course in men's litera-ture, he's not the only humanities professor out there teaching about men. There is, in fact, a whole discipline called Men's Studies, which has taken root at about a hundred North American colleges and universities. But, to quote Rutgers anthropologist Lionel Tiger (who coined the term "male bonding"), Men's Studies is "a wholly owned branch of women's studies," examining maleness through a feminist and social constructionist prism. Robert Heasley, president of the American Men's Studies Association, states unapologetically that "Men's Studies came out of feminist analysis of gender." (Clemens puts it this way: Men's Studies is a "camouflage version of Women's Studies" in which the "operative question" is "Why are we men so awful?") Its founding father and "presiding guru"—to borrow a term from Miles Groth, a sometime key player in the discipline—was Australian sociologist Robert W. Connell, whose 1995 book *Mascu-linities* is the main text in the field. Connell coined the term "hege-monic masculinity," which refers to the supposed fact that society teaches men to dominate women and one another; the concept—which, Connell has acknowledged, derives from "feminist theories of patriarchy"—is at the very heart of Men's Studies.

Given that Connell helped establish an academic discipline the entire point of which is that men are authoritarian bullies, it's not irrelevant that he is now a she: in 2008, it was revealed that Connell had undergone a sex-change operation and was now a woman named Raewyn Connell. Connell's colleagues accepted this change in politically correct fashion, but one must be permitted to ask: what does it mean that the male founder of a discipline called Men's Studies turns out to have been, all along, a transsexual—a person, that is, whose self-image was that of a woman trapped in a man's body, and who viewed that body as alien and abhorrent? Groth, who is chair of the Psychology Department at Wagner College on Staten Island, points out that, astonishing though Connell's transformation is, it "has never been addressed by the Men's Studies group."

Groth was active in the American Men's Studies Association for two years and edited two Men's Studies journals—one about men's health, the other about "boyhood studies." But he lost both editorships when he became involved in a new academic discipline that offers an alternative to Men's Studies. It is called Male Studies, and its leading figure is a psychiatrist, Edward M. Stephens, who established the Foundation for Male Studies in 2010 at a conference at Wagner hosted by Groth. Among the participants was Tiger, who criticized feminism's "denigration of maleness" and dismissed social constructionism, noting that "male and female organisms really are different" and citing the "enormous relation between…biology and…behavior." Other attendees were Christina Hoff Sommers (author of *Who Stole Feminism?* and *The War Against Boys*), who talked about "male-averse attitudes" in American society, and Paul Nathanson, a religious studies scholar at McGill and author of *Spreading Misandry: The Teaching of Contempt for Men in Popular Culture* (2006), who stressed the need to question "some fundamental features of ideological feminism over the last thirty or forty years." When *Inside Higher Ed* asked Heasley what he thought of Male Studies, he called it "a Glenn Beck approach" to the subject; the even more hostile comments about Male Studies by Women's Studies professors make it clear that, in their view, the idea of a nonfeminist approach to the study of maleness is sheer heresy.

New though Male Studies is, it appears to have already divided into at least two streams. Groth now shares Heasley's opinion that the brand of Male Studies represented by Stephens is "reactionary" and "embittered." "The newness of Male Studies," Groth admits, "has drawn to it a variety of individuals with very different motivations." He describes his own motivation in this way: "The national ratio of male-female students is now 39–61, an all-time low.... Boys are failing in elementary school.... They are not drawn to college and if they enroll, they are dropping out in greater and greater numbers.... Graduate programs have only a handful of men in them nationally. They are not entering the professions."

Groth characterizes the goal of Male Studies as follows: having "recognized the spread of misandry in culture," he and his colleagues "are ardent about restoring balance in areas where men are now in a precarious situation"—everything from schooling and child custody to the criminal justice system and media images. He contrasts the concrete and practical approach of Men's Studies with the ideological bent of Women's Studies, which, he maintains, "is not an academic discipline. At universities, where it appears in curricula, it is a congeries of courses that represent ideological feminism." (He distinguishes "ideological feminism" from "egalitarian feminism, which no one would deny was a laudable movement.") He rejects the whole concept of patriarchy, "a shibboleth for blaming all men for the behavior of a few, who have harmed women and *most males*." And he finds Women's Studies courses "fundamentally misandric. My course is among only a few in the country that have successfully run the gauntlet of academic affairs committees to find a place among courses offered for credit. Academe has systematically turned down proposals for such courses for more than thirty years, even while adding more courses in Women's Studies."

At this writing Groth is teaching a course on "The Psychology of Men," in which he and his students examine "theories of male psychological change, the myth of male aggressiveness, masculinities, male sexuality, homoeroticism and male homosexuality, males' relationships with parents, women and children, and male narcissism, spirituality and psychopathology," explore stereotypes about men's "alleged promiscuity and emotional superficiality" and "the illusion of male power in society," and study "manhood in a variety of cultures" and "the mythological elements of masculinity." The reading list includes books with titles like *The Masculine Self, Manhood in the Making: Cultural Concepts of Masculinity*, and *Raising Cain: Protecting the*

Emotional Lives of Boys; Groth also screens such films as *Billy Elliot, Fight Club*, and *Mysterious Skin*.

He started teaching the course in 2003, and every time he's taught it most of his students have been women. Why do they take it? "Because they want to understand men's experience, *about which we know next to nothing*. Men's behavior has been documented and has dominated the history books. But apart from a few standard explanations—testosterone, an irrational desire to dominate women sexually, hunger for power—the deeper story of what motivates men remains untold." As for "the few men who take the course," they tend to "sit quietly. They're glad to see that there's an interest in their lives." He describes them as "struggling to save their self-respect" in a society riddled with male-bashing—such as the every-man-a-potential-rapist rhetoric to which almost all of them are subjected at "date rape seminars" during freshman orientation.

5. "Raced People": Whiteness Studies

Just as Men's Studies isn't really about maleness but about patriarchal oppression, so Whiteness Studies isn't really about whiteness but about racist oppression. As David Horowitz has put it: "Black studies celebrates blackness, Chicano studies celebrates Chicanos, women's studies celebrates women, and white studies attacks white people as evil." It is about "the social construction of whiteness as an ideology tied to social status." To be white, in short, is, by definition, to enjoy a wide variety of privileges of which white people themselves are unaware even though those privileges are blindingly obvious to non-whites. Some readers, far from finding this line of argument fresh, illuminating, and revolutionary—which is what Whiteness Studies represents it as being—may instead be surprised that an entire discipline has been constructed upon a notion that has, after all, been a staple of the rhetoric of racial politics ever since the 1960s.

Among the discipline's founding texts are *The Wages of Whiteness* (1991) by David Roediger, a study of white "working-class racism"; *Playing in the Dark: Whiteness and the Literary Imagina-*

tion (1992), in which Toni Morrison takes on what she considers the "more or less tacit agreement among literary scholars that, because American literature has been clearly the preserve of white male views, genius, and power, those views, genius, and power are without relationship to and removed from the overwhelming presence of black people in the United States"; and *White Women, Race Matters: The Social Construction of Whiteness* (1993), in which Ruth Frankenberg argues that "race shapes white women's lives," that "white people and people of color lead racially structured lives," and that "White people are 'raced,' just as men are gendered." "Whiteness," Frankenberg has said, "is a construct or identity almost impossible to separate from racial domination." In other words, to be white is, in essence, to be by definition an oppressor. Noel Ignatiev has written that the "key to solving the social problems of our age is to abolish the white race—in other words, to abolish the privileges of the white skin." Then there is the anthology *White Privilege: Essential Readings on the Other Side of Racism* (2002), edited by Paula Rothenberg.

The subject has been taught at dozens of American universities, from Princeton to UCLA. And it is, in fact, a very American discipline, many of whose practitioners appear not to recognize that their self-assured postulates about race and identity carry little or no meaning outside of the distinctively American contexts in which they live and work. It is not clear, for example, how "abolish[ing] the privileges of the white skin" would have prevented the Cultural Revolution in China, genocide in Rwanda and Cambodia, or any number of other mass-scale human atrocities that had nothing whatever to do with whiteness. Nor, for that matter, do the practitioners of Whiteness Studies even attempt, in most cases, to provide any explanation of how their works of "scholarship," which consist largely of endlessly repetitive hand-wringing about white privilege, can help in any practical sense to alleviate the social and economic conditions of poor non-whites in the United States or elsewhere.

In 2006, noting that Whiteness Studies had only ten years earlier been "a fringe campus fad" but was "now a vigorously promoted branch of critical race theory," Canadian columnist Barbara Kay described Whiteness Studies as a "case of academic decadence," "a new low in moral vacuity and civilizational self-loathing," and "a particularly far out example of academic pusillanimity"—because it "is all, and only, about white self-hate." According to Whiteness Studies, complained Kay, to be white is to be "branded, literally in the flesh, with evidence of a kind of original sin. You can try to mitigate your evilness, but you can't eradicate it. The goal...is to entrench permanent race consciousness in everyone—eternal victimhood for non-whites, eternal guilt for whites." Kay quoted Jeff Hitchcock, cofounder and executive director of a Whiteness Studies think tank called the Center for White American Culture: "There is no crime that whiteness has not committed against people of color.... We must blame whiteness for the continuing patterns today...which damage and prevent the humanity of those of us within it."

There have been Critical Whiteness Studies conferences, and there is also an annual White Privilege Conference, with its own online journal, *Understanding & Dismantling Privilege*, published at the University of Colorado at Colorado Springs. The 2012 conference, in Albuquerque, was entitled "Intersectionality: Vision, Commitment, and Sustainable Partnerships." The White Privilege Conference describes itself as providing "a challenging, collaborative and comprehensive experience" and as seeking "to empower and equip individuals to work for equity and justice through self and social transformation." Its website proffers some of the movement's favorite truisms, suggesting, for example, that if you're white you're specially privileged because you can "assume that if you work hard and follow the rules, you will get what you deserve" and "go out in public without fear of being harassed or constantly worried about physical safety." The latter claim, of course, utterly upends the realities of interracial crime, which is far more black-on-white than white-on-black. This is one more identity-studies discipline, then, that has less to do with reality than with ideology.

Teachers' unions have reportedly been given federal grants in exchange for agreeing to compel their members to attend White Privilege Conferences—members who, in turn, can be expected to inflict the "ideas" they've acquired on their pupils, from grade school on up.

CHAPTER 7
Is There Hope?

"The situation in our universities, I am confident, will soon right itself once the great silent majority of professors cry 'enough' and challenge what they know to be voguish blather."

So wrote Arthur Schlesinger Jr. in 1998. Alas, he seems to have been mistaken. Since he penned those words, the "voguish blather" has made greater and greater inroads into the study of the humanities and social sciences—and in doing so has increasingly weakened the fabric of American civil society, the shared culture that has made America great.

It has also replaced something that was, in a word, irreplaceable. There is no substitute for a real education in the humanities. To study some things is to prepare for a career; to study the humanities is to prepare for life.

This sounds like a commonplace, a truism, an advertising slogan. It's not. The human race has been around for a couple of million years, human civilization a few thousand. As recently as two or three centuries ago, the idea of young people *en masse* in any country on earth being afforded the chance to devote several years of their lives to reading great books, discussing great ideas, and thinking about the meaning of life would have been inconceivable. All but the most privileged of people in the most prosperous of countries would have considered such an opportunity a luxury with a value beyond reckoning. Consider a letter that John Adams wrote to his wife, Abigail, on May 12, 1780, when she was at home in Massachusetts tending the farm and he was in France in the service of the fledgling American Republic. "To take a Walk in the Gardens of the Palace of the Tuilleries," John wrote to Abigail,

> and describe the Statues there, all in marble, in which the ancient Divinities and Heroes are represented with exquisite Art, would be a very pleasant Amusement, and instructive Entertainment, improving in History, Mythology, Poetry, as well as in Statuary. Another Walk in the Gardens of Versailles, would be usefull and agreable....
>
> I could fill Volumes with Descriptions of Temples and Palaces, Paintings, Sculptures, Tapestry, Porcelaine, &c. &c. &c.—if I could have time. But I could not do this without neglecting my duty.... I must study Politicks and War that my sons may have liberty to study Mathematicks and Philosophy. My sons ought to study Mathematicks and Philosophy, Geography, natural History, Naval Architecture, navigation, Commerce and Agriculture, in order to give their Children a right to study Painting, Poetry, Musick, Architecture, Statuary, Tapestry and Porcelaine.

We are Adams's grandchildren. We stand on his shoulders, and on the shoulders of pioneers and soldiers, entrepreneurs and inventors, factory laborers and farmers, who, over the course of a few extraordinary generations, transformed a wilderness continent into the freest, most dynamic, and most prosperous nation in the history of the human race. One consequence of this freedom, dynamism, and prosperity is that by the late twentieth century virtually every young person in America had the opportunity to acquire a real higher education—to devote precious time not only to training in some practical science or skill, but also to the contemplation of things like painting and poetry, music and architecture.

Unfortunately, very few young Americans nowadays appreciate just how remarkable a blessing this is. This ignorance is not their fault. The simple fact is that they live in an almost historyless society in which nobody has ever explained to them just how fortunate they are to live in the time and place that they do. Nobody has ever helped them to understand just how different their lives are from those of their great-great-grandparents, and why. Nobody has ever told them that only a few generations ago, the lives of most human beings in even the richest countries in the world were poor, nasty, brutish, and short; that most people were illiterate; that there were far more teenagers working themselves to exhaustion in factories or on farms than sitting in classrooms reading Shakespeare.

Indeed, from the beginning of recorded history until a time that is still within living memory, only relatively few people anywhere in the world had the time and the means to sit for hours at a spell, as Socrates and his friends did in the agora in Athens 2,400 years ago, and converse about ideas. Only a few had the privilege of being able to read great books, experience great art and music, and discuss these things seriously with others. Such conversations have been going on ever since the time of Socrates, but to take part in them was the rarest of privileges. It is perhaps the ultimate measure of the success of the American experiment that, at some point in the mid- to late twentieth century, it became possible for almost everyone to participate in those conversations. It is also, alas, a measure of that experiment's success that most young people today simply do not appreciate just how remarkable an opportunity this is. Even now, privileged though they are, many young people are told by their parents or friends or other presumably well-meaning individuals that the humanities are a luxury they cannot afford. Better to study only practical things, to focus laser-like on preparing for a career, than to waste any time on literature, philosophy, art history, or music appreciation. To take such a position is to fail to recognize that the serious study of such subjects *is* a practical matter. It is about learning to think analytically and critically. It is about experiencing wildly different products of the human mind and spirit and making comparisons, recognizing affinities, deciding what one likes and doesn't like, and in the process, over time, refining one's own taste. It is about encountering unfamiliar thoughts, weighing them against one another and against one's own observations of the world, figuring out what one thinks of them, and, in the process, forming one's own philosophy of life. It is about building an understanding of the history of humankind, and of human art and thought and culture, so that one develops, bit by bit, a radically heightened sense of how things got to be the way they are. It is about coming to see the world through increasingly sophisticated eyes, and hence experiencing it in a way far richer than one could ever have imagined at the start of things.

What it's all about, in short, is learning to think, and to think for oneself—to make the fullest and freest use of one's mind. Indeed, it is ultimately about human freedom—the freedom of the individual intellect to do its own work of observing, analyzing, discerning, judging, and thus make its own worthy contribution to the preservation and advancement of human civilization. This is why a real education for all—not just literacy, not just vocational training—is the most American of objectives, and it is why this noblest of goals was met in America before it was met anywhere else. And it is why the replacement of a true education in the humanities by identity studies is a betrayal, in the profoundest sense, of the promise of America.

The discussion that Socrates began millennia ago in Athens, and that has been going on ever since in classrooms and coffeehouses, in the pages of books and magazines and newspapers, and on computer screens, was given a name by the educator Robert Maynard Hutchins (1899–1977). He called it "the Great Conversation."

Multiculturalism, social constructionism, and all the deplorable related "isms" that are part of the postmodern experiment have nothing whatsoever to do with "the great conversation." They do not open the mind—they close it. The Great Conversation is about learning to appreciate, cherish, and pass on to others the glories of Western civilization; the ideologies that have captured—and degraded—the humanities today teach nothing but contempt for that civilization. The Great Conversation is about developing the individual, critical, questioning, adventurous mind; the identity studies and other "studies" that have proliferated in recent years are about propagandizing, making disciples, and excluding heretics.

I can testify to the remarkable extent of the difference that the study of the humanities made in my life. It wasn't the ideal education. It was disorderly. I have often wished that I could go back and redesign it from scratch. Ideally, I wish I had taken a series of Western civilization courses that took me from ancient times up to the present, in which I had read the important works of history, philosophy, biography, theology, and science, the great novels and plays and poetry, and all the important books about the art and architecture and music of every period, all in chronological order, so as to equip me with a broad, full, coherent picture of the great parade of human thought and culture. But few, if any, people get such educations.

To an extent, I was lucky. I was always a self-directed reader, plunging at one point in my teens, for example, into books about Russia, at another point into all the "Inside" books (*Inside USA, Inside Asia*, etc.), published between the late 1930s and early 1970s, in which John Gunther presented richly detailed political and sociocultural portraits of almost every country in the world. But some people aren't so self-directed, and need a nudge, a reading list, tests, deadlines.

Not that I didn't need direction, too. College and graduate school forced me to read things that I probably would never have dipped into otherwise—the more obscure ancient epics, some of the less familiar Elizabethan and Renaissance plays—and that I'm now glad I read. My graduate school reading in nineteenth-and twentieth-century English and American literature was especially thorough, providing me with a wonderfully detailed picture of the subject. I wish my grasp of all history and all literature were as good. I have spent my life trying to fill in some of the many remaining gaps. This is what a humanities education in college should be for: it should be a way of launching young people on that journey, a way of getting them started on—and eager to pursue—a lifelong habit of curiosity about the greatest things that have been thought and written.

This is why the identity studies and other postmodern academic phenomena I have written about in this book are so execrable. They are a perverse betrayal of a rich and beautiful legacy. They throw away a gift we should all be thrilled at the opportunity to enjoy. We have reached the top of the mountain, and they are taking our children by the hand and urging them to jump into the abyss. The people who "teach" these postmodern subjects talk about power, but what they have done as alleged educators is as despicable an abuse of power as one could imagine—because they have used their power to rob young people of their priceless legacy as heirs to the riches of human civilization.

To experience all of this—to attend these people's conferences, read their books, see them teach—can be a dispiriting experience. But there are glimmers of hope. It's promising, for example, that at least some Women's Studies students irritate their professors by expressing concern for the victims of honor killings. It's promising that young women are taking courses in Male Studies in order to learn about their fathers.

Yes, there are many students—alas—who get turned by identity studies into little commissars who see it as their purpose in life to be Thought Police. They don't know enough about the history of the twentieth century to realize that they are the philosophical progeny of the uniformed thugs who led freethinking people off to the gulag in Stalin's Russia and to reeducation camps in Mao's China. They don't know enough about the history of ideas to understand that the ideas to which they have pledged their loyalty are not ideas at all, in any authentic sense, but fierce, rigid, airless, totalitarian orthodoxies.

The fact that at least some college students rebel against these orthodoxies is cheering proof that intelligent young people do have a natural eagerness to learn—to *learn*, not be brainwashed—that cannot easily be quenched. They have a thirst for real knowledge, a thirst to understand the world around them—a natural inquisitiveness about life that is, after all, when it comes down to it, what the humanities are really all about. And they are savvy enough to recognize that identity studies and all these other bogus "studies" do not address any of their questions.

There are other reasons for hope. These "studies" first gained ground—and grew, and grew—because administrators were scared of being called bigots, racists, misogynists, homophobes. But today such accusations have been hurled around so much that they are steadily losing their power. One can only hope this will spell the beginning of the end for "disciplines" founded entirely on guilt-tripping.

Then there is the Internet. It has its pluses and minuses. The minuses are mostly obvious. One plus is that the Internet makes it impossible for propaganda-slinging professors to control the flow of ideas to their students. To Google anything is to discover criticism of it. It is, accordingly, impossible for any teacher to fool a truly curious student into buying, for example, the notion that social constructionism is a universally accepted scientific concept in the same way as the second law of thermodynamics.

And there is yet another cause for hope: the existence of intrepid champions of the *true* humanities who have been struggling against these noxious trends for years.

*   *   *

The time: late one night in 1993. The place: a dorm at the University of Pennsylvania. Eden Jacobowitz, a freshman, is writing a paper in his dorm room when a group of women outside begin singing and chanting so loudly that he finds it difficult to work.

"Shut up, you water buffalo!" he shouts out the window.

The subsequent events occur in rapid succession. The women, who are black, charge Jacobowitz with racist harassment. The university agrees, arguing that the water buffalo is an African animal. (It is Asian.) When Jacobowitz refuses to accept a settlement that would oblige him to plead guilty of racism and attend a racial-sensitivity seminar, the administration decides to prosecute him, an action that could lead to his suspension or expulsion. At this point Jacobowitz engages Alan Charles Kors as his advisor. Kors, in turn, brings in the Pennsylvania ACLU. Intensive research establishes that there is absolutely no record of "water buffalo" ever being used as a racist epithet in English or in any other language. But "water buffalo," it emerges, *is* the English translation of a Hebrew slang word for a thoughtless or rowdy person—a word that was part of Jacobowitz's vocabulary when he was a yeshiva student.

The evidence exculpating Jacobowitz is overwhelming; that against him is nil. The story gains international attention. Newspapers around the world criticize the university's persecution of the innocent student. In the *Wall Street Journal,* Dorothy Rabinowitz calls it "Kafkaesque." On *NBC Nightly News,* John Chancellor comments: "The language police are at work on the campuses of our better schools.... The culture of victimization is hunting for quarry." But university administrators are determined to prove their racial sensitivity by destroying Jacobowitz.

The public criticism mounts. Finally the accusers buckle. Claiming that the media frenzy has made it impossible for them to get justice, they withdraw their charges. Then, and only then, does the university drop what is now known as the "water buffalo" case.

That case had immense repercussions. It led Kors and civil liberties lawyer Harvey Silvergate to establish the Foundation for Individual Rights in Education (FIRE) in 1999. Over the years, FIRE has fought many battles around the United States, successfully challenging "diversity" requirements and political litmus tests for hiring, tenure, and promotion, and defending students' and faculty members' First Amendment rights in cases involving allegedly offensive speech, the stifling of dissent, and much else.

The case also led Kors to devote much of his time to delivering lectures about the dire changes that have transformed the academy in recent decades. Kors spells out the differences between then and now sharply: the pre-sixties secular-humanist university was founded on the ideas of free speech promulgated by John Stuart Mill; the humanities today are founded on the selective censorship advocated by post-sixties icon Herbert Marcuse, who called for "the withdrawal of toleration of speech and assembly from groups and movements which promote aggressive policies, armament, chauvinism, discrimination on the grounds of race or religion, or which oppose the extension of public services, social security, medical care, etc."

Kors chides university administrators who "have given over the humanities, the soft social sciences, and the entire university *in loco parentis* to the zealots of oppression studies and coercive identity politics"—an act that, he writes, has resulted in "a soft tyranny of groupthink, unconscious bias, and self-inflated sense of a mission of demystification." American universities, he charged in a 2006 lecture at the University of Cape Town, believe that blacks, women, gays, and lesbians stand in need of special protections not afforded to others. Where all these groups, in fact, have struggled so fiercely and at such cost for legal equality, our academic leaders believe that they must be protected from arguments or even from the punch lines of jokes, as if these heroic souls were too weak to live with freedom.... The assignment of official group identity always worsens, not betters, human relations at campuses and in the broader society, creating barriers and defensiveness along with injustice.

Kors also criticizes many of his fellow academic historians for their "tendentiousness"—for "seeing their work as an extension of their politics, and merely looking for evidence, however nonrepresentative, to support what they wish to believe. The excitement of being an historian, however, whatever the reason we choose a topic, is precisely to be surprised and forced by evidence to modify our deepest views." For himself,

I don't want disciples of my worldview. I want students who know how to read deeply, how to analyze, how to locate the essential points of similarity and divergence among thinkers, and, indeed, how to understand, with intellectual empathy, how the world looks from the diverse perspectives that constitute the history of European thought. I know that I am not alone, but I also know, alas, that I am in a distinct minority in my pedagogical goals in the humanities and the so-called social sciences.

Twenty minutes or so by foot from the Thirtieth Street Station in Philadelphia is a narrow, tree-lined block of Sansom Street dotted with charming trattorias and bistros. On a hot day in early May 2010, I meet Kors there for a modest lunch and a couple of hours of conversation.

Kors, who with his trim gray beard and suit jacket looks like the distinguished professor that he is, talks about identity politics in the university today. "It's dysfunctional for American education," he says. "It's dysfunctional for the groups it purports to speak for. And it's dysfunctional for intergroup relations—for individuals meeting across group lines. It enforces stereotypes. It tells people 'if you are X, there are certain voices, and *only* those voices, that speak for you.' And if you dissent from those voices that 'speak for you' then you have 'internalized oppression'—the intellectual equivalent of Lenin's 'false consciousness.' You don't really want what you think you want. It's *infantilizing*." He speaks about these issues frequently at college campuses, and he says there's often a pattern to these appearances. "There's a moment in my talk when I see a group sent over by the Multicultural Center or the Women's Center. A hostile group. I look in their direction and I say the following from the marrow of my being: 'It's the right of every free individual to decide the relative importance or unimportance of their race, sex, and sexuality. No one has a right to invade the inner sanctum of your conscience. The promise of this country has been to include everybody in the circle of equal rights. Groups have struggled to enter that circle. No one who tells you that you are too weak to live with freedom is your friend.' When I say that, it's a turning point, and after that I get friendly or probing questions rather than the hostile questions that I might have expected."

He talks about the way in which the American academy "assigns an official group identity" to students, eliminating the distinction "between voluntary association and imposed group identity." For example, "a Jewish student who is totally assimilated—whose Jewish identity is totally unimportant to him—goes to college and is assigned a special Jewish advisor." The academy also distinguishes between people who "own" their sexual, racial, or gender identity and those who, in its view, have "internalized their oppression." For example, Kors says, Walter Olson, a tort reform expert at the Cato Institute who happens to be gay, "is not *really* gay because he doesn't understand the sources of his oppression." Thomas Sowell, an African American author based at the Hoover Institution, "isn't really black." And "Daphne Patai, a founder of Women's Studies at Amherst, isn't really a woman because she identifies with the oppressive culture around her. So in the humanities, when they speak of diversity, the one kind of diversity they *don't* mean is individuated intellectual diversity." On the contrary, there's a process of "vetting *against individuation.* The people who are most discriminated against, then, are not straight white males who just roll over and play along, but rather libertarian and conservative blacks, women who are critics of feminism, and gays and lesbians who are critics of the 'official' gay and lesbian positions on every issue in the world."

As one of those gays, I happen to know that Kors is right. He dismisses, however, the notion that all this academic groupthink is the work of some vast, organized left-wing conspiracy. "There *is* no conspiracy, no network. *That's where the right gets it wrong.* It's an *unofficial consensus.* It's *not* conspiratorial. They look at a [job] candidate who is conservative and they don't say, 'He's conservative,' they say the person isn't bright." Then there's the illusion on the part of many university folk that they're providing some kind of ideological corrective:

> If I put my colleagues on truth serum, they honestly would say that K-12 is one long celebration without criticism of American hegemony and the free-market system. Most faculty send their kids to expensive private schools with progressive agendas or they're in college towns which they think of as aberrations. So they think that what's being taught in ordinary public schools in America is something very different from what their own kids are taught. They think kids are still being told about George Washington chopping down the cherry tree—they see K-12 as a mystification of kids who are further mystified by pop culture, music, movies, TV, ads. All except rap, which they consider transgressive— even though the lyrics are the most misogynistic and antigay around.

Back in 1971, when Kors was an assistant professor, he and another assistant professor, who was gay (Kors is straight), co-founded something called College House. It was intended as "an alternative to the old fraternity or sorority model"; the idea was to give students an opportunity to mix with people unlike themselves. Half of the residents were male and half were female, living on the same floors. "We mixed Black Power advocates with southern whites; Campus Crusaders for Christ with the earliest members of the gay rights movement; Maoists and College Republicans. People rubbed against each other in the wrong way all the time, *and they learned to talk to each other!*"

That first year it was a success. But by the mid- to late seventies, the university had introduced identity politics not just into the curriculum but also into the residential system. "Penn built a Du Bois College House for black students, and we [at College House] lost a huge part of our black student population. Then they built East Asian House, and we lost our East Asian students. They built International House, so we lost our international students. Then there came Arts House, and we lost our musicians. They built Pre Med House, so that premeds who used to live with poets were now just living with one another. The underlying notion was that people are most comfortable being with 'people like themselves.' Then they politicized student life—freshman orientation became a PC ideological boot camp, with people from the LGBT center, the Women's Center—people who haven't *individuated* are presented as Voices of your community.'"

Kors notes that despite pressure to build an LGBT House ("LGBT" stands for Lesbian, Gay, Bisexual, and Transgender), Penn has never done so—though the university *does* have an LGBT Center. Why, Kors asks, was the administration willing to build a special dorm for blacks but not for gays? Because there's a pecking order in the academy: "sexuality trumps neutrality; race trumps sexuality; gender trumps race; and careerism trumps all." (By way of example, Kors notes that a black intellectual who defends homophobic rap is tolerated, as is a feminist who goes after black misogyny.) "So they will *not* test the waters on building a 'gay house'—because of the discomfort it might cause in certain circles. At every university one of the bitterest struggles is over trans students who object to having to choose between men's and women's bathrooms, saying that 'you oppress me every time you ask me to choose between men's and women's bathrooms.' So they *add* gender-neutral bathrooms, while also keeping men's and women's bathrooms."

Pretty much everything that ails the postmodern academy, Kors says, comes down to a simple question: "Is identity individual or is it collective? If the former, then you have to draw a line in the sand about autonomy, rights, and dignity. We know historically that when identity is identified categorically, it's catastrophic for the Other. When the left looks at Western society, it has the sensitivity of the princess and the pea. When it looks at anti-Western societies, all those sensitivities disappear. And yet this is the only country on earth where Hutus and Tutsis"—and he lists a number of other such examples—"can live side by side. It's a historical miracle. What we're seeing now is a revolution of rising expectations. When you're totally oppressed, small things don't bother you. When great progress occurs, the remaining discriminations, however slight, become unbearable. Forty years ago, it was unimaginable that there would be states where gay marriage is legal, and that you'd be able to live openly as gay. Forty years ago, if they'd told you that we'd have two successive blacks as secretary of state, and a black president, you'd have called it a Utopian dream. But the more progress we have, the more unbearable the small slights become." Wrapped up in all this, of course, is the fact that teachers and professors "haven't given students *any* sense of history. These kids don't understand the vast difference between being black or gay or female then—and now."

Founded in 1987, the National Association of Scholars works, in its own words, to "defend the core values of liberal education" from "illiberal ideologies," to "uphold the principle of individual merit" and "the Western intellectual heritage," and to address such issues as "ideological litmus tests in faculty hiring," "trivialized curricula," "hollow baccalaureate requirements," and, not least, "the post-modern evisceration of the humanities." The identity studies establishment views the NAS as an enemy: in 1997, the National Women's Studies Association equated the NAS with the KKK and neo-Nazi groups, arguing that it shared their determination to restore "white, Western, male hegemony." (The NAS's current board of advisors includes such white males as Gertrude Himmelfarb, Christina Hoff Sommers, and Shelby Steele.) The NAS publishes the journal *Academic Questions*, which stands for "humanism," "intellectual freedom," "integrity of scholarship and teaching," and "tolerance and civility on campus."

On a hot day in May 2010, I meet NAS president Steve Balch at the Princeton Junction train station in New Jersey. He drives us to a pleasant restaurant nearby, where we order lunch and he tells me about the organization's history. In the 1970s, as a professor of American government at CUNY's John Jay College of Criminal Justice, Balch became "professionally disillusioned with radical ideologies" (which, he says, found their way into the academy earlier in New York than in some other places) and with "the general atmosphere of laxity" among his fellow academics. What's more, he recognized that these two things—laxity and radicalism—were not unrelated. He was dismayed by "those who saw their teaching as providing cannon fodder for revolution."

So in 1982 he helped found something called the Campus Coalition for Democracy, which would later become the NAS. His cofounders—among them Peter Shaw (a former professor of English at Stony Brook), Herbert London (a professor of humanities at NYU), and literary critic Carol Iannone—were, in his words, "New York neocon types." "At first it was more political," he says of the CCD; over time it became less so, serving as an alternative to increasingly politicized organizations such as the Modern Language Association (MLA). "We see ourselves," Balch says, "as upholding the traditions of the academy as it existed in midcentury—the university as a temple of science, a free marketplace of ideas, a laboratory of investigation and inquiry, a cutting edge of intellectual discovery, a bastion of Western civilization."

The NAS has supported anti-affirmative action initiatives, great books programs, and courses that teach about America's founding ideals. How effective has the NAS been? Balch is frank. It's had "a little bit" of an impact. The problem is that the malady that has infected the academy has also blighted all of American society. Indeed, the post-sixties revolution in the humanities is "partly a leading indicator and partly a driving force." Balch admits that "we haven't gotten the breakthrough I've always wanted. Because the balance is so heavily to the left that administrators are scared to challenge them."

When I mention identity studies, Balch is quick to insist that some admirable work has been produced in these disciplines. Yet on the whole, he says, these fields have been "infected with a spirit at odds with formative notions of the modern university." Balch himself has had research interests that would easily fit into identity studies if those disciplines were more properly conceived: "I was interested in the use of eunuchs in premodern society. They were popular because they could guard harems and couldn't set up dynasties." He still finds it a fascinating subject, certainly one worthy of study. But because of the current tendency of scholars to give their work a politically correct slant, "I would worry nowadays whether a book on that subject was reliable." Indeed, "you need to take the products of these studies with a grain of salt. And it's a shame, because the subjects these fields deal with are *not unimportant subjects!*"

Part of the reason why the humanities have lost their way, he suggests, is that the people who engineered the humanities revolution "conflated things that were not *essentially similar.* They equated natural science with humane sciences"—the latter being his umbrella term for the humanities and social sciences. The difference is that in the "humane sciences," as opposed to the natural sciences, there's no clear way to test a proposition, and "passions aren't involved in the same way." Yes, "scientists do have egos, but scientific struggles are usually not an integral part of broader political issues, the exception being in such cases as evolution and global warming." By contrast, "the humanities are almost all political. They've become so abstracted from anything anyone cares about," and "when they're supported by privately endowed universities, you need systems in which the [people with the] prevailing points of view can't decide on their own who's going to be invited into the guild. You need checks and balances to keep them honest."

Balch wonders aloud, "How much good do the humanities and social sciences really do? If physics and medicine disappeared, we'd be in bad shape. But if sociology disappeared? Even good academic history? Do we understand politics better than the Federalist Papers did? Or are we just creating this new priestly class that wants to shame us and rule us?" But he's hopeful: "ultimately they *can't*" rule us, "because they don't have the stomach for tough politics. They can't stand up to terrorists, and sooner or later this bluff will be called."

*　　*　　*

Based at Boston University, the Association of Literary Scholars, Critics, and Writers (ALSCW, originally ALSC) was founded in 1993 by such distinguished critics as Denis Donoghue, Roger Shattuck, and Christopher Ricks in reaction to the rise of postmodernism in the humanities. The spring 2011 issue of the journal *Academic Questions*, includes an essay, "Rescuing Literature: The Association of Literary Scholars, Critics, and Writers at Sixteen," in which David Rothman laments that theory-besotted English departments have "given up faith in their own field" because it isn't science and "have desperately sought to represent themselves as being stocked with ersatz economists, anthropologists, sociologists, and legal and political theorists."

Rothman is right. If the political upheavals of the 1960s turned the heads of English professors and others laboring in the vineyards of the humanities, the heady advances of mid-twentieth-century science and technology made many of them feel terribly inferior and irrelevant—and that's a key part of the picture of the postmodern humanities.

As a student I was quite aware of the awe, envy, and insecurity with which some of my English professors regarded scientists and their work. Living in an era defined by breathtaking, rapid scientific and technological advances—an era in which science was where the action was—they weren't content with the idea of "simply" being, say, old-fashioned textual scholars or literary critics. Truth be told, some of them weren't all that interested in literature in the first place. In any event, they certainly didn't want to be acolytes—people whose job it was to read other men's and women's masterpieces attentively, even reverentially, and to teach others how to read them attentively, too. No, they wanted to be the stars; they wanted to be perceived as doing something every bit as difficult, and as being every bit as important to the world, as Einstein or Alexander Fleming or Stephen Hawking or Watson and Crick—which meant turning their field into a pseudoscience complete with murky, scientific-sounding jargon and "theories."

If I, as a student, was blessedly immune to such foolishness, it was largely thanks to my father, an internist who'd worked as a medical researcher, as a hospital chief of staff, and, for two decades, as the editor in chief of a medical journal, but who'd also published short stories and had radio plays produced on CBS and NBC. He loved both medicine and literature, and was at once a first-rate diagnostician who could pinpoint an obscure ailment and a top-notch script doctor who could put his finger on exactly why a friend's screenplay didn't work. In our home, science and literature coexisted peacefully: the living room shelves were crowded with fiction, drama, and poetry, the basement shelves with medical and other scientific texts. Neither was better; each had its place and served its purpose. As a child I was powerfully drawn to both art and science; in high school my English professor encouraged my writing even as my chemistry teacher was telling me I should become a chemist. In college I followed a double path, majoring in English and taking premed courses.

I ended up going with English. And I'll never forget the shock I felt on my first day of graduate school, when the director of the Ph.D. program in English looked up from the test scores in my file and asked: "Why aren't you in medical school?" To him, it made no sense that someone with an aptitude for science had opted to study literature. I soon discovered that his feeling of professional and institutional inferiority suffused the humanities. No, it didn't contaminate the very best professors, but it infected many of the others—thereby rendering these disciplines vulnerable to the predations of postmodern pseudoscience.

Which was absurd, of course, because anyone who truly knows and loves both science and literature understands that neither is more "important" than the other; both matter, for different reasons. Those who try to turn the study of literature into a science only prove thereby that they understand neither science nor literature, that their awe of science is matched only by their ignorance of it, and that their interest in being perceived as "relevant" exceeds their attraction to literature itself.

*   *   *

In his tiny, cluttered office, David Clemens tells me about the Great Books program he established at Monterey Peninsula College. At first his proposal for the program was opposed by some administrators, one of whom wanted a more multicultural reading list. But in the end it went through. Clemens teaches students how to read great books, covers the critiques and defenses of the "great books" concept, and discusses reading books versus processing material online.

How, I ask him, has the program been received by students? Clemens says he's been told again and again: "At last! This is what I came to college for." Students, he feels, "have had it up to here" with Theory and multiculturalism.

Months later, looking through the winter 2011 issue of *Literary Matters*, the ALSCW newsletter, I happen to run across an essay by Joshua Converse, a Monterey undergraduate, that is a tribute to Clemens's course, which Converse describes as "earth-shattering (or world-shaping)." Converse says that he and his fellow students were "hungry for something real. We found it in English 1B: Introduction to Literature.'" Converse goes on:

> Over the course of weeks the once-flat landscape of Literature delineated by context, race, class, gender, and the quotidian use of language started to shift beneath us; the World of Ideas opened. We learned how to really read. We were on fire to talk about it..... Within weeks other members of the class and I were meeting on our own time to discuss the Great Books. We read Aristophanes' *Lysistrata*. We read Sappho. We felt and spoke as if we had rediscovered some long-forgotten treasure abandoned by the generation before. Members of the faculty began to attend, and we became an offi-

cially recognized club on campus.... We felt we'd missed out on something essential by not being exposed to these works earlier.

Back in Clemens's office, he and I talk about the proliferation of disciplines with the word *studies* in their names. "Anything with *studies* in it, avoid!" Clemens says. What about Cultural Studies? "That bullshit comes into the classroom in papers." He mentions Monterey's Sign Language Program, which was "founded with the best of intentions" but which actually "promotes deafness" in the name of political correctness. "Just think of not healing a child who can't hear because it's an offense against deaf culture!"

For Clemens, one of the most appalling crimes of today's academy is that it has accustomed students to the idea that teaching is, by definition, an act of political advocacy. Clemens describes himself as a believer in "infusing critical thinking into everything," and explains that when he covers controversial issues in the classroom, "I try to say: what objections might there be to this? Treat it with academic dispassion." Today, alas, "students don't know what dispassion and disinterestedness mean."

He's quick, however, to add a note of hope. "I think there's a change in the post-9/11 generation—a greater seriousness, a greater desire for 'the real deal.' Students feel empty. They've been marinated in multiculturalism since elementary school. They're being taught with technological means that technologize learning." One student told him about a seventh-grade class in which Dante was taught by means of a PowerPoint presentation in which hell, heaven, and purgatory were bullet points. In American education, Clemens complains, there's "no longer an interest in history, in the telling of the American tale"; instead, "it's the black American tale, the feminist American tale," and so on. This is important, because "what we valorize as the salient feature of our past shapes our future": if we focus on class struggle and the history of oppression in teaching American history, then those are the lenses through which our descendants will see our country.

Clemens emphasizes that while the eyes of the mainstream media may be on the Ivy League and other big-name universities, California community colleges such as Monterey "indoctrinate" almost three million people a year with multiculturalism, bogus diversity, and left-wing ideologies that present capitalism as a zero-sum game. Clemens recalls a Korean American student of his who was always being asked: "What is the Asian American viewpoint on this?" "She was a sixth-generation American!" Clemens exclaims. In the academy today, "you're not an individual—and I think people still want to be individuals!"

*   *   *

Yet for all the glimmers of hope, it's not easy to imagine a successful revolt against identity studies and other postmodern academic phenomena anytime soon. The ideologues have transformed the academy—and, to a remarkable extent, driven out the enemy. They've taken over the shop and remade it in their image. And there's no easy route back. After all, there's nothing more entrenched than a tenured professor. Students and their parents, alas, are unwitting accomplices in this protracted siege. Most of them simply aren't aware of what they've gotten into. Some of the parents just don't realize how much things have changed since *they* were students. Indeed, some of them are so young that they, too, were students under the present dispensation—and they think this is what humanities education *is*. And so they instruct their children to avoid the humanities as much as they can and to concentrate on "practical" courses that will lead directly to profitable careers. As a result of which their kids never acquire a real liberal education—and thereby risk the danger of never truly understanding, among other things, what it means to be an American. And with every kid who emerges from college possessing a diploma—and an idea of America derived not from the values of the Declaration and the Constitution but from the preachings of identity studies—the American miracle fades a bit more into the mists of history.

This is a tragedy for America—and for all of humanity. "In a world savagely rent by ethnic and racial antagonisms," wrote Schlesinger, "it is all the more essential that the United States continue as an example of how a highly differentiated society holds itself together."

How to reverse this nightmarish development? First, spread the word. Parents and alumni should educate themselves about what is going on and make noise about it. The people who "teach" this nonsense rely on their ability, when challenged, to silence parents, alumni, and other outsiders with thick clouds of pretentious rhetoric and charges of prejudice and philistinism. Parents and alumni who are aware of what these people are up to and who are not intimidated by their jargon can make a big difference.

A parent who might ordinarily send a child to his or her alma mater should be prepared to do otherwise if it turns out that the study of the humanities in that institution has been hopelessly compromised by postmodernism—and should, moreover, make an issue out of it. A few parents who advertise their readiness to turn their back on a beloved college for such reasons can set off alarms in that institution's highest administrative offices.

There *are*, after all, very fine colleges—not many, but some—at which the humanities have actually been spared the cancer of postmodernism. Parents who want their children to receive an education worth the money they are paying for it are urged to send them to those places. Doing so would send a message to the entire higher educational establishment.

There are other ways to win this war. Clemens's Great Books program provides one example. If the extant departments and programs at a college are a lost cause, run by entrenched ideologues who simply cannot be dislodged, the only solution may be to start a new department or program, as Clemens did, and do an end run around them. In such matters, boards of trustees and administrators have a great deal of power—which they use, alas, all too rarely.

The most ambitious solution of all is to establish new colleges from scratch. One thing that there is no shortage of in the United States these days is unemployed or underemployed people with Ph.D.s in the humanities. Many of them are unemployed or underemployed precisely because they've chosen not to buy into postmodern ideology. Some of them are hardworking adjuncts, teaching several ccurses per term, often at a number of different colleges and universities, invariably for a pittance. Drawing on this pool of talent, an ambitious educator with seed money, drive, and imagination could create a first-rate liberal arts college. The identity studies owe their existence, in very large part, to the munificence of the Ford Foundation. Isn't there a foundation somewhere that is willing to put up the money to counter the madness of the postmodern humanities?

It is staggering how willing many American parents are today to spend outrageous amounts of money on higher educations that are, in many cases, hardly educations at all. What do these parents really want their children to get out of college? Many, for all their generosity, don't put much thought into answering this question. They accept that institutions such as Harvard and Yale are the gold standard of American higher education, simply because the names of these institutions have long since become synonymous with excellence in the popular mind. Coupled with this lazy acceptance is a cynical awareness that millions of other Americans—including their children's potential employers—think exactly the same way, the result being that the sight of Harvard or Yale on a diploma all but guarantees a smooth ride into a successful career.

If everybody thinks this way, however, none of this will ever change for the better. And there's no excuse for *not* trying to make a difference. For with the Internet at one's fingertips, it's not really that difficult for a concerned parent to track down colleges and universities that offer *real* educations—that can, in other words, prepare a young person both for a profitable career *and* for an enriching life.

The future of America hangs in the balance.

ACKNOWLEDGMENTS

I am profoundly indebted to my editor, Adam Bellow, and my agent, John Talbot—two exceptional men and true friends with whom I have now collaborated on several books in what, for me at least, has been a remarkable and invigorating spirit of camaraderie and shared intellectual enthusiasm.

I am also exceedingly grateful to Kathryn Whitenight, Marlena Brown, and Joanna Pinsker, Milan Bozic, William Ruoto, and Jonathan Burnham at HarperCollins for their distinctive contributions to this project and for their many kindnesses.

For their extraordinary friendship, help, advice, and moral support throughout the writing of this book, I wish to extend my deepest thanks to Thor Halvorssen, David Horowitz, Per Birger Sørebø and Mark Smith, Dorothy Heyl and Thomas De Pietro, Mary Hiecke Gioia and Dana Gioia, Fred Litwin, Angelo Pezzana, Nina Rosenwald, David Solway, Brendan McEntee, Alexander Meyer Nilsen, Michael Johannessen, Jenna Bawer, Paula Deitz, Peter Fedorowich, Alex Knepper, Tim Hulsey, Karen Montone, and Valerie Price.

A very special debt is recorded in the dedication of this book.

For their generous interviews, I want to express my sincere appreciation to Shelby Steele, Alan Charles Kors, Stephen H. Balch, Phyllis Chesler, Christina Hoff Sommers, David Clemens, Wayne R. Dynes, Larry Kramer, Miles Groth, David Diaz, and Chon Noriega.

Needless to say, the views here are strictly my own, as are my inevitable errors.

As ever, I am nothing without Tor Andre. And I will never be the same since the loss of my beloved and incomparably devoted cat Henry, who was within arm's reach every day for seventeen years as I sat and wrote.

SELECTED BIBLIOGRAPHY

1. The Victims' Revolution

Barthes, Roland. *Mythologies.*

Benjamin, Walter. "The Work of Art in the Age of Mechanical Reproduction."

Ellis, John M. *Against Deconstruction.*

Fanon, Frantz. *The Wretched of the Earth.*

Freire, Paulo. *Pedagogy of the Oppressed.*

Gramsci, Antonio. *Prison Notebooks.*

Kronman, Anthony T. *Educations End: Why Our Colleges and Universities Have Given Up on the Meaning of Life.*

Patai, Daphne, and Wilfrido Corral. *Theory's Empire: An Anthology of Dissent.*

Patai, Daphne, and Noretta Koertge. *Professing Feminism: Education and Indoctrination in Women's Studies.*

Rose, Gillian. *Feminism and Geography. The Limits of Geographical Knowledge.*

Rotenberg, Paula. *Race, Class, and Gender in the United States.*

Said, Edward. *Orientalism.*

Weber, Max. *The Protestant Ethic and the Spirit of Capitalism.*

Zinn, Howard. *A Peoples History of the United States.*

2. Gilligan's Island: Women's Studies

Anzaldúa, Gloria, ed. *This Bridge Called My Back: Writings by Radical Women of Color.*

Barrett, Michèle. *Women's Oppression Today: The Marxist/Feminist Encounter.*

Baumgardner, Jennifer, and Amy Richards. *Manifesta: Young Women, Feminism, and the Future.*

Beauvoir, Simone de. *The Second Sex.*

Brownmiller, Susan. *Against Our Will: Men, Women and Rape.*

Burman, Stephen. *The State of the American Empire: How the USA Shapes the World.*

Chasin, Barbara H. *Inequality and Violence in the United States: Casualties of Capitalism.*

Chesler, Phyllis. *The Death of Feminism: What's Next in the Struggle for Women's Freedom.*

Cohee, Gail E., Elisabeth Daumer, Theresa D. Kemp, and Paula M. Krebs, eds. *The Feminist Teacher Anthology: Pedagogies and Classroom Strategies.*

Daly, Mary. *Gyn/Ecology: The Metaethics of Radical Feminism.*

——. *Pure Lust: Elemental Feminist Philosophy.*

Dworkin, Andrea. *Intercourse.*

Field Belenky, Mary, Blythe McVicker Clinchy, Nancy Rule Goldberger, and Jill Mattuck Tarule. *Women's Ways of Knowing: The Development of Self Voice, and Mind.*

Friedan, Betty. *The Feminine Mystique.*

Gilbert, Sandra, and Susan Gubar. *The Madwoman in the Attic: The Woman Writer and the Nineteenth-Century Literary Imagination.*Gilligan, Carol. *In a Different Voice: Psychological Theory and Women's Development.*

Greer, Germaine. *The Female Eunuch.*

Haack, Susan. *Manifesto of a Passionate Moderate: Unfashionable Essays.*

Hoff Sommers, Christina. *The War Against Boys: How Misguided Feminism Is Harming Our Young Men.*

——. *Who Stole Feminism? How Women Have Betrayed Women.*

Hooks, Bell. *Ain't I a Woman?*

Howe, Florence, ed. *The Politics of Women's Studies: Testimony from Thirty Founding Mothers.*

Johnson, Allan G. *The Gender Knot: Unraveling Our Patriarchal Legacy.*

Kirk, Gwyn, and Margo Okazawa-Rey. *Women's Lives: Multicultural Perspectives.*

Le Doeuff, Michèle. *The Sex of Knowing.*

Mailer, Norman. *The Prisoner of Sex.*

Mill, John Stuart. *The Subjection of Women.* Millett, Kate. *Sexual Politics.*

Nye, Andrea. *Words of Power: A Feminist Reading of the History of Logic.*

Paglia, Camille. *Sexual Personae: Art and Decadence from Nefertiti to Emily Dickinson.*

Roiphe, Katie. *The Morning After: Sex, Fear and Feminism on Campus.*

Wollstonecraft, Mary. *A Vindication of the Rights of Women.*

3. The Ebony Tower: Black Studies

Du Bois, W. E. B. *The Souls of Black Folic.*

Dyson, Michael Eric. *Is Bill Cosby Right?: Or Has the Black Middle Class Lost Its Mind?*

Ford, Nick Aaron. *Black Studies: Threat or Challenge.*

Franklin, John Hope. *The Color Line: Legacy for the Twenty-first Century.*

Gates, Henry Louis, Jr. *Figures in Black: Words, Signs, and the "Racial" Self*

——. *The Signifying Monkey: A Theory of African-American Literary Criticism.*

Gordon, Lewis R., and Jane Anna Gordon, eds. *A Companion to African-American Studies.*

Karenga, Maulana Ron. *Introduction to Black Studies.*

McWhorter, John. *Authentically Black: Essays for the Black Silent Majority.*

——. *Losing the Race: Self-Sabotage in Black America.*

Reed, Ishmael. *Mumbo Jumbo.*

Rojas, Fabio. *From Black Power to Black Studies: How a Radical Social Movement Became an Academic Discipline.*

Steele, Shelby. *The Content of Our Character: A New Vision of Race in America.*

West, Cornell. *Keeping Faith: Philosophy and Race in America.*

——. *Race Matters.*

4. Visit to a Queer Planet: Queer Studies

Abelove, Henry, Michèle Aina Barale, and David M. Halperin, eds. *The Lesbian and Gay Studies Reader.*

Barnard, Ian. *Queer Race: Cultural Interventions in the Racial Politics of Queer Theory.*

Bawer, Bruce. *A Place at the Table: The Gay Individual in American Society.*

Dynes, Wayne R., ed., *Encyclopedia of Homosexuality.*

——. *Homosexuality: A Research Guide.*

Edelman, Lee. *No Future: Queer Theory and the Death Drive.*

Foucault, Michel. *The History of Sexuality.*

Halperin, David M. *One Hundred Years of Homosexuality: And Other Essays on Greek Love.*

——. *Saint Foucault.*

Halperin, David M., John J. Winkler, and Froma I. Zeitlin, eds. *Before Sexuality: The Construction of Erotic Experience in the Ancient Greek World.*

Katz, Jonathan Ned. *Love Stories: Sex Between Men before Homosexuality.*

Kosofsky Sedgwick, Eve. *A Dialogue on Love.*

——. *Epistemology of the Closet.*

Muñoz, Jose Esteban. *Disidentifications: Queers of Color and the Performance of Politics.*

Sandfort, Theo, Judith Schuyf, Jan Willem Duyvendak, and Jeffrey Weeks, eds. *Lesbian and Gay Studies: An Introductory, Interdisciplinary Approach.*

Sullivan, Andrew. *Virtually Normal: An Argument About Homosexuality.*

Turner, William B. *A Genealogy of Queer Theory.*

Vaid, Urvashi. *Virtual Equality: The Mainstreaming of Gay and Lesbian Liberation.*

Winkler, John J. *The Constraints of Desire: The Anthropology of Sex and Gender in Ancient Greece.*

5. The Dream of Aztlán: Chicano Studies

Acuña, Rodolfo. *Occupied America: A History of Chicanos.*

Alaniz, Yolanda, and Megan Cornish. *Viva la Raza: A History of Chicano Identity and Resistance.*

Diaz, David R. *Barrio Urbanism: Chicanos, Planning and American Cities.*

Garcia, Alma M., ed. *Chicana Feminist Thought: The Basic Historical Writings.*

Gómez-Quiñones, Juan. *Development of the Mexican Working Class North of the Rio Bravo.*

Heidenreich, Linda. *"This Land Was Mexican Once": Histories of Resistance from Northern California.*

Moraga, Cherríe, and Gloria Anzaldúa, eds. *This Bridge Called My Back: Writings by Radical Women of Color.*

Ruiz, Vicki L. *Cannery Women, Cannery Lives: Mexican Women, Unionization, and the California Food Processing Industry, 1930–1950.*

Soldatenko, Michael. *Chicano Studies: The Genesis of a Discipline.*

Torres, Edén. *Chicana Without Apology/Chicana sin vergüenza: The New Chicana Cultural Studies.*

Vásquez, Francisco H. *Latino/a Thought: Culture, Politics, and Society.*

6. Studies, Studies Everywhere

Bacon, Linda. *Health at Every Size: The Surprising Truth about Your Weight.*

Connell, Robert W./Raewyn Connell. *Masculinities.*

Frankenberg, Ruth. *White Women, Race Matters: The Social Construction of Whiteness.*

Morrison, Toni. *Playing in the Dark: Whiteness and the Literary Imagination.*

Nathanson, Paul. *Spreading Misandry: The Teaching of Contempt for Men in Popular Culture.*

Roediger, David R. *The Wages of Whiteness: Race and the Making of the American Working Class.*

Rothblum, Esther, and Sondra Solovay, eds. *The Fat Studies Reader.*

Rothenberg, Paula, ed. *White Privilege: Essential Readings on the Other Side of Racism.*

ABOUT THE AUTHOR

Bruce Bawer is the author of the critically acclaimed books *While Europe Slept*, *Surrender*, *A Place at the Table*, and *Stealing Jesus*. He is also a respected poet and translator who has published several collections of literary and film criticism. A native New Yorker, he has lived in Norway since 1999.